WORKS OF FREI

CAMBRIDGE ED

SCHILLER'S

HISTORICAL DRAMAS

WILLIAM TELL. DON CARLOS. DEMETRIUS.

TRANSLATED FROM THE GERMAN.

ILLUSTRATED.

University Press of the Pacific
Honolulu, Hawaii

Historical Dramas
William Tell. Don Carlos. Demetrius

by
Frederick Schiller

ISBN 0-89875-178-0

University Press of the Pacific
Honolulu, Hawaii
http://www.UniversityPressofthePacific.com

CONTENTS.

WILHELM TELL.

DRAMATIS PERSONÆ.

HERMANN GESSLER, *Governor of Schwytz and Uri.*
WERNER, *Baron of Attinghausen, free noble of Switzerland.*
ULRICH VON RUDENZ, *his Nephew.*

WERNER STAUFFACHER,
CONRAD HUNN,
HANS AUF DER MAUER,
JORG IM HOFE,   } *People of Schwytz.*
ULRICH DER SCHMIDT,
JOST VON WEILER,
ITEL REDING,

WALTER FURST,
WILHELM TELL,
ROSSELMANN, *the Priest,*
PETERMANN, *Sacristan,*   } *People of Uri.*
KUONI, *Herdsman,*
WERNI, *Huntsman,*
RUODI, *Fisherman,*

ARNOLD OF MELCHTHAL,
CONRAD BAUMGARTEN,
MEYER VON SARNEN,
STRUTH VON WINKELRIED, } *People of Unterwald.*
KLAUS VON DER FLUE,
BURKHART AM BUHEL,
ARNOLD VON SEWA,

PFEIFFER OF LUCERNE.
KUNZ OF GERSAU.
JENNI, *Fisherman's Son.*
SEPPI, *Herdsman's Son.*
GERTRUDE, *Stauffacher's Wife.*
HEDWIG, *Wife of Tell, daughter of Furst.*
BERTHA OF BRUNECK, *a rich heiress.*

5

ARMGART,
MECHTHILD,
ELSBETH,   } *Peasant women.*
HILDEGARD,
WALTER,   } *Tell's sons.*
WILHELM,
FRIESSHARDT,   } *Soldiers.*
LEUTHOLD,
RUDOLPH DER HARRAS, *Gessler's master of the horse.*
JOHANNES PARRICIDA, *Duke of Suabia.*
STUSSI, *Overseer.*
THE MAYOR OF URI.
A COURIER.
MASTER STONEMASON, COMPANIONS, AND WORKMEN.
TASKMASTER.
A CRIER.
MONKS OF THE ORDER OF CHARITY.
HORSEMEN OF GESSLER AND LANDENBERG.
MANY PEASANTS; MEN AND WOMEN FROM THE WALDSTETTEN

WILHELM TELL.

ACT I.

SCENE I.

A high, rocky shore of the lake of Lucerne opposite Schwytz. The lake makes a bend into the land; a hut stands at a short distance from the shore; the fisher boy is rowing about in his boat. Beyond the lake are seen the green meadows, the hamlets, and farms of Schwytz, lying in the clear sunshine. On the left are observed the peaks of the Hacken, surrounded with clouds; to the right, and in the remote distance, appear the Glaciers. The Ranz des Vaches, and the tinkling of cattle-bells, continue for some time after the rising of the curtain.

FISHER BOY (*sings in his boat*).

Melody of the Ranz des Vaches.

The clear, smiling lake wooed to bathe in its deep,
A boy on its green shore had laid him to sleep;
    Then heard he a melody
      Flowing and soft,
    And sweet, as when angels
      Are singing aloft.
And as thrilling with pleasure he wakes from his rest,
The waters are murmuring over his breast;
    And a voice from the deep cries,
      " With me thou must go,
    I charm the young shepherd,
      I lure him below."

HERDSMAN (*on the mountains*).

Air. — Variation of the Ranz des Vaches.

    Farewell, ye green meadows,
      Farewell, sunny shore,
    The herdsman must leave you,
      The summer is o'er.

We go to the hills, but you'll see us again,
When the cuckoo is calling, and wood-notes are gay,
When flowerets are blooming in dingle and plain,
And the brooks sparkle up in the sunshine of May.
Farewell, ye green meadows,
Farewell, sunny shore,
The herdsman must leave you,
The summer is o'er.

CHAMOIS HUNTER (*appearing on the top of a cliff*).

Second Variation of the Ranz des Vaches.

On the heights peals the thunder, and trembles the bridge,
The huntsman bounds on by the dizzying ridge,
Undaunted he hies him
O'er ice-covered wild,
Where leaf never budded,
Nor spring ever smiled ;
And beneath him an ocean of mist, where his eye
No longer the dwellings of man can espy;
Through the parting clouds only
The earth can be seen,
Far down 'neath the vapor
The meadows of green.
[*A change comes over the landscape. A rumbling,
cracking noise is heard among the mountains.
Shadows of clouds sweep across the scene.*
[RUODI, *the fisherman, comes out of his cottage.*
WERNI, *the huntsman, descends from the rocks.*
KUONI, *the shepherd, enters, with a milk-pail on
his shoulders, followed by* SEPPI, *his assistant.*
RUODI.   Bestir thee, Jenni, haul the boat on shore.
The grizzly Vale-king * comes, the glaciers
moan,
The lofty Mytenstein† draws on his hood,
And from the Stormcleft chilly blows the wind ;
The storm will burst before we are prepared.

---

* The German is *Thalvogt*, Ruler of the Valley — the name given figura-
tively to a dense gray mist which the south wind sweeps into the valleys from
the mountain tops. It is well known as the precursor of stormy weather.
† A steep rock standing on the north of Rütli, and nearly opposite to
Brumen.

KUONI.   'Twill rain ere long ; my sheep browse eagerly,
          And Watcher there is scraping up the earth.
WERNI.   The fish are leaping, and the water-hen
          Dives up and down.   A storm is coming on.
KUONI (*to his boy*).
          Look, Seppi, if the cattle are not straying.
SEPPI.   There goes brown Liesel, I can hear her bells.
KUONI.   Then all are safe ; she ever ranges farthest.
RUODI.   You've a fine yoke of bells there, master herds-
          man.
WERNI.   And likely cattle, too.   Are they your own ?
KUONI.   I'm not so rich.   They are the noble lord's
          Of Attinghaus, and trusted to my care.
RUODI.   How gracefully yon heifer bears her ribbon !
KUONI.   Ay, well she knows she's leader of the herd,
          And, take it from her, she'd refuse to feed.
RUODI.   You're joking now.   A beast devoid of reason.
WERNI.   That's easy said.   But beasts have reason too —
          And that we know, we men that hunt the
          chamois.
          They never turn to feed — sagacious creatures !
          Till they have placed a sentinel ahead,
          Who pricks his ears whenever we approach,
          And gives alarm with clear and piercing pipe.
RUODI (*to the shepherd*).
          Are you for home ?
KUONI.   The Alp is grazed quite bare.
WERNI.   A safe return, my friend !
KUONI.   The same to you ?
          Men come not always back from tracks like
          yours.
RUODI.   But who comes here, running at topmost speed ?
WERNI.   I know the man ; 'tis Baumgart of Alzellen.
CONRAD BAUMGARTEN (*rushing in breathless*).
          For God's sake, ferryman, your boat !
RUODI.   How now ?
          Why all this haste ?
BAUM.   Cast off ! My life's at stake !
          Set me across !
KUONI.   Why, what's the matter, friend ?
WERNI.   Who are pursuing you ? First tell us that.

BAUM. (*to the fisherman*).
> Quick, quick, even now they're close upon my
>   heels!
> The viceroy's horsemen are in hot pursuit!
> I'm a lost man should they lay hands upon me.

RUODI. Why are the troopers in pursuit of you?

BAUM. First save my life and then I'll tell you all.

WERNI. There's blood upon your garments — how is
>   this?

BAUM. The imperial seneschal, who dwelt at Rossberg.

KUONI. How! What! The Wolfshot?* Is it he pur-
>   sues you?

BAUM. He'll ne'er hunt man again; I've settled him.

ALL (*starting back*).
> Now, God forgive you, what is this you've done!

BAUM. What every free man in my place had done.
> I have but used mine own good household right
> 'Gainst him that would have wronged my wife —
>   my honor.

KUONI. And has he wronged you in your honor, then?

BAUM. That he did not fulfil his foul desire
> Is due to God and to my trusty axe.

WERNI. You've cleft his skull, then, have you, with your
>   axe?

KUONI. Oh, tell us all! You've time enough, before
> The boat can be unfastened from its moorings.

BAUM. When I was in the forest, felling timber,
> My wife came running out in mortal fear
> "The seneschal," she said, "was in my house,
> Had ordered her to get a bath prepared,
> And thereupon had taken unseemly freedoms,
> From which she rid herself and flew to me."
> Armed as I was I sought him, and my axe
> Has given his bath a bloody benediction.

WERNI. And you did well; no man can blame the deed.

KUONI. The tyrant! Now he has his just reward!
> We men of Unterwald have owed it long.

---

* In German, *Wolfenschiessen* — a young man of noble family, and a
native of Unterwalden, who attached himself to the house of Austria and
was appointed *Burgvogt*, or seneschal, of the castle of Rossberg. He was
killed by Baumgarten in the manner and for the cause mentioned in the
text.

BAUM. The deed got wind, and now they're in pursuit.
Heavens! whilst we speak, th etime is flying fast.
[It begins to thunder.

KUONI. Quick, ferrymen, and set the good man over.

RUODI. Impossible! a storm is close at hand,
Wait till it pass! You must.

BAUM. Almighty heavens!
I cannot wait; the least delay is death.

KUONI (*to the fisherman*).
Push out. God with you! We should help our
neighbors;
The like misfortune may betide us all.
[Thunder and the roaring of the wind.

RUODI. The south wind's up!* See how the lake is
rising!
I cannot steer against both storm and wave.

BAUM. (*clasping him by the knees*).
God so help you, as now you pity me!

WERNI. His life's at stake. Have pity on him, man!

KUONI. He is a father: has a wife and children.
[Repeated peals of thunder.

RUODI. What! and have I not, then, a life to lose,
A wife and child at home as well as he?
See, how the breakers foam, and toss, and whirl,
And the lake eddies up from all its depths!
Right gladly would I save the worthy man,
But 'tis impossible, as you must see.

BAUM. (*still kneeling*).
Then must I fall into the tyrant's hands,
And with the port of safety close in sight!
Yonder it lies! My eyes can measure it,
My very voice can echo to its shores.
There is the boat to carry me across,
Yet must I lie here helpless and forlorn.

KUONI. Look! who comes here?

---

* Literally, the *Föhn* is loose! "When," says Müller, in his History of
Switzerland, "the wind called the Föhn is high the navigation of the lake
becomes extremely dangerous. Such is its vehemence that the laws of the
country require that the fires shall be extinguished in the houses while it
lasts, and the night watches are doubled. The inhabitants lay heavy stones
upon the roofs of their houses to prevent their being blown away."

RUODI.   'Tis Tell, brave Tell, of Bürglen.*
                    [*Enter* TELL, *with a crossbow.*
TELL.   Who is the man that here implores for aid ?
KUONI.   He is from Alzellen, and to guard his honor
             From touch of foulest shame, has slain the Wolf-
                 shot !
             The imperial seneschal, who dwelt at Rossberg.
             The viceroy's troopers are upon his heels ;
             He begs the boatman here to take him over,
             But he, in terror of the storm, refuses.
RUODI.   Well, there is Tell can steer as well as I.
             He'll be my judge, if it be possible.
                    [*Violent peals of thunder — the lake becomes*
                        more tempestuous.
             Am I to plunge into the jaws of hell?
             I should be mad to dare the desperate act.
TELL.   The brave man thinks upon himself the last.
             Put trust in God, and help him in his need !
RUODI.   Safe in the port, 'tis easy to advise.
             There is the boat, and there the lake ! Try you !
TELL.   The lake may pity, but the viceroy will not.
             Come, venture, man !
SHEPHERD *and* HUNTSMAN.
                    Oh, save him! save him! save him!
RUODI.   Though 'twere my brother, or my darling child,
             I would not go. It is St. Simon's day,
             The lake is up, and calling for its victim.
TELL.   Naught's to be done with idle talking here.
             Time presses on — the man must be assisted.
             Say, boatman, will you venture?
RUODI.   No ; not I.
TELL.   In God's name, then, give me the boat ! I will
             With my poor strength, see what is to be done !
KUONI.   Ha, noble Tell !
WERNI.   That's like a gallant huntsman !
BAUM.   You are my angel, my preserver, Tell.
TELL.   I may preserve you from the viceroy's power
             But from the tempest's rage another must.

---

* Bürglen, the birthplace and residence of Tell. A chapel erected in
1522 remains on the spot formerly occupied by his house.

Yet you had better fall into God's hands,
Than into those of men.   [*To the herdsman.*
                        Herdsman, do thou
Console my wife, should aught of ill befall me.
I do but what I may not leave undone.
                        [*He leaps into the boat.*

KUONI (*to the fisherman*).
        A pretty man to be a boatman, truly!
        What Tell could risk you dared not venture on.
RUODI. Far better men than I would not ape Tell.
        There does not live his fellow 'mong the moun-
                tains.
WERNI (*who has ascended a rock*).
        He pushes off. God help thee now, brave sailor!
        Look how his bark is reeling on the waves!
KUONI (*on the shore*).
        The surge has swept clean over it. And now
        Tis out of sight. Yet stay, there 'tis again!
        Stoutly he stems the breakers, noble fellow!
SEPPI. Here come the troopers hard as they can ride!
KUONI. Heavens! so they do! Why, that was help,
                indeed.
                        [*Enter a troop of horsemen.*
1ST H. Give up the murderer! You have him here!
2D H.   This way he came! 'Tis useless to conceal him!
RUODI *and* KUONI.
        Whom do you mean?
FIRST HORSEMAN (*discovering the boat*).
                        The devil! What do I see?
WERNI (*from above*).
        Is't he in yonder boat ye seek? Ride on,
        If you lay to, you may o'ertake him yet.
2D H.   Curse on you, he's escaped!
FIRST HORSEMAN (*to the shepherd and fisherman*).
                        You helped him off,
        And you shall pay for it. Fall on their herds!
        Down with the cottage! burn it! beat it down!
                        [*They rush off.*
SEPPI (*hurrying after them*). Oh, my poor lambs!
KUONI (*following him*). Unhappy me, my herds!
WERNI. The tyrants!

RUODI (*wringing his hands*).
     Righteous Heaven !   Oh, when will come
  Deliverance to this devoted land ?
            [*Exeunt severally.*

SCENE II.

A lime-tree in front of STAUFFACHER'S *house at Steinen,
 in Schwytz, upon the public road, near a bridge.*

 WERNER STAUFFACHER *and* PFEIFFER, *of Lucerne,
  enter into conversation.*

PFEIFF. Ay, ay, friend Stauffacher, as I have said,
   Swear not to Austria, if you can help it.
   Hold by the empire stoutly as of yore,
   And God preserve you in your ancient freedom !
    [*Presses his hand warmly and is going.*
STAUFF. Wait till my mistress comes. Now do ! You are
   My guest in Schwytz — I in Lucerne am yours.
PFEIFF. Thanks ! thanks ! But I must reach Gersau to-
   day.
   Whatever grievances your rulers' pride
   And grasping avarice may yet inflict,
   Bear them in patience — soon a change may
   come.
   Another emperor may mount the throne.
   But Austria's once, and you are hers forever.
            [*Exit.*
   [STAUFFACHER *sits down sorrowfully upon a
    bench under the lime tree. Gertrude, his
    wife, enters, and finds him in this posture.
    She places herself near him, and looks at
    him for some time in silence.*
GERT. So sad, my love ! I scarcely know thee now.
   For many a day in silence I have marked
   A moody sorrow furrowing thy brow.
   Some silent grief is weighing on thy heart ;
   Trust it to me.   I am thy faithful wife,
   And I demand my half of all thy cares.
   [STAUFEACHER *gives her his hand and is silent.*
   Tell me what can oppress thy spirits thus ?

Thy toil is blest — the world goes well with
    thee —
Our barns are full — our cattle many a score;
Our handsome team of sleek and well-fed steeds,
Brought from the mountain pastures safely home,
To winter in their comfortable stalls.
There stands thy house—no nobleman's more fair!
'Tis newly built with timber of the best,
All grooved and fitted with the nicest skill;
Its many glistening windows tell of comfort!
'Tis quartered o'er with scutcheons of all hues,
And proverbs sage, which passing travellers
Linger to read, and ponder o'er their meaning.

STAUFF. The house is strongly built, and handsomely,
    But, ah! the ground on which we built it totters.

GERT. Tell me, dear Werner, what you mean by that?

STAUFF. No later since than yesterday, I sat
    Beneath this linden, thinking with delight,
    How fairly all was finished, when from Küss-
        nacht
    The viceroy and his men came riding by.
    Before this house he halted in surprise:
    At once I rose, and, as beseemed his rank,
    Advanced respectfully to greet the lord,
    To whom the emperor delegates his power,
    As judge supreme within our Canton here.
    " Who is the owner of this house?" he asked,
    With mischief in his thoughts, for well he knew.
    With prompt decision, thus I answered him :
    "The emperor, your grace — my lord and yours,
    And held by me in fief."   On this he answered,
    " I am the emperor's viceregent here,
    And will not that each peasant churl should build
    At his own pleasure, bearing him as freely
    As though he were the master in the land.
    I shall make bold to put a stop to this! "
    So saying he, with menaces, rode off,
    And left me musing, with a heavy heart,
    On the fell purpose that his words betrayed.

GERT. Mine own dear lord and husband! Wilt thou
    take ·

A word of honest counsel from thy wife?
I boast to be the noble Iberg's child,
A man of wide experience. Many a time,
As we sat spinning in the winter nights,
My sisters and myself, the people's chiefs
Were wont to gather round our father's hearth,
To read the old imperial charters, and
To hold sage converse on the country's weal.
Then heedfully I listened, marking well
What or the wise men thought, or good man
    wished,
And garnered up their wisdom in my heart.
Hear then, and mark me well; for thou wilt see,
I long have known the grief that weighs thee
    down.
The viceroy hates thee, fain would injure thee,
For thou hast crossed his wish to bend the Swiss
In homage to this upstart house of princes,
And kept them stanch, like their good sires of
    old,
In true allegiance to the empire. Say.
Is't not so, Werner? Tell me, am I wrong?

STAUFF. 'Tis even so. For this doth Gessler hate me.

GERT. He burns with envy, too, to see thee living
Happy and free on thy inheritance,
For he has none. From the emperor himself
Thou holdest in fief the lands thy fathers left
    thee.
There's not a prince in the empire that can show
A better title to his heritage;
For thou hast over thee no lord but one,
And he the mightiest of all Christian kings.
Gessler, we know, is but a younger son,
His only wealth the knightly cloak he wears;
He therefore views an honest man's good fortune
With a malignant and a jealous eye.
Long has he sworn to compass thy destruction
As yet thou art uninjured. Wilt thou wait
Till he may safely give his malice scope?
A wise man would anticipate the blow.

STAUFF. What's to be done?

GERT.   Now hear what I advise.
Thou knowest well, how here with us in Schwytz,
All worthy men are groaning underneath
This Gessler's grasping, grinding tyranny.
Doubt not the men of Unterwald as well,
And Uri, too, are chafing like ourselves,
At this oppressive and heart-wearying yoke.
For there, across the lake, the Landenberg
Wields the same iron rule as Gessler here —
No fishing-boat comes over to our side
But brings the tidings of some new encroach-
        ment,
Some outrage fresh, more grievous than the last.
Then it were well that some of you — true men —
Men sound at heart, should secretly devise
How best to shake this hateful thraldom off.
Well do I know that God would not desert you,
But lend his favor to the righteous cause.
Hast thou no friend in Uri, say, to whom
Thou frankly may'st unbosom all thy thoughts?
STAUFF. I know full many a gallant fellow there,
And nobles, too, — great men, of high repute,
In whom I can repose unbounded trust. [*Rising.*
    Wife! What a storm of wild and perilous
        thoughts
Hast thou stirred up within my tranquil breast?
The darkest musings of my bosom thou
Hast dragged to light, and placed them full be-
        fore me,
And what I scarce dared harbor e'en in thought,
Thou speakest plainly out, with fearless tongue.
But hast thou weighed well what thou urgest
        thus?
Discord will come, and the fierce clang of arms,
To scare this valley's long unbroken peace,
If we, a feeble shepherd race, shall dare
Him to the fight that lords it o'er the world.
Even now they only wait some fair pretext
For setting loose their savage warrior hordes,
To scourge and ravage this devoted land,
To lord it o'er us with the victor's rights,

And 'neath the show of lawful chastisement,
Despoil us of our chartered liberties.

GERT. You, too, are men; can wield a battle-axe
As well as they.   God ne'er deserts the brave.

STAUFF. Oh wife ! a horrid, ruthless fiend is war,
That strikes at once the shepherd and his flock.

GERT. Whate'er great heaven inflicts we must endure ;
No heart of noble temper brooks injustice.

STAUFF. This house — thy pride — war, unrelenting war,
Will burn it down.

GERT.   And did I think this heart
Enslaved and fettered to the things of earth,
With my own hand I'd hurl the kindling torch.

STAUFF. Thou hast faith in human kindness, wife ; but war
Spares not the tender infant in its cradle.

GERT. There is a friend to innocence in heaven !
Look forward, Werner — not behind you, now !

STAUFF. We men may perish bravely, sword in hand ;
But oh, what fate, my Gertrude, may be thine ?

GERT. None are so weak, but one last choice is left.
A spring from yonder bridge, and I am free !

STAUFF. (embracing her).
Well may he fight for hearth and home that
    clasps
A heart so rare as thine against his own !
What are the hosts of emperors to him !
Gertrude, farewell !   I will to Uri straight.
There lives my worthy comrade, Walter Furst,
His thoughts and mine upon these times are one.
There, too, resides the noble Banneret
Of Attinghaus.   High though of blood he be,
He loves the people, honors their old customs.
With both of these I will take counsel how
To rid us bravely of our country's foe.
Farewell ! and while I am away, bear thou
A watchful eye in management at home.
The pilgrim journeying to the house of God,
And pious monk, collecting for his cloister,
To these give liberally from purse and garner.
Stauffacher's house would not be hid.   Right
    out

Upon the public way it stands, and offers
To all that pass an hospitable roof.
[*While they are retiring,* TELL *enters with* BAUMGARTEN.
TELL.   Now, then, you have no further need of me.
Enter yon house. 'Tis Werner Stauffacher's,
A man that is a father to distress.
See, there he is himself! Come, follow me.
[*They retire up. Scene changes.*

SCENE III.

*A common near Altdorf. On an eminence in the background a
castle in progress of erection, and so far advanced that the
outline of the whole may be distinguished. The back part is
finished; men are working at the front. Scaffolding, on which
the workmen are going up and down. A slater is seen upon the
highest part of the roof. All is bustle and activity.*

TASKMASTER, MASON, WORKMEN, *and* LABORERS.

TASK. (*with a stick, urging on the workmen*).
Up, up! You've rested long enough. To work!
The stones here, now the mortar, and the lime!
And let his lordship see the work advanced
When next he comes. These fellows crawl like
snails!
[*To two laborers with loads.*
What! call ye that a load? Go, double it.
Is this the way ye earn your wages, laggards?
1st W.   'Tis very hard that we must bear the stones,
To make a keep and dungeon for ourselves!
TASK.   What's that you mutter? 'Tis a worthless
race,
And fit for nothing but to milk their cows,
And saunter idly up and down the mountains.
OLD MAN (*sinks down exhausted*).
I can no more.
TASK. (*shaking him*).
Up, up, old man, to work!
1st W.   Have you no bowels of compassion, thus
To press so hard upon a poor old man,
That scarce can drag his feeble limbs along?

MASTER MASON *and* WORKMEN.

        Shame, shame upon you — shame! It cries to
        heaven!

TASK.   Mind your own business. I but do my duty.

1ST W.   Pray, master, what's to be the name of this
        Same castle when 'tis built?

TASK.   The keep of Uri;
        For by it we shall keep you in subjection.

WORK.   The keep of Uri.

TASK.   Well, why laugh at that?

2D W.   So you'll keep Uri with this paltry place!

1ST W.   How many molehills such as that must first
        Be piled above each other ere you make
        A mountain equal to the least in Uri?
            [TASKMASTER *retires up the stage.*

MAS. M.   I'll drown the mallet in the deepest lake,
        That served my hand on this accursed pile.
            [*Enter* TELL *and* STAUFFACHER.

STAUFF.   Oh, that I had not lived to see this sight!

TELL.   Here 'tis not good to be. Let us proceed.

STAUFF.   Am I in Uri, in the land of freedom?

MAS. M.   Oh, sir, if you could only see the vaults
        Beneath these towers. The man that tenants
        them
        Will never hear the cock crow more.

STAUFF.   O God!

MASON.   Look at these ramparts and these buttresses,
        That seem as they were built to last forever.

TELL.   Hands can destroy whatever hands have reared.
            [*Pointing to the mountains.*
        That house of freedom God hath built for us.
        [*A drum is heard. People enter bearing a cap*
          upon a pole, followed by a crier. Women
          and children thronging tumultuously after
          them.

1ST W.   What means the drum? Give heed!

MASON.   Why here's a mumming!
        And look, the cap, — what can they mean by
        that?

CRIER.   In the emperor's name, give ear!

WORK.   Hush! silence! hush!

CRIER. Ye men of Uri, ye do see this cap!
It will be set upon a lofty pole
In Altdorf, in the market-place: and this
Is the lord governor's good will and pleasure,
The cap shall have like honor as himself,
And all shall reverence it with bended knee,
And head uncovered; thus the king will know
Who are his true and loyal subjects here:
His life and goods are forfeit to the crown,
That shall refuse obedience to the order.
[*The people burst out into laughter. The
drum beats, and the procession passes on.*

1ST W. A strange device to fall upon, indeed!
Do reverence to a cap! a pretty farce!
Heard ever mortal anything like this?

MAS. M. Down to a cap on bended knee, forsooth!
Rare jesting this with men of sober sense!

1ST W. Nay, were it but the imperial crown, indeed!
But 'tis the cap of Austria! I've seen it
Hanging above the throne in Gessler's hall.

MASON. The cap of Austria! Mark that! A snare
To get us into Austria's power, by heaven!

WORK. No freeborn man will stoop to such disgrace.

MAS. M. Come — to our comrades, and advise with them!
[*They retire up.*

TELL (*to* STAUFFACHER).
You see how matters stand. Farewell, my friend!

STAUFF. Whither away? Oh, leave us not so soon.

TELL. They look for me at home. So fare ye well.

STAUFF. My heart's so full, and has so much to tell you.

TELL. Words will not make a heart that's heavy light.

STAUFF. Yet words may possibly conduct to deeds.

TELL. All we can do is to endure in silence.

STAUFF. But shall we bear what is not to be borne?

TELL. Impetuous rulers have the shortest reigns.
When the fierce south wind rises from his chasms,
Men cover up their fires, the ships in haste
Make for the harbor, and the mighty spirit
Sweeps o'er the earth, and leaves no trace behind.
Let every man live quietly at home;
Peace to the peaceful rarely is denied.

STAUFF. And is it thus you view our grievances?
TELL. The serpent stings not till it is provoked.
Let them alone; they'll weary of themselves,
Whene'er they see we are not to be roused.
STAUFF. Much might be done — did we stand fast
together.
TELL. When the ship founders, he will best escape
Who seeks no other's safety but his own.
STAUFF. And you desert the common cause so coldly?
TELL. A man can safely count but on himself!
STAUFF. Nay, even the weak grow strong by union.
TELL. But the strong man is the strongest when alone.
STAUFF. Your country, then, cannot rely on you
If in despair she rise against her foes.
TELL. Tell rescues the lost sheep from yawning gulfs:
Is he a man, then, to desert his friends?
Yet, whatsoe'er you do, spare me from council!
I was not born to ponder and select;
But when your course of action is resolved,
Then call on Tell; you shall not find him fail.
    [*Exeunt severally. A sudden tumult is
    heard around the scaffolding.*
MASON (*running in*). What's wrong?
FIRST WORKMAN (*running forward*).
            The slater's fallen from the roof.
BERTHA (*rushing in*).
    Is he dashed to pieces? Run — save him, help!
    If help be possible, save him! Here is gold.
        [*Throws her trinkets among the people.*
MASON. Hence with your gold, — your universal charm,
And remedy for ill! When you have torn
Fathers from children, husbands from their wives,
And scattered woe and wail throughout the land,
You think with gold to compensate for all.
Hence! Till we saw you we were happy men;
With you came misery and dark despair.
BERTHA (*to the* TASKMASTER, *who has returned*).
    Lives he?
                [TASKMASTER *shakes his head.*
        Ill-fated towers, with curses built,
And doomed with curses to be tenanted! [*Exit.*

Scene IV.

The House of Walter Furst. Walter Furst *and* Arnold Von Melchthal *enter simultaneously at different sides.*

Melch. Good Walter Furst.
Furst.   If we should be surprised!
    Stay where you are. We are beset with spies.
Melch. Have you no news for me from Unterwald?
    What of my father? 'Tis not to be borne,
    Thus to be pent up like a felon here!
    What have I done of such a heinous stamp,
    To skulk and hide me like a murderer?
    I only laid my staff across the fingers
    Of the pert varlet, when before my eyes,
    By order of the governor, he tried
    To drive away my handsome team of oxen.
Furst. You are too rash by far. He did no more
    Than what the governor had ordered him.
    You had transgressed, and therefore should have
     paid
    The penalty, however hard, in silence.
Melch. Was I to brook the fellow's saucy words?
    " That if the peasant must have bread to eat,
    " Why, let him go and draw the plough him-
     self! "
    It cut me to the very soul to see
    My oxen, noble creatures, when the knave
    Unyoked them from the plough. As though
     they felt
    The wrong, they lowed and butted with their
     horns.
    On this I could contain myself no longer,
    And, overcome by passion, struck him down.
Furst. Oh, we old men can scarce command ourselves!
    And can we wonder youth shall break its bounds?
Melch. I'm only sorry for my father's sake!
    To be away from him, that needs so much
    My fostering care! The governor detests him,
    Because he hath, whene'er occasion served,
    Stood stoutly up for right and liberty.

Therefore they'll bear him hard — the poor old
    man!
And there is none to shield him from their
    gripe.
Come what come may, I must go home again.

FURST. Compose yourself, and wait in patience till
We get some tidings o'er from Unterwald.
Away! away! I hear a knock! Perhaps
A message from the viceroy! Get thee in!
You are not safe from Landenberger's * arm
In Uri, for these tyrants pull together.

MELCH. They teach us Switzers what we ought to do.

FURST. Away! I'll call you when the coast is clear.
                       [MELCHTHAL *retires.*

Unhappy youth! I dare not tell him all
The evil that my boding heart predicts!
Who's there? The door ne'er opens but I look
For tidings of mishap. Suspicion lurks
With darkling treachery in every nook.
Even to our inmost rooms they force their way,
These myrmidons of power; and soon we'll
    need
To fasten bolts and bars upon our doors.
    [*He opens the door and steps back in surprise
    as* WERNER STAUFFACHER *enters.*
What do I see? You, Werner? Now, by
    Heaven!
A valued guest, indeed. No man e'er set
His foot across this threshold more esteemed.
Welcome! thrice welcome, Werner, to my roof!
What brings you here? What seek you here
    in Uri?

STAUFF. (*shakes* FURST *by the hand*).
The olden times and olden Switzerland.

FURST. You bring them with you. See how I'm rejoiced,
My heart leaps at the very sight of you.
Sit down — sit down, and tell me how you left

---

* Berenger von Landenberg, a man of noble family in Thurgau, and governor of Unterwald, infamous for his cruelties to the Swiss, and particularly to the venerable Henry of the Halden. He was slain at the battle of Morgarten in 1315.

Your charming wife, fair Gertrude? Iberg's
    child,
And clever as her father. Not a man,
That wends from Germany, by Meinrad's Cell, *
To Italy, but praises far and wide
Your house's hospitality. But say,
Have you came here direct from Flüelen,
And have you noticed nothing on your way,
Before you halted at my door?

STAUFF. (*sits down*).   I saw
A work in progress, as I came along,
I little thought to see — that likes me ill.

FURST. O friend! you've lighted on my thought at once.

STAUFF. Such things in Uri ne'er were known before.
Never was prison here in man's remembrance,
Nor ever any stronghold but the grave.

FURST. You name it well. It is the grave of freedom.

STAUFF. Friend, Walter Furst, I will be plain with you.
No idle curiosity it is
That brings me here, but heavy cares. I left
Thraldom at home, and thraldom meets me here.
Our wrongs, e'en now, are more than we can
    bear.
And who shall tell us where they are to end?
From eldest time the Switzer has been free,
Accustomed only to the mildest rule.
Such things as now we suffer ne'er were known
Since herdsmen first drove cattle to the hills.

FURST. Yes, our oppressions are unparalleled !
Why, even our own good lord of Attinghaus,
Who lived in olden times, himself declares
They are no longer to be tamely borne.

STAUFF. In Unterwalden yonder 'tis the same ;
And bloody has the retribution been.
The imperial seneschal, the Wolfshot, who
At Rossberg dwelt, longed for forbidden fruit —
Baumgarten's wife, that lives at Alzellen,
He wished to overcome in shameful sort,
On which the husband slew him with his axe.

* A cell built in the ninth century by Meinrad, Count Hohenzollern, the
founder of the Convent of Einsiedeln, subsequently alluded to in the text.

FURST. Oh, Heaven is just in all its judgments still!
  Baumgarten, say you? A most worthy man.
  Has he escaped, and is he safely hid?

STAUFF. Your son-in-law conveyed him o'er the lake,
  And he lies hidden in my house at Steinen.
  He brought the tidings with him of a thing
  That has been done at Sarnen, worse than all,
  A thing to make the very heart run blood!

FURST (*attentively*).
  Say on. What is it?

STAUFF.   There dwells in Melchthal, then,
  Just as you enter by the road from Kearns,
  An upright man, named Henry of the Halden,
  A man of weight and influence in the Diet.

FURST. Who knows him not? But what of him?
  Proceed.

STAUFF. The Landenberg, to punish some offence,
  Committed by the old man's son, it seems,
  Had given command to take the youth's best
    pair
  Of oxen from his plough: on which the lad
  Struck down the messenger and took to flight.

FURST. But the old father — tell me, what of him?

STAUFF. The Landenberg sent for him, and required
  He should produce his son upon the spot;
  And when the old man protested, and with
    truth,
  That he knew nothing of the fugitive,
  The tyrant called his torturers.

FURST (*springs up and tries to lead him to the other side*).
        Hush, no more!

STAUFFACHER (*with increasing warmth*).
    " And though thy son," he cried, " Has escaped
    me now,
    I have thee fast, and thou shalt feel my
    vengeance."
  With that they flung the old man to the earth,
  And plunged the pointed steel into his eyes.

FURST. Merciful heavens!

MELCH. (*rushing out*).
      Into his eyes, his eyes?

STAUFF. (*addresses himself in astonishment to* WALTER
    FURST).
        Who is this youth ?
MELCH. (*grasping him convulsively*).
                Into his eyes ?   Speak, speak !
FURST. Oh, miserable hour !
STAUFF.   Who is it, tell me ?
            [STAUFFACHER *makes a sign to him.*
        It is his son ! All righteous heaven !
MELCH.   And I
        Must be from thence ! What ! into both his eyes ?
FURST. Be calm, be calm ; and bear it like a man !
MELCH. And all for me — for my mad wilful folly !
        Blind, did you say ?   Quite blind — and both his
            eyes ?
STAUFF. Even so.   The fountain of his sight's dried up.
        He ne'er will see the blessed sunshine more.
FURST. Oh, spare his anguish !
MELCH.   Never, never more !
        [*Presses his hands upon his eyes and is silent
            for some moments ; then turning from one
            to the other, speaks in a subdued tone, broken
            by sobs.*
        O the eye's light, of all the gifts of heaven,
        The dearest, best ! From light all beings live —
        Each fair created thing — the very plants
        Turn with a joyful transport to the light,
        And he — he must drag on through all his days
        In endless darkness !   Never more for him
        The sunny meads shall glow, the flowerets
            bloom ;
        Nor shall he more behold the roseate tints
        Of the iced mountain top !   To die is nothing,
        But to have life, and not have sight — oh, that
        Is misery indeed !   Why do you look
        So piteously at me ?   I have two eyes,
        Yet to my poor blind father can give neither !
        No, not one gleam of that great sea of light,
        That with its dazzling splendor floods my gaze.
STAUFF. Ah, I must swell the measure of your grief,
        Instead of soothing it.   The worst, alas !

Remains to tell. They've stripped him of his all ;
Naught have they left him, save his staff, on which,
Blind and in rags, he moves from door to door.

MELCH. Naught but his staff to the old eyeless man !
Stripped of his all — even of the light of day,
The common blessing of the meanest wretch.
Tell me no more of patience, of concealment !
Oh, what a base and coward thing am I,
That on mine own security I thought
And took no care of thine ! Thy precious head
Left as a pledge within the tyrant's grasp !
Hence, craven-hearted prudence, hence ! And all
My thoughts be vengeance, and the despot's blood !   [now —
I'll seek him straight — no power shall stay me
And at his hands demand my father's eyes.
I'll beard him 'mid a thousand myrmidons !
What's life to me, if in his heart's best blood
I cool the fever of this mighty anguish.
                                    [*He is going.*

FURST. Stay, this is madness, Melchthal !   What avails
Your single arm against his power ?   He sits
At Sarnen high within his lordly keep,
And, safe within its battlemented walls,
May laugh to scorn your unavailing rage.

MELCH. And though he sat within the icy domes
Of yon far Schreckhorn — ay, or higher, where
Veiled since eternity, the Jungfrau soars,
Still to the tyrant would I make my way ;
With twenty comrades minded like myself,
I'd lay his fastness level with the earth !
And if none follow me, and if you all,
In terror for your homesteads and your herds,
Bow in submission to the tyrant's yoke,
I'll call the herdsmen on the hills around me,
And there beneath heaven's free and boundless roof,
Where men still feel as men, and hearts are true
Proclaim aloud this foul enormity !

STAUFF. (*to* FURST).
    'Tis at its height — and are we then to wait
    Till some extremity ——
MELCHTHAL.   What extremity
    Remains for apprehension, where men's eyes
    Have ceased to be secure within their sockets?
    Are we defenceless? Wherefore did we learn
    To bend the crossbow — wield the battle-axe?
    What living creature, but in its despair,
    Finds for itself a weapon of defence?
    The baited stag will turn, and with the show
    Of his dread antlers hold the hounds at bay;
    The chamois drags the huntsman down the
        abyss; •
    The very ox, the partner of man's toil,
    The sharer of his roof, that meekly bends
    The strength of his huge neck beneath the yoke,
    Springs up, if he's provoked, whets his strong
        horn,
 •   And tosses his tormenter to the clouds.
FURST.   If the three Cantons thought as we three do,
    Something might, then, be done, with good effect.

STAUFF. When Uri calls, when Unterwald replies,
    Schwytz will be mindful of her ancient league.*

---

* The League, or Bond, of the Three Cantons was of very ancient origin. They met and renewed it from time to time, especially when their liberties were threatened with danger. A remarkable instance of this occurred in the end of the thirteenth century, when Albert of Austria became emperor, and when, possibly, for the first time, the bond was reduced to writing. As it is important to the understanding of many passages of the play, a translation is subjoined of the oldest known document relating to it. The original, which is in Latin and German, is dated in August, 1291, and is under the seals of the whole of the men of Schwytz, the commonalty of the vale of Uri, and the whole of the men of the upper and lower vales of Stanz.

THE BOND.

Be it known to every one, that the men of the Dale of Uri, the Community of Schwytz, as also the men of the mountains of Unterwald, in consideration of the evil times, have full confidently bound themselves, and sworn to help each other with all their power and might, property and people, against all who shall do violence to them, or any of them. That is our Ancient Bond.

Whoever hath a Seignior, let him obey according to the conditions of his service.

We are agreed to receive into these dales no Judge who is not a countryman and indweller, or who hath bought his place.

Every controversy amongst the sworn confederates shall be determined

MELCH. I've many friends in Unterwald, and none
        That would not gladly venture life and limb
        If fairly backed and aided by the rest.
        Oh, sage and reverend fathers of this land,
        Here do I stand before your riper years,
        An unskilled youth whose voice must in the Diet
        Still be subdued into respectful silence.
        Do not, because that I am young and want
        Experience, slight my counsel and my words.
        'Tis not the wantonness of youthful blood
        That fires my spirit; but a pang so deep
        That even the flinty rocks must pity me.
        You, too, are fathers, heads of families,
        And you must wish to have a virtuous son
        To reverence your gray hairs and shield your eyes
        With pious and affectionate regard.
        Do not, I pray, because in limb and fortune
        You still are unassailed, and still your eyes
        Revolve undimmed and sparkling in their
                spheres;
        Oh, do not, therefore, disregard our wrongs!
        Above you, too, doth hang the tyrant's sword.
        You, too, have striven to alienate the land
        From Austria. This was all my father's crime:
        You share his guilt and may his punishment.
STAUFFACHER (to FURST).
        Do thou resolve! I am prepared to follow.
FURST.   First let us learn what steps the noble lords
        Von Sillinen and Attinghaus propose.
        Their names would rally thousands in the cause.
MELCH. Is there a name within the Forest Mountains

by some of the sagest of their number, and if any one shall challenge their
judgment, then shall he be constrained to obey it by the rest.
     Whoever intentionally or deceitfully kills another shall be executed, and
whoever shelters him shall be banished.
     Whoever burns the property of another shall no longer be regarded as a
countryman, and whoever shelters him shall make good the damage done.
     Whoever injures another, or robs him, and hath property in our country,
shall make satisfaction out of the same.
     No one shall distrain a debtor without a judge, nor any one who is not his
debtor, or the surety for such debtor.
     Every one in these dales shall submit to the judge, or we, the sworn con-
federates, all will take satisfaction for all the injury occasioned by his con-
tumacy. And if in any internal division the one party will not accept
justice, all the rest shall help the other party. These decrees shall, God
willing, endure eternally for our general advantage.

That carries more respect than thine — and
    thine?
To names like these the people cling for help
With confidence — such names are household
    words.
Rich was your heritage of manly virtue,
And richly have you added to its stores.
What need of nobles? Let us do the work
Ourselves. Although we stood alone, methinks
We should be able to maintain our rights.

STAUFF. The nobles' wrongs are not so great as ours.
The torrent that lays waste the lower grounds
Hath not ascended to the uplands yet.
But let them see the country once in arms
They'll not refuse to lend a helping hand.

FURST. Were there an umpire 'twixt ourselves and
    Austria,
Justice and law might then decide our quarrel.
But our oppressor is our emperor, too,
And judge supreme. 'Tis God must help us,
    then,
And our own arm! Be yours the task to rouse
The men of Schwytz; I'll rally friends in Uri.
But whom are we to send to Unterwald?

MELCH. Thither send me. Whom should it more
    concern?

FURST. No, Melchthal, no; thou art my guest, and I
Must answer for thy safety.

MELCHTHAL.   Let me go.
I know each forest track and mountain pass;
Friends too I'll find, be sure, on every hand,
To give me willing shelter from the foe.

STAUFF. Nay, let him go; no traitors harbor there:
For tyranny is so abhorred in Unterwald
No minions can be found to work her will.
In the low valleys, too, the Alzeller
Will gain confederates and rouse the country.

MELCH. But how shall we communicate, and not
Awaken the suspicion of the tyrants?

STAUFF. Might we not meet at Brunnen or at Treib,
Hard by the spot where merchant-vessels land?

FURST.   We must not go so openly to work.
            Hear my opinion.   On the lake's left bank,
            As we sail hence to Brunnen, right against
            The Mytenstein, deep-hidden in the wood
            A meadow lies, by shepherds called the Rootli,
            Because the wood has been uprooted there.
            'Tis where our Canton boundaries verge on
                yours ; —   [*To* MELCHTHAL.
            Your boat will carry you across from Schwytz.
                                        [*To* STAUFFACHER.
            Thither by lonely by-paths let us wend
            At midnight and deliberate o'er our plans.
            Let each bring with him there ten trusty men,
            All one at heart with us; and then we may
            Consult together for the general weal,
            And, with God's guidance, fix our onward
                course.

STAUFF. So let it be.   And now your true right hand !
            Yours, too, young man ! and as we now three
                men
            Among ourselves thus knit our hands together
            In all sincerity and truth, e'en so
            Shall we three Cantons, too, together stand
            In victory and defeat, in life and death.

FURST *and* MELCHTHAL.
            In life and death.
                    [*They hold their hands clasped together for
                    some moments in silence.*

MELCHTHAL.   Alas, my old blind father !
            Thou canst no more behold the day of freedom ;
            But thou shalt hear it.   When from Alp to Alp
            The beacon-fires throw up their flaming signs,
            And the proud castles of the tyrants fall,
            Into thy cottage shall the Switzer burst,
            Bear the glad tidings to thine ear, and o'er
            Thy darkened way shall Freedom's radiance
                pour.

ACT II.

Scene I.

The Mansion of the BARON OF ATTINGHAUSEN. *A Gothic hall, decorated with escutcheons and helmets. The* BARON, *a gray-headed man, eighty-five years old, tall, and of a commanding mien, clad in a furred pelisse, and leaning on a staff tipped with chamois horn.* KUONI *and six hinds standing round him, with rakes and scythes.* ULRICH OF RUDENZ *enters in the costume of a knight.*

RUD. Uncle, I'm here! Your will?

ATTINGHAUSEN.   First let me share,
        After the ancient custom of our house,
        The morning-cup with these my faithful ser-
              vants!
            [*He drinks from a cup, which is then passed
              round.*
        Time was I stood myself in field and wood,
        With mine own eyes directing all their toil,
        Even as my banner led them in the fight,
        Now I am only fit to play the steward;
        And, if the genial sun come not to me,
        I can no longer seek it on the mountains.
        Thus slowly, in an ever-narrowing sphere,
        I move on to the narrowest and the last,
        Where all life's pulses cease. I now am but
        The shadow of my former self, and that
        Is fading fast — 'twill soon be but a name.

KUONI (*offering* RUDENZ *the cup*).
        A pledge, young master!
                    [RUDENZ *hesitates to take the cup.*
                    Nay, sir, drink it off!
        One cup, one heart! You know our proverb, sir!

ATTING. Go, children, and at eve, when work is done,
        We'll meet and talk the country's business over.
                        [*Exeunt Servants.*
        Belted and plumed, and all thy bravery on!
        Thou art for Altdorf — for the castle, boy?

RUD. Yes, uncle. Longer may I not delay ——

ATTINGHAUSEN (*sitting down*).
        Why in such haste? Say, are thy youthful hours

Doled in such niggard measure that thou must
Be chary of them to thy aged uncle?

RUD.   I see, my presence is not needed here,
I am but as a stranger in this house.

ATTINGHAUSEN (*gazes fixedly at him for a considerable
time*).
Alas, thou art indeed! Alas, that home
To thee has grown so strange! Oh, Uly! Uly!
I scarce do know thee now, thus decked in
silks,
The peacock's feather* flaunting in thy cap,
And purple mantle round thy shoulders flung;
Thou lookest upon the peasant with disdain,
And takest with a blush his honest greeting.

RUD.   All honor due to him I gladly pay,
But must deny the right he would usurp.

ATTING.   The sore displeasure of the king is resting
Upon the land, and every true man's heart
Is full of sadness for the grievous wrongs
We suffer from our tyrants. Thou alone
Art all unmoved amid the general grief.
Abandoning thy friends, thou takest thy stand
Beside thy country's foes, and, as in scorn
Of our distress, pursuest giddy joys,
Courting the smiles of princes, all the while
Thy country bleeds beneath their cruel scourge.

RUD.   The land is sore oppressed; I know it, uncle.
But why? Who plunged it into this distress?
A word, one little easy word, might buy
Instant deliverance from such dire oppression,
And win the good-will of the emperor.
Woe unto those who seal the people's eyes,
And make them adverse to their country's good;
The men who, for their own vile, selfish ends,
Are seeking to prevent the Forest States
From swearing fealty to Austria's house,
As all the countries round about have done.
It fits their humor well, to take their seats

---

* The Austrian knights were in the habit of wearing a plume of peacocks'
feathers in their helmets. After the overthrow of the Austrian dominion in
Switzerland it was made highly penal to wear the peacock's feather at any
public assembly there.

Amid the nobles on the Herrenbank ; *
They'll have the Cæsar for their lord, forsooth,
That is to say, they'll have no lord at all.

ATTING. Must I hear this, and from thy lips, rash boy!

RUD. You urged me to this answer. Hear me out.
What, uncle, is the character you've stooped
To fill contentedly through life? Have you
No higher pride, than in these lonely wilds
To be the Landamman or Banneret,†
The petty chieftain of a shepherd race?
How! Were it not a far more glorious choice
To bend in homage to our royal lord,
And swell the princely splendors of his court,
Than sit at home, the peer of your own vassals,
And share the judgment-seat with vulgar clowns?

ATTING. Ah, Uly, Uly; all too well I see,
The tempter's voice has caught thy willing ear,
And poured its subtle poison in thy heart.

RUD. Yes, I conceal it not. It doth offend
My inmost soul to hear the stranger's gibes,
That taunt us with the name of "Peasant Nobles."
Think you the heart that's stirring here can brook,
While all the young nobility around
Are reaping honor under Hapsburg's banner,
That I should loiter, in inglorious ease,
Here on the heritage my fathers left,
And, in the dull routine of vulgar toil,
Lose all life's glorious spring? In other lands
Deeds are achieved. A world of fair renown
Beyond these mountains stirs in martial pomp.
My helm and shield are rusting in the hall;
The martial trumpet's spirit-stirring blast,
The herald's call, inviting to the lists,
Rouse not the echoes of these vales, where naught
Save cowherd's horn and cattle-bell is heard,
In one unvarying, dull monotony.

ATTING. Deluded boy, seduced by empty show!
Despise the land that gave thee birth! Ashamed

---

* The bench reserved for the nobility.
† The Landamman was an officer chosen by the Swiss Gemeinde, or Diet,
to preside over them. The Banneret was an officer intrusted with the keeping of the state banner, and such others as were taken in battle.

Of the good ancient customs of thy sires!
The day will come, when thou, with burning
    tears,
Wilt long for home, and for thy native hills,
And that dear melody of tuneful herds,
Which now, in proud disgust, thou dost despise!
A day when thou wilt drink its tones in sadness,
Hearing their music in a foreign land.
Oh! potent is the spell that binds to home!
No, no, the cold, false world is not for thee.
At the proud court, with thy true heart thou wilt
Forever feel a stranger among strangers.
The world asks virtues of far other stamp
Than thou hast learned within these simple vales.
But go — go thither; barter thy free soul,
Take land in fief, become a prince's vassal,
Where thou might'st be lord paramount, and prince
    prince
Of all thine own unburdened heritage!
O, Uly, Uly, stay among thy people!
Go not to Altdorf. Oh, abandon not
The sacred cause of thy wronged native land!
I am the last of all my race. My name
Ends with me. Yonder hang my helm and
    shield;
They will be buried with me in the grave.*
And must I think, when yielding up my breath,
That thou but wait'st the closing of mine eyes,
To stoop thy knee to this new feudal court,
And take in vassalage from Austria's hands
The noble lands, which I from God received
Free and unfettered as the mountain air!

RUD.   'Tis vain for us to strive against the king.
The world pertains to him: — shall we alone,
In mad, presumptuous obstinacy strive
To break that mighty chain of lands, which he
Hath drawn around us with his giant grasp.
His are the markets, his the courts; his too
The highways; nay, the very carrier's horse,

* According to the custom by which, when the last male descendant of a
noble family died, his sword, helmet, and shield were buried with him.

That traffics on the Gotthardt, pays him toll.
By his dominions, as within a net,
We are enclosed, and girded round about.
— And will the empire shield us? Say, can it
Protect itself 'gainst Austria's growing power?
To God, and not to emperors, must we look!
What store can on their promises be placed,
When they, to meet their own necessities,
Can pawn, and even alienate the towns
That flee for shelter 'neath the eagle's wings?*
No, uncle. It is wise and wholesome prudence,
In times like these, when faction's all abroad,
To own attachment to some mighty chief.
The imperial crown's transferred from line to
line,†
It has no memory for faithful service:
But to secure the favor of these great
Hereditary masters, were to sow
Seed for a future harvest.

ATTINGHAUSEN. Art so wise?
Wilt thou see clearer than thy noble sires,
Who battled for fair freedom's costly gem,
With life, and fortune, and heroic arm?
Sail down the lake to Lucerne, there inquire,
How Austria's rule doth weigh the Cantons down.
Soon she will come to count our sheep, our cattle,
To portion out the Alps, e'en to their summits,
And in our own free woods to hinder us
From striking down the eagle or the stag;
To set her tolls on every bridge and gate,
Impoverish us to swell her lust of sway,
And drain our dearest blood to feed her wars.
No, if our blood must flow, let it be shed
In our own cause! We purchase liberty
More cheaply far than bondage.

RUDENZ. What can we,
A shepherd race, against great Albert's hosts?

---

* This frequently occurred. But in the event of an imperial city being mortgaged for the purpose of raising money it lost its freedom, and was considered as put out of the realm.
† An allusion to the circumstance of the imperial crown not being hereditary, but conferred by election on one of the counts of the empire.

ATTING. Learn, foolish boy, to know this shepherd race!
    I know them, I have led them on in fight —
    I saw them in the battle at Favenz.
    Austria will try, forsooth, to force on us
    A yoke we are determined not to bear!
    Oh, learn to feel from what a race thou'rt sprung!
    Cast not, for tinsel trash and idle show,
    The precious jewel of thy worth away.
    To be the chieftain of a freeborn race,
    Bound to thee only by their unbought love,
    Ready to stand — to fight — to die with thee,
    Be that thy pride, be that thy noblest boast!
    Knit to thy heart the ties of kindred — home —
    Cling to the land, the dear land of thy sires,
    Grapple to that with thy whole heart and soul!
    Thy power is rooted deep and strongly here,
    But in yon stranger world thou'lt stand alone,
    A trembling reed beat down by every blast.
    Oh come! 'tis long since we have seen thee, Uly!
    Tarry but this one day. Only to-day
    Go not to Altdorf. Wilt thou? Not to-day!
    For this one day bestow thee on thy friends.
                        [*Takes his hand.*
RUD. I gave my word. Unhand me! I am bound.
ATTING. (*drops his hand and says sternly*).
    Bound, didst thou say? Oh yes, unhappy boy,
    Thou art, indeed. But not by word or oath.
    Tis by the silken mesh of love thou'rt bound.
                    [RUDENZ *turns away.*
    Ay, hide thee, as thou wilt. 'Tis she, I know,
    Bertha of Bruneck, draws thee to the court;
    'Tis she that chains thee to the emperor's service.
    Thou think'st to win the noble, knightly maid,
    By thy apostacy. Be not deceived.
    She is held out before thee as a lure;
    But never meant for innocence like thine.
RUD. No more; I've heard enough. So fare you well.
                              [*Exit.*
ATTING. Stay, Uly! Stay! Rash boy, he's gone! I can
    Nor hold him back, nor save him from de-
       struction.

And so the Wolfshot has deserted us; —
Others will follow his example soon.
This foreign witchery, sweeping o'er our hills,
Tears with its potent spell our youth away:
O luckless hour, when men and manners strange
Into these calm and happy valleys came,
To warp our primitive and guileless ways.
The new is pressing on with might. The old,
The good, the simple, fleeteth fast away.
New times come on. A race is springing up,
That think not as their fathers thought before!
What do I here? All, all are in the grave
With whom erewhile I moved and held converse;
My age has long been laid beneath the sod:
Happy the man who may not live to see
What shall be done by those that follow me!

Scene II.

A meadow surrounded by high rocks and wooded ground. On the rocks are tracks, with rails and ladders, by which the peasants are afterwards seen descending. In the background the lake is observed, and over it a moon rainbow in the early part of the scene. The prospect is closed by lofty mountains, with glaciers rising behind them. The stage is dark, but the lake and glaciers glisten in the moonlight.

Melchthal, Baumgarten, Winkelried, Meyer von Sarnen, Burkhart am Buhel, Arnold von Sewa, Klaus von der Flue, *and four other peasants, all armed.*

Melchthal (*behind the scenes*).
   The mountain pass is open. Follow me
   I see the rock, and little cross upon it:
   This is the spot; here is the Rootli.
        [*They enter with torches.*
Winkelried.   Hark!
Sewa. The coast is clear.
Meyer.   None of our comrades come?
   We are the first, we Unterwaldeners.
Melch. How far is't in the night?

BAUM.   The beacon watch
Upon the Selisberg has just called two.
                [*A bell is heard at a distance.*

MEYER. Hush! Hark!

BUHEL.   The forest chapel's matin bell
Chimes clearly o'er the lake from Switzerland.

VON F. The air is clear, and bears the sound so far.

MELCH. Go, you and you, and light some broken boughs,
Let's bid them welcome with a cheerful blaze.
                [*Two peasants exeunt.*

SEWA. The moon shines fair to-night. Beneath its
        beams
The lake reposes, bright as burnished steel.

BUHEL. They'll have an easy passage.

WINK. (*pointing to the lake*).   Ha! look there!
See you nothing?

MEYER.   What is it? Ay, indeed!
A rainbow in the middle of the night.

MELCH. Formed by the bright reflection of the moon!

VON F. A sign most strange and wonderful, indeed!
Many there be who ne'er have seen the like.

SEWA. 'Tis doubled, see, a paler one above!

BAUM. A boat is gliding yonder right beneath it.

MELCH. That must be Werner Stauffacher! I knew
The worthy patriot would not tarry long.
        [*Goes with* BAUMGARTEN *towards the shore.*

MEYER. The Uri men are like to be the last.

BUHEL. They're forced to take a winding circuit through
The mountains; for the viceroy's spies are out.
        [*In the meanwhile the two peasants have
          kindled a fire in the centre of the stage.*

MELCH. (*on the shore*).
     Who's there? The word?

STAUFF. (*from below*).   Friends of the country.
        [*All retire up the stage, towards the party
          landing from the boat. Enter* STAUFF-
          ACHER, ITEL, REDING, HANS AUF DER
          MAUER, JORG IM HOFE, CONRAD HUNN,
          ULRICH DER SCHMIDT, JOST VON WEILER,
          and three other peasants, armed.

ALL.   Welcome!

[*While the rest remain behind exchanging greetings,* MELCHTHAL *comes forward with* STAUFFACHER.

MELCH. Oh, worthy Stauffacher, I've looked but now
On him, who could not look on me again.
I've laid my hands upon his rayless eyes,
And on their vacant orbits sworn a vow
Of vengeance, only to be cooled in blood.

STAUFF. Speak not of vengeance. We are here to meet
The threatened evil, not to avenge the past.
Now tell me what you've done, and what secured,
To aid the common cause in Unterwald.
How stands the peasantry disposed, and how
Yourself escaped the wiles of treachery?

MELCH. Through the Surenen's fearful mountain chain,
Where dreary ice-fields stretch on every side,
And sound is none, save the hoarse vulture's cry,
I reached the Alpine pasture, where the herds
From Uri and from Engelberg resort,
And turn their cattle forth to graze in common.
Still as I went along, I slaked my thirst
With the coarse oozings of the lofty glacier,
That through the crevices come foaming down,
And turned to rest me in the herdsman's cots,*
Where I was host and guest, until I gained
The cheerful homes and social haunts of men.
Already through these distant vales had spread
The rumor of this last atrocity ;
And wheresoe'er I went, at every door,
Kind words and gentle looks were there to
     greet me.
I found these simple spirits all in arms
Against our rulers' tyrannous encroachments.
For as their Alps through each succeeding year
Yield the same roots, — their streams flow
     ever on
In the same channels, — nay, the clouds and winds

---

* These are the cots, or shealings, erected by the herdsmen for shelter while pasturing their herds on the mountains during the summer. These are left deserted in winter, during which period Melchthal's journey was taken.

The selfsame course unalterably pursue,
So have old customs there, from sire to son,
Been handed down, unchanging and unchanged ;
Nor will they brook to swerve or turn aside
From the fixed, even tenor of their life.
With grasp of their hard hands they welcomed
      me —
Took from the walls their rusty falchions down —
And from their eyes the soul of valor flashed
With joyful lustre, as I spoke those names,
Sacred to every peasant in the mountains,
Your own and Walter Fürst's.   Whate'er your
      voice
Should dictate as the right they swore to do ;
And you they swore to follow e'en to death.
So sped I on from house to house, secure
In the guest's sacred privilege — and when
I reached at last the valley of my home,
Where dwell my kinsmen, scattered far and
      near —
And when I found my father stripped and blind,
Upon the stranger's straw, fed by the alms
Of charity——

STAUFFACHER.   Great heaven !
MELCHTHAL.   Yet wept I not !
No — not in weak and unavailing tears
Spent I the force of my fierce, burning anguish;
Deep in my bosom, like some precious treasure,
I locked it fast, and thought on deeds alone.
Through every winding of the hills I crept —
No valley so remote but I explored it;
Nay, even at the glacier's ice-clad base,
I sought and found the homes of living men ;
And still, where'er my wandering footsteps
      turned,
The self-same hatred of these tyrants met me.
For even there, at vegetation's verge,
Where the numbed earth is barren of all fruits,
There grasping hands had been stretched forth
      for plunder.
Into the hearts of all this honest race.

The story of my wrongs struck deep, and now
They to a man are ours ; both heart and hand.

STAUFF. Great things, indeed, you've wrought in little
time.

MELCH. I did still more than this. The fortresses,
Rossberg and Sarnen, are the country's dread ;
For from behind their rocky walls the foe
Swoops, as the eagle from his eyrie, down,
And, safe himself, spreads havoc o'er the land.
With my own eyes I wished to weigh its
strength,
So went to Sarnen, and explored the castle.

STAUFF. How ! Risk thyself even in the tiger's den ?

MELCH. Disguised in pilgrim's weeds I entered it ;
I saw the viceroy feasting at his board —
Judge if I'm master of myself or no !
I saw the tyrant, and I slew him not !

STAUFF. Fortune, indeed, has smiled upon your boldness.
[*Meanwhile the others have arrived and join*
MELCHTHAL *and* STAUFFACHER.
Yet tell me now, I pray, who are the friends,
The worthy men, who came along with you?
Make me acquainted with them, that we may
Speak frankly, man to man, and heart to heart.

MEYER. In the three Cantons, who, sir, knows not you?
Meyer of Sarnen is my name ; and this
Is Struth of Winkelried, my sister's son.

STAUFF. No unknown name. A Winkelried it was
Who slew the dragoon in the fen at Weiler,
And lost his life in the encounter, too.

WINK. That, Master Stauffacher, was my grandfather.

MELCH. (*pointing to two peasants*).
These two are men belonging to the convent
Of Engelberg, and live behind the forest.
You'll not think ill of them, because they're
serfs,
And sit not free upon the soil, like us.
They love the land, and bear a good repute.

STAUFFACHER (*to them*).
Give me your hands. He has good cause for
thanks.

That unto no man owes his body's service.
But worth is worth, no matter where 'tis found.
HUNN.   That is Herr Reding, sir, our old Landamman.
MEYER.   I know him well.   There is a suit between us,
About a piece of ancient heritage.
Herr Reding, we are enemies in court,
Here we are one.   *[Shakes his hand.*
STAUFFACHER.   That's well and bravely said.
WINK.   Listen! They come.   Hark to the horn of Uri!
          *[On the right and left armed men are seen
          descending the rocks with torches.*
MAUER.   Look, is not that God's pious servant there?
A worthy priest!   The terrors of the night,
And the way's pains and perils scare not him,
A faithful shepherd caring for his flock.
BAUM.   The Sacrist follows him, and Walter Fürst.
But where is Tell?   I do not see him there.
          *[WALTER FURST, ROSSELMANN the Pastor,
          PETERMANN the Sacrist, KUONI the Shep-
          herd, WERNI the Huntsman, RUODI the
          Fisherman, and five other countrymen,
          thirty-three in all, advance and take their
          places round the fire.*
FURST.   Thus must we, on the soil our fathers left us,
Creep forth by stealth to meet like murderers,
And in the night, that should their mantle lend
Only to crime and black conspiracy,
Assert our own good rights, which yet are clear
As is the radiance of the noonday sun.
MELCH.   So be it.   What is woven in gloom of night
Shall free and boldly meet the morning light.
ROSSEL.   Confederates! listen to the words which God
Inspires my heart withal.   Here we are met
To represent the general weal.   In us
Are all the people of the land convened.
Then let us hold the Diet, as of old,
And as we're wont in peaceful times to do.
The time's necessity be our excuse
If there be aught informal in this meeting.
Still, wheresoe'er men strike for justice, there
Is God, and now beneath his heaven we stand.

STAUFF. 'Tis well advised. Let us, then, hold the Diet
According to our ancient usages.
Though it be night there's sunshine in our cause.

MELCH. Few though our numbers be, the hearts are here
Of the whole people; here the best are met.

HUNN. The ancient books may not be near at hand,
Yet are they graven in our inmost hearts.

ROSSEL. 'Tis well. And now, then, let a ring be formed,
And plant the swords of power within the
ground.*

MAUER. Let the Landamman step into his place,
And by his side his secretaries stand.

SACRIST. There are three Cantons here. Which hath the
right
To give the head to the united council?
Schwytz may contest the dignity with Uri,
We Unterwaldeners enter not the field.

MELCH. We stand aside. We are not suppliants here,
Invoking aid from our more potent friends.

STAUFF. Let Uri have the sword. Her banner takes
In battle the precedence of our own.

FURST. Schwytz, then, must share the honor of the
sword;
For she's the honored ancestor of all.

ROSSEL. Let me arrange this generous controversy.
Uri shall lead in battle — Schwytz in council.

FURST (*gives* STAUFFACHER *his hand*).
Then take your place.

STAUFFACHER. Not I. Some older man.

HOFE. Ulrich, the smith, is the most aged here.

MAUER. A worthy man, but he is not a freeman;
No bondman can be judge in Switzerland.

STAUFF. Is not Herr Reding here, our old Landamman?
Where can we find a worthier man than he?

FURST. Let him be Amman and the Diet's chief?
You that agree with me hold up your hands!
[*All hold up their right hands.*

REDING (*stepping into the centre*).
I cannot lay my hands upon the books;

* It was the custom at the meetings of the Landes Gemeinde, or Diet, to set swords upright in the ground as emblems of authority.

But by yon everlasting stars I swear
Never to swerve from justice and the right.
[*The two swords are placed before him, and a*
    circle formed; Schwytz in the centre, Uri
    on his right, Unterwald on his left.

REDING (*resting on his battle-sword*).
Why, at the hour when spirits walk the earth,
Meet the three Cantons of the mountains here,
Upon the lake's inhospitable shore?
And what the purport of the new alliance
We here contract beneath the starry heaven?

STAUFFACHER (*entering the circle*).
No new alliance do we now contract,
But one our fathers framed, in ancient times,
We purpose to renew! For know, confederates,
Though mountain ridge and lake divide our
    bounds,
And every Canton's ruled by its own laws,
Yet are we but one race, born of one blood,
And all are children of one common home.

WINK. Then is the burden of our legends true,
That we came hither from a distant land?
Oh, tell us what you know, that our new league
May reap fresh vigor from the leagues of old.

STAUFF. Hear, then, what aged herdsmen tell. There
    dwelt
A mighty people in the land that lies
Back to the north. The scourge of famine came;
And in this strait 'twas publicly resolved,
That each tenth man, on whom the lot might fall
Should leave the country. They obeyed — and
    forth,
With loud lamentings, men and women went,
A mighty host; and to the south moved on,
Cutting their way through Germany by the
    sword,
Until they gained that pine-clad hills of ours;
Nor stopped they ever on their forward course,
Till at the shaggy dell they halted, where
The Müta flows through its luxuriant meads.
No trace of human creature met their eye,

Save one poor hut upon the desert shore,
Where dwelt a lonely man, and kept the ferry.
A tempest raged — the lake rose mountains high
And barred their further progress. Thereupon
They viewed the country; found it rich in wood,
Discovered goodly springs, and felt as they
Were in their own dear native land once more.
Then they resolved to settle on the spot;
Erected there the ancient town of Schwytz;
And many a day of toil had they to clear
The tangled brake and forest's spreading roots.
Meanwhile their numbers grew, the soil became
Unequal to sustain them, and they crossed
To the black mountain, far as Weissland, where,
Concealed behind eternal walls of ice,
Another people speak another tongue.
They built the village Stanz, beside the Kern-
        wald :
The village Altdorf, in the vale of Reuss ;
Yet, ever mindful of their parent stem,
The men of Schwytz, from all the stranger race,
That since that time have settled in the land,
Each other recognize.   Their hearts still know,
And beat fraternally to kindred blood.
            [*Extends his hand right and left.*
MAUER. Ay, we are all one heart, one blood, one race !
ALL (*joining hands*).
        We are one people, and will act as one.
STAUFF. The nations round us bear a foreign yoke ;
For they have yielded to the conqueror.
Nay, even within our frontiers may be found
Some that owe villein service to a lord,
A race of bonded serfs from sire to son.
But we, the genuine race of ancient Swiss,
Have kept our freedom from the first till now,
Never to princes have we bowed the knee ;
Freely we sought protection of the empire.
ROSSEL. Freely we sought it — freely it was given.
'Tis so set down in Emperor Frederick's charter.
STAUFF. For the most free have still some feudal lord.
There must be still a chief, a judge supreme,

To whom appeal may lie in case of strife.
And therefore was it that our sires allowed
For what they had recovered from the waste,
This honor to the emperor, the lord
Of all the German and Italian soil;
And, like the other freemen of his realm,
Engaged to aid him with their swords in war;
And this alone should be the freeman's duty,
To guard the empire that keeps guard for him.

MELCH. He's but a slave that would acknowledge more.

STAUFF. They followed, when the Heribann * went forth,
The imperial standard, and they fought its
    battles!
To Italy they marched in arms, to place
The Cæsars' crown upon the emperor's head.
But still at home they ruled themselves in peace,
By their own laws and ancient usages.
The emperor's only right was to adjudge
The penalty of death; he therefore named
Some mighty noble as his delegate,
That had no stake or interest in the land.
He was called in, when doom was to be passed,
And, in the face of day, pronounced decree,
Clear and distinctly, fearing no man's hate.
What traces here, that we are bondsmen?
    Speak,
If there be any can gainsay my words!

HOFE. No! You have spoken but the simple truth;
We never stooped beneath a tyrant's yoke.

STAUFF. Even to the emperor we refused obedience,
When he gave judgment in the church's favor;
For when the Abbey of Einsiedlen claimed
The Alp our fathers and ourselves had grazed,
And showed an ancient charter, which bestowed
The land on them as being ownerless —
For our existence there had been concealed —
What was our answer? This: "The grant is
    void,
No emperor can bestow what is our own:

---

* The Heribann was a muster of warriors similar to the *arrière ban*
in France.

And if the empire shall deny us justice,
We can, within our mountains, right ourselves! "
Thus spake our fathers! And shall we endure
The shame and infamy of this new yoke,
And from the vassal brook what never king
Dared in the fulness of his power attempt?
This soil we have created for ourselves,
By the hard labor of our hands; we've changed
The giant forest, that was erst the haunt
Of savage bears, into a home for man;
Extirpated the dragon's brood, that wont
To rise, distent with venom, from the swamps;
Rent the thick misty canopy that hung
Its blighting vapors on the dreary waste;
Blasted the solid rock; o'er the abyss
Thrown the firm bridge for the wayfaring man :
By the possession of a thousand years
The soil is ours. And shall an alien lord,
Himself a vassal, dare to venture here,
On our own hearths insult us, — and attempt
To forge the chains of bondage for our hands,
And do us shame on our own proper soil?
Is there no help against such wrong as this?
       [*Great sensation among the people.*
Yes! there's a limit to the despot's power!
When the oppressed looks round in vain for
    justice,
When his sore burden may no more be borne,
With fearless heart he makes appeal to Heaven,
And thence brings down his everlasting rights,
Which there abide, inalienably his,
And indestructible as are the stars.
Nature's primeval state returns again,
Where man stands hostile to his fellow-man;
And if all other means shall fail his need,
One last resource remains — his own good sword.
Our dearest treasures call to us for aid
Against the oppressor's violence; we stand
For country, home, for wives, for children here!
ALL (*clashing their swords*).
    Here stand we for our homes, our wives, and
    children.

ROSSELMANN (*stepping into the circle*).
   Bethink ye well before ye draw the sword.
   Some peaceful compromise may yet be made;
   Speak but one word, and at your feet you'll
    see
   The men who now oppress you. Take the terms
   That have been often tendered you; renounce
   The empire, and to Austria swear allegiance!
MAUER. What says the priest? To Austria allegiance?
BUHEL. Hearken not to him!
WINKELRIED.   'Tis a traitor's counsel,
   His country's foe!
REDING.   Peace, peace, confederates!
SERVA. Homage to Austria, after wrongs like these!
FLUE. Shall Austria exort from us by force
   What we denied to kindness and entreaty?
MEYER. Then should we all be slaves, deservedly.
MAUER. Yes! Let him forfeit all a Switzer's rights
   Who talks of yielding to the yoke of Austria!
   I stand on this, Landamman. Let this be
   The foremost of our laws!
MELCHTHAL.   Even so! Whoever
   Shall talk of tamely bearing Austria's yoke,
   Let him be stripped of all his rights and honors;
   And no man hence receive him at his hearth!
ALL (*raising their right hands*).
   Agreed! Be this the law!
REDING (*after a pause*).   The law it is.
ROSSEL. Now you are free — by this law you are free.
   Never shall Austria obtain by force
   What she has failed to gain by friendly suit.
WEIL. On with the order of the day! Proceed!
REDING. Confederates! Have all gentler means been
   tried?
   Perchance the emperor knows not of our wrongs,
   It may not be his will that thus we suffer:
   Were it not well to make one last attempt,
   And lay our grievances before the throne,
   Ere we unsheath the sword? Force is at best
   A fearful thing even in a righteous cause;
   God only helps when man can help no more.

STAUFF. (*to* CONRAD HUNN).
Here you can give us information. Speak!
HUNN. I was at Rheinfeld, at the emperor's palace,
Deputed by the Cantons to complain
Of the oppression of these governors,
And claim the charter of our ancient freedom,
Which each new king till now has ratified.
I found the envoys there of many a town,
From Suabia and the valley of the Rhine,
Who all received their parchments as they wished
And straight went home again with merry heart.
They sent for me, your envoy, to the council,
Where I was soon dismissed with empty comfort;
" The emperor at present was engaged ;
Some other time he would attend to us ! "
I turned away, and passing through the hall,
With heavy heart in a recess I saw
The Grand Duke John * in tears, and by his side
The noble lords of Wart and Tegerfeld,
Who beckoned me, and said, " Redress your-
selves.
Expect not justice from the emperor.
Does he not plunder his own brother's child,
And keep from him his just inheritance ?
The duke claims his maternal property,
Urging he's now of age, and 'tis full time
That he should rule his people and dominions ;
What is the answer made to him ? The king
Places a chaplet on his head : " Behold,
The fitting ornament," he cries, " of youth ! "
MAUER. You hear. Expect not from the emperor
Or right, or justice. Then redress yourselves!
REDING. No other course is left us. Now, advise
What plan most likely to insure success.
FURST. To shake a thraldom off that we abhor,
To keep our ancient rights inviolate,
As we received them from our forefathers — this,
Not lawless innovation, is our aim.
Let Cæsar still retain what is his due ;

---

* The Duke of Suabia, who soon afterwards assassinated his uncle, for
withholding his patrimony from him.

And he that is a vassal let him pay
The service he is sworn to faithfully.
MEYER. I hold my land of Austria in fief.
FURST. Continue, then, to pay your feudal service.
WEIL. I'm tenant of the lords of Rapperswell.
FURST. Continue, then, to pay them rent and tithe.
ROSSEL. Of Zurich's lady, I'm the humble vassal.
FURST. Give to the cloister what the cloister claims.
STAUFF. The empire only is my feudal lord.
FURST. What needs must be, we'll do, but nothing fur-
     ther.
     We'll drive these tyrants and their minions
     hence,
     And raze their towering strongholds to the
     ground,
     Yet shed, if possible, no drop of blood.
     Let the emperor see that we were driven to cast
     The sacred duties of respect away;
     And when he finds we keep within our bounds,
     His wrath, belike, may yield to policy;
     For truly is that nation to be feared,
     That, when in arms, is temperate in its wrath.
REDING. But, prithee, tell us how may this be done?
     The enemy is armed as well as we,
     And, rest assured, he will not yield in peace.
STAUFF. He will, whene'er he sees us up in arms;
     We shall surprise him, ere he is prepared.
MEYER. 'Tis easily said, but not so easily done.
     Two fortresses of strength command the country.
     They shield the foe, and should the king in-
     vade us,
     The task would then be dangerous indeed.
     Rossberg and Sarnen both must be secured,
     Before a sword is drawn in either Canton.
STAUFF. Should we delay, the foe will soon be warned;
     We are too numerous for secrecy.
MEYER. There is no traitor in the Forest States.
ROSSEL. But even zeal may heedlessly betray.
FURST. Delay it longer, and the keep at Altdorf
     Will be complete, — the governor secure.
MEYER. You think but of yourselves.

SACRISTAN.   You are unjust!
MEYER. Unjust! said you? Dares Uri taunt us so?
REDING. Peace, on your oath!
MEYER.   If Schwytz be leagued with Uri,
        Why then, indeed, we must perforce be silent.
REDING. And let me tell you, in the Diet's name,
        Your hasty spirit much disturbs the peace.
        Stand we not all for the same common cause?
WINK.   What, if we delay till Christmas? 'Tis then
        The custom for the serfs to throng the castle,
        Bringing the governor their annual gifts.
        Thus may some ten or twelve selected men
        Assemble unobserved within its walls,
        Bearing about their persons pikes of steel,
        Which may be quickly mounted upon staves,
        For arms are not admitted to the fort.
        The rest can fill the neighboring wood, prepared
        To sally forth upon a trumpet's blast,
        Whene'er their comrades have secured the gate;
        And thus the castle will be ours with ease.
MELCH. The Rossberg I will undertake to scale,
        I have a sweetheart in the garrison,
        Whom with some tender words I could persuade
        To lower me at night a hempen ladder.
        Once up, my friends will not be long behind.
REDING. Are all resolved in favor of delay?
                        [*The majority raise their hands.*
STAUFF. (*counting them*).
        Twenty to twelve is the majority.
FURST. If on the appointed day the castles fall,
        From mountain on to mountain we shall pass
        The fiery signal: in the capital
        Of every Canton quickly rouse the Landsturm.*
        Then, when these tyrants see our martial front,
        Believe me, they will never make so bold
        As risk the conflict, but will gladly take
        Safe conduct forth beyond our boundaries.
STAUFF. Not so with Gessler. He will make a stand.
        Surrounded with his dread array of horse,
        Blood will be shed before he quits the field.

                * A sort of national militia.

And even expelled he'd still be terrible.
'Tis hard, indeed 'tis dangerous, to spare him.

BAUM. Place me where'er a life is to be lost;
I owe my life to Tell, and cheerfully
Will pledge it for my country. I have cleared
My honor, and my heart is now at rest.

REDING. Counsel will come with circumstance. Be
patient.
Something must still be trusted to the moment.
Yet, while by night we hold our Diet here,
The morning, see, has on the mountain-tops
Kindled her glowing beacon. Let us part,
Ere the broad sun surprise us.

FURST.   Do not fear.
The night wanes slowly from these vales of ours.
[*All have involuntarily taken off their caps,
and contemplate the breaking of day, absorbed in silence.*

ROSSEL. By this fair light, which greeteth us, before
Those other nations, that, beneath us far,
In noisome cities pent, draw painful breath,
Swear we the oath of our confederacy!
We swear to be a nation of true brothers,
Never to part in danger or in death!
[*They repeat his words with three fingers raised.*
We swear we will be free, as were our sires,
And sooner die than live in slavery!
[*All repeat as before.*
We swear to put our trust in God Most High,
And not to quail before the might of man!
[*All repeat as before, and embrace each other.*

STAUFF. Now every man pursue his several way
Back to his friends his kindred, and his home.
Let the herd winter up his flock and gain
In silence, friends, for our confederacy!
What for a time must be endured, endure.
And let the reckoning of the tyrants grow,
Till the great day arrive, when they shall pay
The general and particular debt at once.
Let every man control his own just rage,
And nurse his vengeance for the public wrongs;

For he whom selfish interest now engage
Defrauds the general weal of what to it belongs.
[*As they are going off in profound silence, in
three different directions, the orchestra
plays a solemn air. The empty scene remains open for some time, showing the
rays of the sun rising over the glaciers.*

ACT III.

Scene I.

Court before TELL'S *house.* TELL *with an axe.* HEDWIG *engaged
in her domestic duties.* WALTER *and* WILHELM *in the background playing with a little cross-bow.*

WALTER (*sings*).

With his cross-bow and his quiver
    The huntsman speeds his way,
Over mountain, dale, and river
    At the dawning of the day.

As the eagle, on wild pinion,
    Is the king in realms of air ;
So the hunter claims dominion
    Over crag and forest lair.

Far as ever bow can carry
    Through the trackless, airy space,
All he sees he makes his quarry,
    Soaring bird and beast of chase.

WILHELM (*runs forward*).
    My string has snapped ! Wilt mend it for me,
    father ?
TELL.   Not I ; a true-born archer helps himself.
                                    [*Boys retire.*
HEDW.   The boys begin to use the bow betimes.
TELL.   'Tis early practice only makes the master.
HEDW.   Ah ! Would to heaven they never learnt the art !
TELL.   But they shall learn it, wife, in all its points.
    Whoe'er would carve an independent way
    Through life must learn to ward or plant a blow.

HEDW.   Alas, alas! and they will never rest
        Contentedly at home.
TELL   No more can I!
        I was not framed by nature for a shepherd.
        Restless I must pursue a changing course;
        I only feel the flush and joy of life
        In starting some fresh quarry every day.
HEDW.   Heedless the while of all your wife's alarms
        As she sits watching through long hours at
            home.
        For my soul sinks with terror at the tales
        The servants tell about your wild adventures.
        Whene'er we part my trembling heart forebodes
        That you will ne'er come back to me again.
        I see you on the frozen mountain steeps,
        Missing, perchance, your leap from cliff to cliff;
        I see the chamois, with a wild rebound,
        Drag you down with him o'er the precipice.
        I see the avalanche close o'er your head,
        The treacherous ice give way, and you sink down
        Entombed alive within its hideous gulf.
        Ah! in a hundred varying forms does death
        Pursue the Alpine huntsman on his course.
        That way of life can surely ne'er be blessed,
        Where life and limb are perilled every hour.
TELL.   The man that bears a quick and steady eye,
        And trusts to God and his own lusty sinews,
        Passes, with scarce a scar, through every danger.
        The mountain cannot awe the mountain child.
          [*Having finished his work, he lays aside his*
             tools.
        And now, methinks, the door will hold awhile.
        The axe at home oft saves the carpenter.
                    [*Takes his cap.*
HEDW.   Whither away!
TELL.   To Altdorf, to your father.
HEDW.   You have some dangerous enterprise in view?
        Confess!
TELL.   Why think you so?
HEDWIG.   Some scheme's on foot,
        Against the governors. There was a Diet

	Held on the Rootli — that I know — and you Are one of the confederacy I'm sure.
TELL.	I was not there. Yet will I not hold back Whene'er my country calls me to her aid.
HEDW.	Wherever danger is, will you be placed. On you, as ever, will the burden fall.
TELL.	Each man shall have the post that fits his powers.
HEDW.	You took — ay, 'mid the thickest of the storm — The man of Unterwald across the lake. 'Tis a marvel you escaped. Had you no thought Of wife and children then?
TELL.	Dear wife, I had; And therefore saved the father for his children.
HEDW.	To brave the lake in all its wrath ; 'Twas not To put your trust in God ! 'Twas tempting him.
TELL.	The man that's over-cautious will do little.
HEDW.	Yes, you've a kind and helping hand for all; But be in straits and who will lend you aid?
TELL.	God grant I ne'er may stand in need of it ! [*Takes up his crossbow and arrows.*
HEDW.	Why take your crossbow with you? Leave it here.
TELL.	I want my right hand when I want my bow. [*The boys return.*
WALT.	Where, father, are you going?
TELL.	To grand-dad, boy — To Altdorf. Will you go?
WALTER.	Ay, that I will !
HEDW.	The viceroy's there just now. Go not to Altdorf.
TELL.	He leaves to-day.
HEDWIG.	Then let him first be gone, Cross not his path. You know he bears us grudge.
TELL.	His ill-will cannot greatly injure me. I do what's right, and care for no man's hate.
HEDW.	'Tis those who do what's right whom he most hates.
TELL.	Because he cannot reach them. Me, I ween, His knightship will be glad to leave in peace.

HEDW.   Ay!   Are you sure of that?
TELL.   Not long ago,
As I was hunting through the wild ravines
Of Shechenthal, untrod by mortal foot, —
There, as I took my solitary way
Along a shelving ledge of rocks, where 'twas
Impossible to step on either side;
For high above rose, like a giant wall,
The precipice's side, and far below
The Shechen thundered o'er its rifted bed; —
    [*The boys press towards him, looking upon
       him with excited curiosity.*
There, face to face, I met the viceroy.   He
Alone with me — and I myself alone —
Mere man to man, and near us the abyss.
And when his lordship had perused my face,
And knew the man he had severely fined
On some most trivial ground not long before;
And saw me, with my sturdy bow in hand,
Come striding towards him, then his cheek grew
    pale,
His knees refused their office, and I thought
He would have sunk against the mountain side.
Then, touched with pity for him, I advanced,
Respectfully, and said, " 'Tis I, my lord."
But ne'er a sound could he compel his lips
To frame an answer.   Only with his hand
He beckoned me in silence to proceed.
So I passed on, and sent his train to seek him.
HEDW.   He trembled then before you?   Woe the while
You saw his weakness; that he'll not forgive.
TELL.   I shun him, therefore, and he'll not seek me.
HEDW.   But stay away to day.   Go hunting rather!
TELL.   What do you fear?
HEDWIG.   I am uneasy.   Stay.
TELL.   Why thus distress yourself without a cause?
HEDW.   Because there is no cause.   Tell, Tell! stay here!
TELL.   Dear wife, I gave my promise I would go.
HEDW.   Must you, — then go.   But leave the boys with
    me.
WALT.   No, mother dear, I'm going with my father.

HEDW. How, Walter! Will you leave your mother
     then ?

WALT. I'll bring you pretty things from grandpapa.
                            [Exit with his father.

WILH. Mother, I'll stay with you!

HEDWIG *(embracing him)*.   Yes, yes! thou art
     My own dear child. Thou'rt all that's left to me.
      [She goes to the gate of the court, and looks
        anxiously after TELL *and her son for a con-*
        siderable time.

SCENE II.

A retired part of the Forest. Brooks dashing in spray over
the rocks.

Enter BERTHA *in a hunting dress. Immediately after-*
wards RUDENZ.

BERTHA. He follows me. Now to explain myself!

RUDENZ *(entering hastily)*.
     At length, dear lady, we have met alone
     In this wild dell, with rocks on every side,
     No jealous eye can watch our interview.
     Now let my heart throw off this weary silence.

BERTHA. But are you sure they will not follow us?

RUD. See, yonder goes the chase. Now, then, or
     never!
     I must avail me of the precious moment, —
     Must hear my doom decided by thy lips,
     Though it should part me from thy side forever.
     Oh, do not arm that gentle face of thine
     With looks so stern and harsh! Who — who
     am I,
     That dare aspire so high as unto thee?
     Fame hath not stamped me yet; nor may I take
     My place amid the courtly throng of knights,
     That, crowned with glory's lustre, woo thy
     smiles.
     Nothing have I to offer but a heart
     That overflows with truth and love for thee.

BERTHA *(sternly and with severity)*.
     And dare you speak to me of love — of truth?

You, that are faithless to your nearest ties!
You, that are Austria's slave — bartered and
    sold
To her — an alien, and your country's tyrant!

RUD.   How! This reproach from thee! Whom do I
    seek
On Austria's side, my own beloved, but thee?

BERTHA. Think you to find me in the traitor's ranks?
Now, as I live, I'd rather give my hand
To Gessler's self, all despot though he be,
Than to the Switzer who forgets his birth,
And stoops to be the minion of a tyrant.

RUD.   Oh heaven, what must I hear!

BERTHA.   Say! what can lie
Nearer the good man's heart than friends and
    kindred?
What dearer duty to a noble soul
Than to protect weak, suffering innocence,
And vindicate the rights of the oppressed?
My very soul bleeds for your countrymen;
I suffer with them, for I needs must love them;
They are so gentle, yet so full of power;
They draw my whole heart to them. Every day
I look upon them with increased esteem.
But you, whom nature and your knightly vow,
Have given them as their natural protector,
Yet who desert them and abet their foes,
In forging shackles for your native land,
You — you it is, that deeply grieve and wound me.
I must constrain my heart, or I shall hate you.

RUD.   Is not my country's welfare all my wish?
What seek I for her but to purchase peace
'Neath Austria's potent sceptre?

BERTHA.   Bondage, rather!
You would drive freedom from the last strong-
    hold
That yet remains for her upon the earth.
The people know their own true interests better:
Their simple natures are not warped by show,
But round your head a tangling net is wound.

RUD.   Bertha, you hate me — you despise me!

BERTHA.   Nay!
    And if I did, 'twere better for my peace.
    But to see him despised and despicable, —
    The man whom one might love.
RUDENZ.   Oh, Bertha! You
    Show me the pinnacle of heavenly bliss,
    Then, in a moment, hurl me to despair!
BERTH. No, no! the noble is not all extinct
    Within you. It but slumbers, — I will rouse it.
    It must have cost you many a fiery struggle
    To crush the virtues of your race within you.
    But, heaven be praised, 'tis mightier than
      yourself,
    And you are noble in your own despite!
RUD. You trust me, then? Oh, Bertha, with thy love
    What might I not become?
BERTHA.   Be only that
    For which your own high nature destined you.
    Fill the position you were born to fill; —
    Stand by your people and your native land·
    And battle for your sacred rights!
RUDENZ.   Alas!
    How can I hope to win you — to possess you,
    If I take arms against the emperor?
    Will not your potent kinsman interpose,
    To dictate the disposal of your hand?
BERTH. All my estates lie in the Forest Cantons;
    And I am free, when Switzerland is free.
RUD. Oh! what a prospect, Bertha, hast thou shown
    me!
BERTH. Hope not to win my hand by Austria's favor;
    Fain would they lay their grasp on my estates,
    To swell the vast domains which now they hold.
    The selfsame lust of conquest that would rob
    You of your liberty endangers mine.
    Oh, friend, I'm marked for sacrifice; — to be
    The guerdon of some parasite, perchance!
    They'll drag me hence to the imperial court
    That hateful haunt of falsehood and intrigue;
    There do detested marriage bonds await me.
    Love, love alone, — your love can rescue me.

RUD.   And thou could'st be content, love, to live here,
        In my own native land to be my own?
        Oh, Bertha, all the yearnings of my soul
        For this great world and its tumultuous strife,
        What were they, but a yearning after thee?
        In glory's path I sought for thee alone,
        And all my thirst of fame was only love.
        But if in this calm vale thou canst abide
        With me, and bid earth's pomps and pride adieu,
        Then is the goal of my ambition won ;
        And the rough tide of the tempestuous world
        May dash and rave around these firm-set hills!
        No wandering wishes more have I to send
        Forth to the busy scene that stirs beyond.
        Then may these rocks that girdle us extend
        Their giants walls impenetrably round,
        And this sequestered happy vale alone
        Look up to heaven, and be my paradise!

BERTH. Now art thou all my fancy dreamed of thee.
        My trust has not been given to thee in vain.

RUD.   Away, ye idle phantoms of my folly!
        In mine own home I'll find my happiness.
        Here where the gladsome boy to manhood grew,
        Where every brook, and tree, and mountain
            peak,
        Teems with remembrances of happy hours,
        In mine own native land thou wilt be mine.
        Ah, I have ever loved it well, I feel
        How poor without it were all earthly joys.

BERTH. Where should we look for happiness on earth,
        If not in this dear land of innocence?
        Here, where old truth hath its familiar home,
        Where fraud and guile are strangers, envy ne'er
        Shall dim the sparkling fountain of our bliss,
        And ever bright the hours shall o'er us glide.
        There do I see thee, in true manly worth,
        The foremost of the free and of thy peers,
        Revered with homage pure and unconstrained,
        Wielding a power that kings might envy thee.

RUD.   And thee I see, thy sex's crowning gem,
        With thy sweet woman grace and wakeful love,

Building a heaven for me within my home,
And, as the springtime scatters forth her flowers,
Adorning with thy charms my path of life,
And spreading joy and sunshine all around.

BERTH. And this it was, dear friend, that caused my grief,
To see thee blast this life's supremest bliss,
With thine own hand. Ah! what had been my fate,
Had I been forced to follow some proud lord,
Some ruthless despot, to his gloomy castle!
Here are no castles, here no bastioned walls
Divide me from a people I can bless.

RUD. Yet, how to free myself; to loose the coils
Which I have madly twined around my head?

BERTH. Tear them asunder with a man's resolve.
Whatever the event, stand by the people.
It is thy post by birth.
      [*Hunting horns are heard in the distance.*
But hark! The chase!
Farewell, — 'tis needful we should part — away!
Fight for thy land; thou fightest for thy love.
One foe fills all our souls with dread; the blow
That makes one free emancipates us all.
      [*Exeunt severally.*

SCENE III.

A meadow near Altdorf. Trees in the foreground. At the back of the stage a cap upon a pole. The prospect is bounded by the Bannberg, which is surmounted by a snow-capped mountain.

FRIESHARDT *and* LEUTHOLD *on guard.*

FRIESS. We keep our watch in vain. There's not a soul
Will pass and do obeisance to the cap.
But yesterday the place swarmed like a fair;
Now the whole green looks like a very desert,
Since yonder scarecrow hung upon the pole.

LEUTH. Only the vilest rabble show themselves,
And wave their tattered caps in mockery at us.
All honest citizens would sooner make
A tedious circuit over half the town
Than bend their backs before our master's cap.

FRIESS. They were obliged to pass this way at noon,
         As they were coming from the council house.
         I counted then upon a famous catch,
         For no one thought of bowing to the cap.
         But Rosselmann, the priest, was even with me :
         Coming just then from some sick penitent,
         He stands before the pole — raises the Host —
         The Sacrist, too, must tinkle with his bell —
         When down they dropped on knee — myself and
             all
         In reverence to the Host, but not the cap.

LEUTH.   Hark ye, companion, I've a shrewd suspicion,
         Our post's no better than the pillory.
         It is a burning shame, a trooper should
         Stand sentinel before an empty cap,
         And every honest fellow must despise us,
         To do obeisance to a cap, too ! Faith,
         I never heard an order so absurd !

FRIESS. Why not, an't please thee, to an empty cap.
         Thou'st ducked, I'm sure, to many an empty
             sconce.
                   [HILDEGARD, MECHTHILD, *and* ELSBETH
                       *enter with their children and station
                       themselves around the pole.*

LEUTH.   And thou art an officious sneaking knave,
         That's fond of bringing honest folks to trouble.
         For my part, he that likes may pass the cap :
         I'll shut my eyes and take no note of him.

MECH.   There hangs the viceroy ! Your obeisance, chil-
             dren !

ELS.   I would to God he'd go, and leave his cap !
         The country would be none the worse for it.

FRIESSHARDT (*driving them away*).
         Out of the way ! Confounded pack of gossips !
         Who sent for you ? Go, send your husbands
             here,
         If they have courage to defy the order.
                   [TELL *enters with his crossbow, leading his
                       son* WALTER *by the hand. They pass
                       the hat without noticing it, and advance
                       to the front of the stage.*

WALTER (*pointing to the Bannberg*).
    Father, is't true, that on the mountain there,
    The trees, if wounded with a hatchet, bleed?
TELL.   Who says so, boy?
WALTER.   The master herdsman, father!
    He tells us there's a charm upon the trees,
    And if a man shall injure them, the hand
    That struck the blow will grow from out the
        grave.
TELL.   There is a charm about them, that's the truth.
    Dost see those glaciers yonder, those white horns,
    That seem to melt away into the sky?
WALT.   They are the peaks that thunder so at night,
    And send the avalanches down upon us.
TELL.   They are; and Altdorf long ago had been
    Submerged beneath these avalanches' weight,
    Did not the forest there above the town
    Stand like a bulwark to arrest their fall.
WALTER (*after musing a little*).
    And are there countries with no mountains,
        father?
TELL.   Yes, if we travel downwards from our heights,
    And keep descending in the rivers' courses,
    We reach a wide and level country, where
    Our mountain torrents brawl and foam no more,
    And fair, large rivers glide serenely on.
    All quarters of the heaven may there be scanned
    Without impediment. The corn grows there
    In broad and lovely fields, and all the land
    Is fair as any garden to the view.
WALT.   But, father, tell me, wherefore haste we not
    Away to this delightful land, instead
    Of toiling here, and struggling as we do?
TELL.   The land is fair and bountiful as Heaven;
    But they who till it never may enjoy
    The fruits of what they sow.
WALTER.   Live they not free,
    As you do, on the land their fathers left them?
TELL.   The fields are all the bishop's or the king's.
WALT.   But they may freely hunt among the woods?
TELL.   The game is all the monarch's — bird and beast.

WALT.   But they, at least, may surely fish the streams?
TELL.   Stream, lake, and sea, all to the king belong.
WALT.   Who is this king, of whom they're so afraid?
TELL.   He is the man who fosters and protects them.
WALT.   Have they not courage to protect themselves?
TELL.   The neighbor there dare not his neighbor trust.
WALT.   I should want breathing room in such a land,
        I'd rather dwell beneath the avalanches.
TELL.   'Tis better, child, to have these glacier peaks
        Behind one's back than evil-minded men!
                                [They are about to pass on.

WALT.   See, father, see the cap on yonder pole!
TELL.   What is the cap to us?   Come, let's be gone.
                [As he is going, FRIESSHARDT, *presenting his
                pike, stops him.*
FRIESS.   Stand, I command you, in the emperor's name.
TELL. (*seizing the pike*).
        What would ye? Wherefore do ye stop my path?
FRIESS.   You've broke the mandate, and must go with us.
LEUTH.   You have not done obeisance to the cap.
TELL.   Friend, let me go.
FRIESS.   Away, away to prison!
WALT.   Father to prison!   Help!
                          [Calling to the side scene.
                        This way, you men!
        Good people, help! They're dragging him to
        prison!
                *[*ROSSELMANN, *the priest, and the* SACRISTAN,
                with three other men, enter.
SACRIS.   What's here amiss?
ROSS.   Why do you seize this man?
FRIESS.   He is an enemy of the king — a traitor!
TELL. (*seizing him with violence*).
        A traitor, I!
ROSSELMANN.   Friend, thou art wrong.   'Tis Tell,
        An honest man, and worthy citizen.
WALTER (*descries* FURST, *and runs up to him*).
        Grandfather, help! they want to seize my father!
FRIESS.   Away to prison!
FURST (*running in*).   Stay! I offer bail.
        For God's sake, Tell, what is the matter here?
                *[*MELCHTHAL *and* STAUFFACHER *enter.*

LEUTH.   He has contemned the viceroy's sovereign power,
          Refusing flatly to acknowledge it.
STAUFF. Has Tell done this?
MELCHTHAL.   Villain, thou knowest 'tis false!
LEUTH.   He has not made obeisance to the cap.
FURST.   And shall for this to prison?   Come, my friend,
          Take my security, and let him go.
FRIESS.   Keep your security for yourself — you'll need it.
          We only do our duty.   Hence with him.
MELCHTHAL (*to the country people*).
          This is too bad—shall we stand by, and see them.
          Drag him away before our very eyes?
SACRIS.   We are the strongest.   Don't endure it, friends.
          Our countrymen will back us to a man.
FRIESS.   Who dares resist the governor's commands?
OTHER THREE PEASANTS (*running in*).
          We'll help you.   What's the matter?   Down
            with them!
          [HILDEGARD, MECHTHILD, *and* ELSBETH *return.*
TELL.   Go, go, good people, I can help myself.
          Think you, had I a mind to use my strength,
          These pikes of theirs should daunt me?
MELCHTHAL (*to* FRIESSHARDT).   Only try —
          Try, if you dare, to force him from amongst us.
FURST *and* STAUFFACHER.
          Peace, peace, friends!
FRIESSHARDT (*loudly*).   Riot! Insurrection, ho!
          [*Hunting horns without.*
WOMEN. The governor!
FRIESSHARDT (*raising his voice*).   Rebellion!   Mutiny!
STAUFF. Roar, till you burst, knave!
ROSSELMANN *and* MELCHTHAL.   Will you hold your
            tongue?
FRIESSHARDT (*calling still louder*).
          Help, help, I say, the servants of the law!
FURST.   The viceroy here!   Then we shall smart for this!
          [*Enter* GESSLER *on horseback, with a falcon*
            on his wrist; RUDOLPH DER HARRAS,
            BERTHA, *and* RUDENZ, *and a numerous*
            train of armed attendants, who form a
            circle of lances around the whole stage.

HAR.   Room for the viceroy!

GESSLER.   **Drive the clowns apart.**
Why throng the people thus? Who calls for
    help?   [*General silence.*
Who was it? I will know.
               [FRIESSHARDT *steps forward.*
                     And who art thou?
And why hast thou this man in custody?
        [*Gives his falcon to an attendant.*

FRIESS.   Dread sir, I am a soldier of your guard,
And stationed sentinel beside the cap;
This man I apprehended in the act
Of passing it without obeisance due,
So I arrested him, as you gave order,
Whereon the people tried to rescue him.

GESSLER (*after a pause*).
And do you, Tell, so lightly hold your king,
And me, who act as his vicegerent here,
That you refuse the greeting to the cap
I hung aloft to test your loyalty?
I read in this a disaffected spirit.

TELL.   Pardon me, good my lord! The action sprung
From inadvertence, — not from disrespect.
Were I discreet, I were not William Tell.
Forgive me now — I'll not offend again.

GESSLER (*after a pause*).
I hear, Tell, you're a master with the bow, —
And bear the palm away from every rival.

WALT.   That must be true, sir! At a hundred yards
He'll shoot an apple for you off the tree.

GESSL.   Is that boy thine, Tell?

TELL.   Yes, my gracious lord.

GESSL.   Hast any more of them?

TELL.   Two boys, my lord.

GESSL.   And, of the two, which dost thou love the most?

TELL.   Sir, both the boys are dear to me alike.

GESSL.   Then, Tell, since at a hundred yards thou canst
Bring down the apple from the tree, thou shalt
Approve thy skill before me. Take thy bow —
Thou hast it there at hand — and make thee
    ready

To shoot an apple from the stripling's head!
But take this counsel, — look well to thine aim,
See that thou hittest the apple at the first,
For, shouldst thou miss, thy head shall pay the
    forfeit.   [*All give signs of horror.*

TELL.   What monstrous thing, my lord, is this you ask?
That I, from the head of mine own child!—No, no!
It cannot be, kind sir, you meant not that —
God in His grace forbid! You could not ask
A father seriously to do that thing!

GESSL.   Thou art to shoot an apple from his head!
I do desire — command it so.

TELL.   What, I!
Level my crossbow at the darling head
Of mine own child? No — rather let me die!

GESSL.   Or thou must shoot, or with thee dies the boy.

TELL.   Shall I become the murderer of my child!
You have no children, sir — you do not know
The tender throbbings of a father's heart.

GESSL.   How now, Tell, so discreet upon a sudden
I had been told thou wert a visionary, —
A wanderer from the paths of common men.
Thou lovest the marvellous. So have I now
Culled out for thee a task of special daring.
Another man might pause and hesitate;
Thou dashest at it, heart and soul, at once.

BERTH.   Oh, do not jest, my lord, with these poor souls!
See, how they tremble, and how pale they look,
So little used are they to hear thee jest.

GESSL.   Who tells thee that I jest?
                [*Grasping a branch above his head.*
                Here is the apple.
Room there, I say! And let him take his dis-
    tance —
Just eighty paces — as the custom is —
Not an inch more or less! It was his boast,
That at a hundred he could hit his man.
Now, archer, to your task, and look you miss not!

HAK.   Heavens! this grows serious — down, boy, on
    your knees,
And beg the governor to spare your life.

FURST. (*aside to* MELCHTHAL, *who can scarcely restrain his impatience*).

    Command yourself — be calm, I beg of you!

BERTHA (*to the governor*).

    Let this suffice you, sir! It is inhuman
    To trifle with a father's anguish thus.
    Although this wretched man had forfeited
    Both life and limb for such a slight offence,
    Already has he suffered tenfold death.
    Send him away uninjured to his home;
    He'll know thee well in future; and this hour
    He and his children's children will remember.

GESSL.   Open a way there — quick! Why this delay?
    Thy life is forfeited; I might despatch thee,
    And see I graciously repose thy fate
    Upon the skill of thine own practised hand.
    No cause has he to say his doom his harsh,
    Who's made the master of his destiny.
    Thou boastest of thy steady eye. 'Tis well!
    Now is a fitting time to show thy skill.
    The mark is worthy, and the prize is great.
    To hit the bull's-eye in the target; that
    Can many another do as well as thou;
    But he, methinks, is master of his craft
    Who can at all times on his skill rely,
    Nor lets his heart disturb or eye or hand.

FURST.   My lord, we bow to your authority;
    But, oh, let justice yield to mercy here.
    Take half my property, nay, take it all,
    But spare a father this unnatural doom!

WALT.   Grandfather, do not kneel to that bad man!
    Say, where am I to stand? I do not fear;
    My father strikes the bird upon the wing,
    And will not miss now when 'twould harm his boy!

STAUFF. Does the child's innocence not touch your heart?

ROSSEL. Bethink you, sir, there is a God in heaven,
    To whom you must account for all your deeds.

GESSLER (*pointing to the boy*).

    Bind him to yonder lime tree straight!

WALTER. Bind me?
No, I will not be bound! I will be still,
Still as a lamb — nor even draw my breath!
But if you bind me I cannot be still.
Then I shall writhe and struggle with my bonds.
HAR. But let your eyes at least be bandaged, boy!
WALT. And why my eyes? No! Do you think I fear
An arrow from my father's hand? Not I!
I'll wait it firmly, nor so much as wink!
Quick, father, show them that thou art an
archer!
He doubts thy skill — he thinks to ruin us.
Shoot then and hit though but to spite the tyrant!
[*He goes to the lime tree, and an apple is
placed on his head.*

MELCHTHAL (*to the country people*).
What! Is this outrage to be perpetrated
Before our very eyes? Where is our oath?
STAUFF. 'Tis all in vain. We have no weapons here;
And see the wood of lances that surrounds us!
MELCH. Oh! would to heaven that we had struck at
once!
God pardon those who counselled the delay!
GESSLER (*to* TELL).
Now, to thy task! Men bear not arms for
naught.
'Tis dangerous to carry deadly weapons,
And on the archer oft his shaft recoils.
This right these haughty peasant-churls assume
Trenches upon their master's privileges.
None should be armed but those who bear com-
mand.
.It pleases you wear the bow and bolt;
Well, be it so. I will provide the mark.
TELL (*bends the bow and fixes the arrow*).
A lane there! Room!
STAUFFACHER. What, Tell? You would — no, no!
You shake — your hand's unsteady — your knees
tremble!
TELL (*letting the bow sink down*).
There's something swims before mine eyes!

WOMEN.   Great Heaven!

TELL.   Release me from this shot!   Here is my heart!
                                    [*Tears open his breast.*
           Summon your troopers — let them strike me
              down!

GESSL.   I do not want thy life, Tell, but the shot.
           Thy talent's universal!   Nothing daunts thee!
           Thou canst direct the rudder like the bow!
           Storms fright not thee when there's a life at
              stake.
           Now, savior, help thyself, — thou savest all!
              [TELL *stands fearfully agitated by contending*
                 emotions, his hands moving convulsively,
                 and his eyes turning alternately to the
                 governor and heaven.   Suddenly he takes
                 a second arrow from his quiver and sticks
                 it in his belt.   The governor watches all
                 these motions.

WALTER (*beneath the lime tree*).
           Come, father, shoot!   I'm not afraid!

TELL.   It must be!
                  [*Collects himself and levels the bow.*

RUDENZ (*who all the while has been standing in a state*
              of violent excitement, and has with difficulty
              restrained himself, advances).
           My lord, you will not urge this matter further.
           You will not.   It was surely but a test.
           You've gained your object.   Rigor pushed too
              far
           Is sure to miss its aim, however good,
           As snaps the bow that's all too straightly bent.

GESSL.   Peace, till your counsel's asked for!

RUDENZ.   I will speak!
           Ay, and I dare!   I reverence my king;
           But acts like these must make his name abhorred.
           He sanctions not this cruelty.   I dare
           Avouch the fact.   And you outstep your powers
           In handling thus an unoffending people.

GESSL.   Ha! thou growest bold methinks!

RUDENZ.   I have been dumb
           To all the oppressions I was doomed to see.

I've closed mine eyes that they might not behold
   them,
Bade my rebellious, swelling heart be still,
And pent its struggles down within my breast.
But to be silent longer were to be
A traitor to my king and country both.

BERTHA (*casting herself between him and the governor*).
Oh, heavens! you but exasperate his rage!

RUD.   My people I forsook, renounced my kindred —
Broke all the ties of nature that I might
Attach myself to you. I madly thought
That I should best advance the general weal,
By adding sinews to the emperor's power.
The scales have fallen from mine eyes — I see
The fearful precipice on which I stand.
You've led my youthful judgment far astray, —
Deceived my honest heart. With best intent,
I had well nigh achieved my country's ruin.

GESSL.   Audacious boy, this language to thy lord?

RUD.   The emperor is my lord, not you! I'm free
As you by birth, and I can cope with you
In every virtue that beseems a knight.
And if you stood not here in that king's name,
Which I respect e'en where 'tis most abused,
I'd throw my gauntlet down, and you should give
An answer to my gage in knightly fashion.
Ay, beckon to your troopers! Here I stand ;
But not like these   [*Pointing to the people.*
   — unarmed. I have a sword,
And he that stirs one step ——

STAUFFACHER (*exclaims*).   The apple's down!
   [*While the attention of the crowd has been
   directed to the spot where* BERTHA *had cast
   herself between* RUDENZ *and* GESSLER,
   TELL *has shot.*

ROSSEL. The boy's alive!

MANY VOICES.   The apple has been struck !
   [WALTER FURST *staggers, and is about to fall.*
   BERTHA *supports him.*

GESSLER (*astonished*).
How ? Has he shot? The madman !

BERTHA.   Worthy father!
        Pray you compose yourself.   The boy's alive!
WALTER (*runs in with the apple*).
        Here is the apple, father!   Well I knew
        You would not harm your boy.
                [TELL *stands with his body bent forwards,*
                as though he would follow the arrow. His
                bow drops from his hand.   When he sees
                the boy advancing, he hastens to meet him
                with open arms, and embracing him pas-
                sionately sinks down with him quite ex-
                hausted. All crowd round them deeply
                affected.

BERTHA.   Oh, ye kind heavens!
FURST (*to father and son*).   My children, my dear
                children!
STAUFFACHER.   God be praised!
LEUTH.   Almighty powers!   That was a shot indeed!
        It will be talked of to the end of time.
HAR.   This feat of Tell, the archer, will be told
        While yonder mountains stand upon their base.
                        [*Hands the apple to* GESSLER.
GESSL.   By heaven! the apple's cleft right through the
                core.
        It was a master shot I must allow.
ROSSEL. The shot was good.   But woe to him who drove
        The man to tempt his God by such a feat!
STAUFF. Cheer up, Tell, rise!   You've nobly freed your-
                self,
        And now may go in quiet to your home.
ROSSEL. Come, to the mother let us bear her son!
                        [*They are about to lead him off.*
GESSL.   A word, Tell.
TELL.   Sir, your pleasure?
GESSLER.   Thou didst place
        A second arrow in thy belt — nay, nay!
        I saw it well — what was thy purpose with it?
TELL (*confused*).   It is the custom with all archers, sir.
GESSL.   No, Tell, I cannot let that answer pass.
        There was some other motive, well I know.
        Frankly and cheerfully confess the truth; —

Whate'er it be I promise thee thy life,
Wherefore the second arrow?

TELL.   Well, my lord,
Since you have promised not to take my life,
I will, without reserve, declare the truth.
[*He draws the arrow from his belt, and fixes
his eyes sternly upon the governor.*
If that my hand had struck my darling child,
This second arrow I had aimed at you,
And, be assured, I should not then have missed.

GESSL. Well, Tell, I promised thou shouldst have thy
                life;
I gave my knightly word, and I will keep it.
Yet, as I know the malice of thy thoughts,
I will remove thee hence to sure confinement,
Where neither sun nor moon shall reach thine
                eyes,
Thus from thy arrows I shall be secure.
Seize on him, guards, and bind him.
                                    [*They bind him.*

STAUFFACHER.   How, my lord —
How can you treat in such a way a man
On whom God's hand has plainly been revealed?

GESSL. Well, let us see if it will save him twice!
Remove him to my ship; I'll follow straight.
In person I will see him lodged at Küssnacht.

ROSSEL. You dare not do it. Nor durst the emperor's self,
So violate our dearest chartered rights.

GESSL. Where are they? Has the emperor confirmed
                them?
He never has. And only by obedience
Need you expect to win that favor from him.
You are all rebels 'gainst the emperor's power —
And bear a desperate and rebellious spirit.
I know you all — I see you through and through.
Him do I single from amongst you now,
But in his guilt you all participate.
The wise will study silence and obedience.
                [*Exit, followed by* BERTHA, RUDENZ, HARRAS,
                and attendants. FRIESSHARDT *and* LEU-
                THOLD *remain.*

FURST (*in violent anguish*).
     All's over now ! He is resolved to bring
     Destruction on myself and all my house.
STAUFF. (*to* TELL). Oh, why did you provoke the tyrant's
       rage ?
TELL.   Let him be calm who feels the pangs I felt.
STAUFF. Alas ! Alas ! Our hope is gone.
     With you we all are fettered and enchained.
COUNTRY PEOPLE (*surrounding* TELL).
     Our last remaining comfort goes with you !
LEUTH. (*approaching him*).
     I'm sorry for you, Tell, but must obey.
TELL.   Farewell !
WALTER TELL (*clinging to him in great agony*).
     Oh, father, father, my dear father !
TELL (*pointing to heaven*).
     Thy father is on high — appeal to him !
STAUFF. Hast thou no message, Tell, to send thy wife ?
TELL (*clasping the boy passionately to his breast*).
     The boy's uninjured ; God will succor me !
       [*Tears himself suddenly away, and follows*
          the soldiers of the guard.

ACT IV.

SCENE I.

Eastern shore of the lake of Lucerne; rugged and singularly
shaped rocks close the prospect to the west. The lake is agitated,
violent roaring and rushing of wind, with thunder and lightning
at intervals.

    KUNZ OF GERSAU, FISHERMAN, *and* BOY.

KUNZ.   I saw it with these eyes ! Believe me, friend,
       It happened all precisely as I've said.
FISHER. Tell, made a prisoner and borne off to Küssnacht ?
       The best man in the land, the bravest arm,
       Had we resolved to strike for liberty !
KUNZ.   The viceroy takes him up the lake in person :
       They were about to go on board as I
       Left Flüelen ; but still the gathering storm,

That drove me here to land so suddenly,
Perchance has hindered their abrupt departure.

FISHER. Our Tell in chains, and in the viceroy's power!
Oh, trust me, Gessler will entomb him where
He never more shall see the light of day;
For, Tell once free, the tyrant well may dread
The just revenge of one so deep incensed.

KUNZ. The old Landamman, too — von Attinghaus —
They say, is lying at the point of death.

FISHER. Then the last anchor of our hopes gives way!
He was the only man who dared to raise
His voice in favor of the people's rights.

KUNZ. The storm grows worse and worse. So, fare ye
well!
I'll go and seek out quarters in the village.
There's not a chance of getting off to-day.
[*Exit.*

FISHER. Tell dragged to prison, and the baron dead!
Now, tyranny, exalt thy insolent front —
Throw shame aside! The voice of truth is
silenced,
The eye that watched for us in darkness closed,
The arm that should have struck thee down in
chains!

BOY. 'Tis hailing hard — come, let us to the cottage!
This is no weather to be out in, father!

FISHER. Rage on, ye winds! Ye lightnings, flash your
fires!
Burst, ye swollen clouds! Ye cataracts of
heaven,
Descend, and drown the country! In the germ,
Destroy the generations yet unborn!
Ye savage elements, be lords of all!
Return, ye bears; ye ancient wolves, return
To this wide, howling waste! The land is yours.
Who would live here when liberty is gone?

BOY. Hark! How the wind whistles and the whirl-
pool roars;
I never saw a storm so fierce as this!

FISHER. To level at the head of his own child!
Never had father such command before.

And shall not nature, rising in wild wrath,
Revolt against the deed? I should not marvel,
Though to the lake these rocks should bow
    their heads,
Though yonder pinnacles, yon towers of ice,
That, since creation's dawn, have known no thaw,
Should, from their lofty summits, melt away;
Though yonder mountains, yon primeval cliffs,
Should topple down, and a new deluge whelm
Beneath its waves all living men's abodes!
                            [Bells heard.

BOY.   Hark! they are ringing on the mountain yonder!
They surely see some vessel in distress,
And toll the bell that we may pray for it.
                            [Ascends a rock.

FISHER. Woe to the bark that now pursues its course,
Rocked in the cradle of these storm-tossed waves.
Nor helm nor steersman here can aught avail;
The storm is master. Man is like a ball,
Tossed 'twixt the winds and billows. Far or near,
No haven offers him its friendly shelter!
Without one ledge to grasp, the sheer, smooth
    rocks
Look down inhospitably on his despair,
And only tender him their flinty breasts.

BOY (*calling from above*).
    Father, a ship; and bearing down from Flüelen.

FISHER. Heaven pity the poor wretches! When the storm
Is once entangled in this strait of ours,
It rages like some savage beast of prey,
Struggling against its cage's iron bars.
Howling, it seeks an outlet — all in vain;
For the rocks hedge it round on every side,
Walling the narrow pass as high as heaven.
                         [He ascends a cliff.

BOY.   It is the governor of Uri's ship;
By its red poop I know it, and the flag.

FISHER. Judgments of Heaven! Yes, it is he himself.
It is the governor! Yonder he sails,
And with him bears the burden of his crimes!
Soon has the arm of the avenger found him;

Now over him he knows a mightier lord.
These waves yield no obedience to his voice,
These rocks bow not their heads before his cap.
Boy, do not pray; stay not the Judge's arm!

BOY.   I pray not for the governor; I pray
For Tell, who is on board the ship with him.

FISHER.   Alas, ye blind, unreasoning elements!
Must ye, in punishing one guilty head,
Destroy the vessel and the pilot too?

BOY.   See, see, they've cleared the Buggisgrat;* but
now
The blast, rebounding from the Devil's Minster,*
Has driven them back on the Great Axenberg.*
I cannot see them now.

FISHERMAN.   The Hakmesser *
Is there, that's foundered many a gallant ship.
If they should fail to double that with skill,
Their bark will go to pieces on the rocks
That hide their jagged peaks below the lake.
They have on board the very best of pilots;
If any man can save them, Tell is he;
But he is manacled, both hand and foot.

> [*Enter* WILLIAM TELL, *with his crossbow. He
> enters precipitately, looks wildly round, and
> testifies the most violent agitation. When
> he reaches the centre of the stage, he throws
> himself upon his knees, and stretches out
> his hands, first towards the earth, then
> towards heaven.*

BOY (*observing him*).
See, father! Who is that man, kneeling yonder?

FISHER.   He clutches at the earth with both his hands,
And looks as though he were beside himself.

BOY (*advancing*).
What do I see? Father, come here, and look!

FISHERMAN (*approaches*).
Who is it? God in heaven! What! William Tell,
How came you hither? Speak, Tell!

BOY.   Were you not
In yonder ship, a prisoner, and in chains?

* Rocks on the shore of the Lake of Lucerne.

FISHER. Were they not bearing you away to Küssnacht?

TELL (*rising*). I am released.

FISHERMAN *and* BOY. Released, oh miracle!

BOY. Whence came you here?

TELL. From yonder vessel!

FISHERMAN. What?

BOY. Where is the viceroy?

TELL. Drifting on the waves.

FISHER. Is't possible? But you! How are you here?
How 'scaped you from your fetters and the
storm?

TELL. By God's most gracious providence. Attend.

FISHER *and* BOY. Say on, say on!

TELL. You know what passed at Altdorf?

FISHER. I do — say on!

TELL. How I was seized and bound,
And ordered by the governor to Küssnacht.

FISHER. And how with you at Flüelen he embarked.
All this we know. Say, how have you escaped?

TELL. I lay on deck, fast bound with cords, disarmed,
In utter hopelessness. I did not think
Again to see the gladsome light of day,
Nor the dear faces of my wife and children;
And eyed disconsolate the waste of waters——

FISHER. Oh, wretched man!

TELL. Then we put forth; the viceroy,
Rudolph der Harras, and their suite. My bow
And quiver lay astern beside the helm;
And just as we had reached the corner, near
The Little Axen,* heaven ordained it so,
That from the Gotthardt's gorge, a hurricane
Swept down upon us with such headlong force,
That every rower's heart within him sank,
And all on board looked for a watery grave.
Then heard I one of the attendant train,
Turning to Gessler, in this strain accost him:
"You see our danger, and your own, my lord
And that we hover on the verge of death.
The boatmen there are powerless from fear,
Nor are they confident what course to take;

* A rock on the shore of the lake of Lucerne.

Now, here is Tell, a stout and fearless man,
And knows to steer with more than common
 skill.
How if we should avail ourselves of him
In this emergency?" The viceroy then
Addressed me thus : "If thou wilt undertake
To bring us through this tempest safely, Tell,
I might consent to free thee from thy bonds."
I answered, " Yes, my lord, with God's assistance,
I'll see what can be done, and help us heaven!"
On this they loosed me from my bonds, and I
Stood by the helm and fairly steered along;
Yet ever eyed my shooting-gear askance,
And kept a watchful eye upon the shore,
To find some point where I might leap to
 land :
And when I had descried a shelving crag,
That jutted, smooth atop, into the lake ——

FISHER. I know it. 'Tis at foot of the Great Axen ;
But looks so steep, I never could have dreamed
'Twere possible to leap it from the boat.

TELL. I bade the men put forth their utmost might,
Until we came before the shelving crag.
For there, I said, the danger will be past!
Stoutly they pulled, and soon we neared the
 point ;
One prayer to God for his assisting grace,
And straining every muscle, I brought round
The vessel's stern close to the rocky wall ;
Then snatching up my weapons, with a bound
I swung myself upon the flattened shelf,
And with my feet thrust off, with all my might,
The puny bark into the hell of waters.
There let it drift about, as heaven ordains!
Thus am I here, delivered from the might
Of the dread storm, and man, more dreadful
 still.

FISHER. Tell, Tell, the Lord has manifestly wrought
A miracle in thy behalf! I scarce
Can credit my own eyes. But tell me, now,
Whither you purpose to betake yourself?

For you will be in peril should the viceroy
Chance to escape this tempest with his life.

TELL.   I heard him say, as I lay bound on board,
His purpose was to disembark at Brunnen;
And, crossing Schwytz, convey me to his castle.

FISHER. Means he to go by land?

TELL.   So he intends.

FISHER. Oh, then, conceal yourself without delay!
Not twice will heaven release you from his
    grasp.

TELL.   Which is the nearest way to Arth and Küss-
    nacht?

FISHER. The public road leads by the way of Steinen,
But there's a nearer road, and more retired,
That goes by Lowerz, which my boy can show
    you.

TELL (*gives him his hand*).

May heaven reward your kindness!   Fare ye
    well!

                    [*As he is going he comes back.*
Did not you also take the oath at Rootli?
I heard your name, methinks.

FISHERMAN.   Yes, I was there,
And took the oath of the confederacy;

TELL.   Then do me this one favor; speed to Bürglen —
My wife is anxious at my absence — tell her
That I am free, and in secure concealment.

FISHER. But whither shall I tell her you have fled?

TELL.   You'll find her father with her, and some more,
Who took the oath with you upon the Rootli;
Bid them be resolute, and strong of heart, —
For Tell is free and master of his arm;
They shall hear further news of me ere long.

FISHER. What have you, then, in view?   Come, tell me
    frankly!

TELL.   When once 'tis done 'twill be in every mouth.
                                                    [*Exit.*

FISHER. Show him the way, boy. Heaven be his support!
Whate'er he has resolved, he'll execute.
                                                    [*Exit.*

Scene II.

Baronial mansion of Attinghausen. The BARON *upon a couch dying.* WALTER FURST, STAUFFACHER, MELCHTHAL, *and* BAUMGARTEN *attending round him.* WALTER TELL *kneeling before the dying man.*

FURST. All now is over with him. He is gone.
STAUFF. He lies not like one dead. The feather, see,
        Moves on his lips! His sleep is very calm,
        And on his features plays a placid smile.
                    [BAUMGARTEN *goes to the door and speaks*
                        with some one.
FURST. Who's there?
BAUGMARTEN (*returning*).
                    Tell's wife, your daughter; she insists
        That she must speak with you, and see her boy.
                    [WALTER TELL *rises.*
FURST. I who need comfort — can I comfort her?
        Does every sorrow centre on my head?
HEDWIG (*forcing her way in*).
        Where is my child? Unhand me! I must see
        him.
STAUFF. Be calm! Reflect you're in the house of death!
HEDWIG (*falling upon her boy's neck*).
        My Walter! Oh, he yet is mine!
WALTER.   Dear mother!
HEDW. And is it surely so? Art thou unhurt?
                    [*Gazing at him with anxious tenderness.*
        And is it possible he aimed at thee?
        How could he do it? Oh, he has no heart —
        And he could wing an arrow at his child!
FURST. His soul was racked with anguish when he did it.
        No choice was left him, but to shoot or die!
HEDW. Oh, if he had a father's heart, he would
        Have sooner perished by a thousand deaths!
STAUFF. You should be grateful for God's gracious care,
        That ordered things so well.
HEDWIG.   Can I forget
        What might have been the issue. God of
        heaven!
        Were I to live for centuries, I still

Should see my boy tied up, — his father's mark,—
And still the shaft would quiver in my heart!
MELCH. You know not how the viceroy taunted him!
HEDW. ⸢ Oh, ruthless heart of man! Offend his pride,
And reason in his breast forsakes her seat;
In his blind wrath he'll stake upon a cast
A child's existence, and a mother's heart!
BAUM. Is then your husband's fate not hard enough,
That you embitter it by such reproaches?
Have you no feeling for his sufferings?
HEDWIG (*turning to him and gazing full upon him*).
Hast thou tears only for thy friend's distress?
Say, where were you when he — my noble Tell,
Was bound in chains? Where was your friend-
ship, then?
The shameful wrong was done before your eyes;
Patient you stood, and let your friend be dragged,
Ay, from your very hands. Did ever Tell
Act thus to you? Did he stand whining by
When on your heels the viceroy's horsemen
pressed,
And full before you roared the storm-tossed lake?
Oh, not with idle tears he showed his pity;
Into the boat he sprung, forgot his home,
His wife, his children, and delivered thee!
FURST. It had been madness to attempt his rescue,
Unarmed, and few in numbers as we were.
HEDWIG (*casting herself upon his bosom*).
Oh, father, and thou, too, hast lost my Tell!
The country — all have lost him! All lament
His loss; and, oh, how he must pine for us!
Heaven keep his soul from sinking to despair!
No friend's consoling voice can penetrate
His dreary dungeon walls. Should he fall sick!
Ah! In the vapors of the murky vault
He must fall sick. Even as the Alpine rose
Grows pale and withers in the swampy air,
There is no life for him, but in the sun,
And in the balm of heaven's refreshing breeze.
Imprisoned? Liberty to him is breath;
He cannot live in the rank dungeon air!

STAUFF. Pray you be calm! And, hand in hand, we'll all
Combine to burst his prison doors.

HEDWIG. Without him,
What have you power to do? While Tell was
free,
There still, indeed, was hope — weak innocence
Had still a friend, and the oppressed a stay.
Tell saved you all! You cannot all combined
Release him from his cruel prison bonds.
[*The* BARON *wakes.*

BAUM. Hush, hush! He starts!

ATTINGHAUSEN (*sitting up*). Where is he?

STAUFFACHER. Who?

ATTINGHAUSEN. He leaves me, —
In my last moments he abandons me.

STAUFF. He means his nephew. Have they sent for
him?

FURST. He has been summoned. Cheerily, sir! Take
comfort!
He has found his heart at last, and is our own.

ATTING. Say, has he spoken for his native land?

STAUFF. Ay, like a hero!

ATTINGHAUSEN. Wherefore comes he not,
That he may take my blessing ere I die?
I feel my life fast ebbing to a close.

STAUFF. Nay, talk not thus, dear sir! This last short sleep
Has much refreshed you, and your eye is bright.

ATTING. Life is but pain, and even that has left me;
My sufferings, like my hopes, have passed away.
[*Observing the boy.*
What boy is that?

FURST. Bless him. Oh, good my lord!
He is my grandson, and is fatherless.
[HEDWIG *kneels with the boy before the
dying man.*

ATTING. And fatherless — I leave you all, ay, all!
Oh, wretched fate, that these old eyes should
see
My country's ruin, as they close in death.
Must I attain the utmost verge of life,
To feel my hopes go with me to the grave.

STAUFFACHER (*to* FURST).
> Shall he depart 'mid grief and gloom like this?
> Shall not his parting moments be illumed
> By hope's delightful beams? My noble lord,
> Raise up your drooping spirit! We are not
> Forsaken quite — past all deliverance.

ATTING. Who shall deliver you?

FURST.   Ourselves. For know
> The Cantons three are to each other pledged
> To hunt the tyrants from the land. The league
> Has been concluded, and a sacred oath
> Confirms our union. Ere another year
> Begins its circling course — the blow shall fall.
> In a free land your ashes shall repose.

ATTING. The league concluded! Is it really so?

MELCH. On one day shall the Cantons rise together.
> All is prepared to strike — and to this hour
> The secret closely kept though hundreds share
>   it;
> The ground is hollow 'neath the tyrant's feet;
> Their days of rule are numbered, and ere long
> No trace of their dominion shall remain.

ATTING. Ay, but their castles, how to master them?

MELCH. On the same day they, too, are doomed to fall.

ATTING. And are the nobles parties to this league?

STAUFF. We trust to their assistance should we need
>   it;
> As yet the peasantry alone have sworn.

ATTING. (*raising himself up in great astonishment*).
> And have the peasantry dared such a deed
> On their own charge without their nobles' aid —
> Relied so much on their own proper strength?
> Nay then, indeed, they want our help no more;
> We may go down to death cheered by the
>   thought
> That after us the majesty of man
> Will live, and be maintained by other hands.
>   [*He lays his hand upon the head of the child,
>   who is kneeling before him.*
> From this boy's head, whereon the apple lay,
> Your new and better liberty shall spring;

The old is crumbling down — the times are
    changing —
And from the ruins blooms a fairer life.

STAUFF*A*THER (*to* FURST).

See, see, what splendor streams around his eye!
This is not nature's last expiring flame,
It is the beam of renovated life.

ATTING*O* From their old towers the nobles are descending,
And swearing in the towns the civic oath.
In Uechtland and Thurgau the work's begun;
The noble Bern lifts her commanding head,
And Freyburg is a stronghold of the free;
The stirring Zurich calls her guilds to arms;
And now, behold! the ancient might of kings
Is shivered against her everlasting walls.

[*He speaks what follows with a prophetic
tone; his utterance rising into enthusiasm.*

I see the princes and their haughty peers,
Clad all in steel, come striding on to crush
A harmless shepherd race with mailed hand.
Desperate the conflict: 'tis for life or death;
And many a pass will tell to after years
Of glorious victories sealed in foemen's blood.*
The peasant throws himself with naked breast,
A willing victim on their serried lances.
They yield — the flower of chivalry's cut down,
And freedom waves her conquering banner
    high!

[*Grasps the hands of* WALTER FURST
and STAUFFACHER.

Hold fast together, then — forever fast!
Let freedom's haunts be one in heart and
    mind!
Set watches on your mountain-tops, that league

* An allusion to the gallant self-devotion of Arnold Struthan of Winkelried, at the battle of Sempach (9th July, 1386), who broke the Austrian
phalanx by rushing on their lances, grasping as many of them as he could
reach, and concentrating them upon his breast. The confederates rushed
forward through the gap thus opened by the sacrifice of their comrade, broke
and cut down their enemy's ranks, and soon became the masters of the field.
"Dear and faithful confederates, I will open you a passage. Protect my
wife and children," were the words of Winkelried as he rushed to death.

May answer league, when comes the hour to
    strike.
Be one — be one — be one ——
    [*He falls back upon the cushion. His life-
    less hands continue to grasp those of
    FURST and STAUFFACHER, who regard
    him for some moments in silence, and
    then retire, overcome with sorrow. Mean-
    while the servants have quietly pressed
    into the chamber, testifying different
    degrees of grief. Some kneel down beside
    him and weep on his body : while this
    scene is passing the castle bell tolls.*

RUDENZ (*entering hurriedly*).
    Lives he? Oh, say, can he still hear my voice?
FURST (*averting his face*).
    You are our seignior and protector now ;
    Henceforth this castle bears another name.
RUDENZ (*gazing at the body with deep emotion*).
    Oh, God! Is my repentance, then, too late?
    Could he not live some few brief moments more,
    To see the change that has come o'er my heart?
    Oh, I was deaf to his true counselling voice
    While yet he walked on earth. Now he is gone ;
    Gone and forever, — leaving me the debt, —
    The heavy debt I owe him — undischarged !
    Oh, tell me! did he part in anger with me?
STAUFF. When dying he was told what you had done,
    And blessed the valor that inspired your words!
RUDENZ (*kneeling down beside the dead body*).
    Yes, sacred relics of a man beloved !
    Thou lifeless corpse! Here, on thy death-cold
        hand,
    Do I abjure all foreign ties forever !
    And to my country's cause devote myself.
    I am a Switzer, and will act as one
    With my whole heart and soul.   [*Rises.*
                        Mourn for our friend,
    Our common parent, yet be not dismayed !
    'Tis not alone his lands that I inherit, —
    His heart — his spirit have devolved on me ;

And my young arm shall execute the task
For which his hoary age remained your debtor.
Give me your hands, ye venerable fathers !
Thine, Melchthal, too ! Nay, do not hesitate,
Nor from me turn distrustfully away.
Accept my plighted vow — my knightly oath !

FURST.   Give him your hands, my friends ! A heart like his
That sees and owns its error claims our trust.

MELCH.   You ever held the peasantry in scorn;
What surety have we that you mean us fair ?

RUD.   Oh, think not of the error of my youth !

STAUFFACHER (*to* MELCHTHAL).
Be one ! They were our father's latest words.
See they be not forgotten !

MELCH.   Take my hand, —
A peasant's hand, — and with it, noble sir,
The gage and the assurance of a man !
Without us, sir, what would the nobles be ?
Our order is more ancient, too, than yours !

RUD.   I honor it, and with my sword will shield it !

MELCH.   The arm, my lord, that tames the stubborn earth,
And makes its bosom blossom with increase,
Can also shield a man's defenceless breast.

RUD.   Then you shall shield my breast and I will yours ;
Thus each be strengthened by the others' aid !
Yet wherefore talk we while our native land
Is still to alien tyranny a prey ?
First let us sweep the foeman from the soil,
Then reconcile our difference in peace !
                    [*After a moment's pause.*
How ! You are silent ! Not a word for me ?
And have I yet no title to your trust ?
Then must I force my way, despite your will,
Into the league you secretly have formed.
You've held a Diet on the Rootli, — I
Know this, — know all that was transacted
there !
And though I was not trusted with your secret,
I still have kept it like a sacred pledge.

Trust me, I never was my country's foe,
Nor would I ever have ranged myself against
    you!
Yet you did wrong to put your rising off.
Time presses! We must strike, and swiftly,
    too!
Already Tell has fallen a sacrifice
To your delay.

STAUFF.   We swore to wait till Christmas.

RUD.   I was not there, — I did not take the oath.
If you delay I will not!

MELCHTHAL.   What! You would ——

RUD.   I count me now among the country's fathers,
And to protect you is my foremost duty.

FURST.   Within the earth to lay these dear remains,
That is your nearest and most sacred duty.

RUD.   When we have set the country free, we'll place
Our fresh, victorious wreaths upon his bier.
Oh, my dear friends, 'tis not your cause alone!
I have a cause to battle with the tyrants
That more concerns myself. Know, that my
    Bertha
Has disappeared, — been carried off by stealth,
Stolen from amongst us by their ruffian hands!

STAUFF. And has the tyrant dared so fell an outrage
Against a lady free and nobly born?

RUD.   Alas! my friends, I promised help to you,
And I must first implore it for myself?
She that I love is stolen — is forced away,
And who knows where the tyrant has concealed
    her.
Or with what outrages his ruffian crew
May force her into nuptials she detests?
Forsake me not! Oh help me to her rescue!
She loves you! Well, oh well, has she deserved
That all should rush to arms in her behalf.

STAUFF. What course do you propose?

RUDENZ.   Alas! I know not.
In the dark mystery that shrouds her fate,
In the dread agony of this suspense,
Where I can grasp at naught of certainty,

One single ray of comfort beams upon me.
From out the ruins of the tyrant's power
Alone can she be rescued from the grave.
Their strongholds must be levelled! Every one,
Ere we can pierce into her gloomy prison.

MELCH. Come, lead us on! We follow! Why defer
Until to-morrow what to-day may do?
Tell's arm was free when we at Rootli swore,
This foul enormity was yet undone.
And change of circumstance brings change of law.
Who such a coward as to waver still?

RUDENZ (*to* WALTER FURST).
Meanwhile to arms, and wait in readiness
The fiery signal on the mountain-tops.
For swifter than a boat can scour the lake
Shall you have tidings of our victory;
And when you see the welcome flames ascend,
Then, like the lightning, swoop upon the foe,
And lay the despots and their creatures low!

SCENE III.

*The pass near Küssnacht, sloping down from behind, with rocks
on either side. The travellers are visible upon the heights, before
they appear on the stage. Rocks all round the stage. Upon
one of the foremost a projecting cliff overgrown with brushwood.*

TELL (*enters with his crossbow*).
Here through this deep defile he needs must pass;
There leads no other road to Küssnacht; here
I'll do it; the opportunity is good.
Yon alder tree stands well for my concealment,
Thence my avenging shaft will surely reach him.
The straitness of the path forbids pursuit.
Now, Gessler, balance thine account with Heaven!
Thou must away from earth, thy sand is run.

I led a peaceful, inoffensive life;
My bow was bent on forest game alone,
And my pure soul was free from thoughts of
murder.
But thou hast scared me from my dream of peace;
The milk of human kindness thou hast turned

To rankling poison in my breast, and made
Appalling deeds familiar to my soul.
He who could make his own child's head his mark
Can speed his arrow to his foeman's heart.

My children dear, my loved and faithful wife,
Must be protected, tyrant, from thy fury!
When last I drew my bow, with trembling hand,
And thou, with murderous joy, a father forced
To level at his child; when, all in vain,
Writhing before thee, I implored thy mercy,
Then in the agony of my soul I vowed
A fearful oath, which met God's ear alone,
That when my bow next winged an arrow's flight
Its aim should be thy heart.   The vow I made
Amid the hellish torments of that moment
I hold a sacred debt, and I will pay it.

Thou art my lord, my emperor's delegate,
Yet would the emperor not have stretched his
     power
So far as thou.   He sent thee to these Cantons
To deal forth law, stern law, for he is angered;
But not to wanton with unbridled will
In every cruelty, with fiendlike joy :
There is a God to punish and avenge.

Come forth, thou bringer once of bitter pangs,
My precious jewel now, my chiefest treasure;
A mark I'll set thee, which the cry of grief
Could never penetrate, but thou shalt pierce it.
And thou, my trusty bowstring, that so oft
Has served me faithfully in sportive scenes,
Desert me not in this most serious hour —
Only be true this once, my own good cord,
That has so often winged the biting shaft : —
For shouldst thou fly successless from my hand,
I have no second to send after thee.
              [*Travellers pass over the stage.*
I'll sit me down upon this bench of stone,
Hewn for the wayworn traveller's brief repose —
For here there is no home.   Each hurries by

The other, with quick step and careless look,
Nor stays to question of his grief. Here goes
The merchant, full of care — the pilgrim next,
With slender scrip — and then the pious monk,
The scowling robber, and the jovial player,
The carrier with his heavy-laden horse,
That comes to us from the far haunts of men ;
For every road conducts to the world's end.
They all push onwards — every man intent
On his own several business — mine is murder.
                              [*Sits down.*
Time, was, my dearest children, when with joy
You hailed your father's safe return to home
From his long mountain toils; for when he came
He ever brought some little present with him.
A lovely Alpine flower — a curious bird —
Or elf-boat found by wanderers on the hills.
But now he goes in quest of other game :
In the wild pass he sits, and broods on murder ;
And watches for the life-blood of his foe,
But still his thoughts are fixed on you alone,
Dear children.   'Tis to guard your innocence,
To shield you from the tyrant's fell revenge,
He bends his bow to do a deed of blood !
                              [*Rises.*
Well — I am watching for a noble prey —
Does not the huntsman, with severest toil,
Roam for whole days amid the winter's cold,
Leap with a daring bound from rock to rock, —
And climb the jagged, slippery steeps, to which
His limbs are glued by his own streaming blood ;
And all this but to gain a wretched chamois.
A far more precious prize is now my aim —
The heart of that dire foe who would destroy me.
       [*Sprightly music heard in the distance,
             which comes gradually nearer.*
From my first years of boyhood I have used
The bow — been practised in the archer's feats ;
The bull's-eye many a time my shafts have hit,
And many a goodly prize have I brought home,
Won in the games of skill.   This day I'll make

My master-shot, and win the highest prize
Within the whole circumference of the mountains.
> [*A marriage train passes over the stage,*
> *and goes up the pass.* TELL *gazes at*
> *it, leaning on his bow.* He is joined
> *by* STUSSI, *the Ranger.*

STUSSI. There goes the bridal party of the steward
Of Mörlischachen's cloister. He is rich!
And has some ten good pastures on the Alps.
He goes to fetch his bride from Imisee,
There will be revelry to-night at Küssnacht.
Come with us — every honest man's invited.

TELL.   A gloomy guest fits not a wedding feast.

STUSSI. If grief oppress you, dash it from your heart!
Bear with your lot. The times are heavy now,
And we must snatch at pleasure while we can.
Here 'tis a bridal, there a burial.

TELL.   And oft the one treads close upon the other.

STUSSI. So runs the world at present. Everywhere
We meet with woe and misery enough.
There's been a slide of earth in Glarus, and
A whole side of the Glärnisch has fallen in.

TELL.   Strange! And do even the hills begin to totter?
There is stability for naught on earth.

STUSSI. Strange tidings, too, we hear from other parts.
I spoke with one but now, that came from Baden,
Who said a knight was on his way to court,
And as he rode along a swarm of wasps
Surrounded him, and settling on his horse,
So fiercely stung the beast that it fell dead,
And he proceeded to the court on foot.

TELL.   Even the weak are furnished with a sting.

ARMGART (*enters with several children, and places her-*
self at the entrance of the pass).

STUSSI. 'Tis thought to bode disaster to the country, —
Some horrid deed against the course of nature.

TELL.   Why, every day brings forth such fearful deeds;
There needs no miracle to tell their coming.

STUSSI. Too true!   He's blessed who tills his field in
peace,
And sits untroubled by his own fireside.

TELL.   The very meekest cannot rest in quiet,
         Unless it suits with his ill neighbor's humor.
              [TELL *looks frequently with restless expecta-*
                  tion towards the top of the pass.
STUSSI. So fare you well! You're waiting some one
              here?
TELL.   I am.
STUSSI.   A pleasant meeting with your friends!
         You are from Uri, are you not? His grace
         The governor's expected thence to-day.
TRAVELLER (*entering*).
         Look not to see the governor to-day.
         The streams are flooded by the heavy rains,
         And all the bridges have been swept away.
                                        [TELL *rises.*
ARMGART (*coming forward*).
         The viceroy not arrived?
STUSSI.   And do you seek him?
ARM.   Alas, I do!
STUSSI.   But why thus place yourself
         Where you obstruct his passage down the pass?
ARM.   Here he cannot escape me. He must hear me.
FRIESS. (*coming hastily down the pass, and calls upon*
                    the stage).
         Make way, make way! My lord, the governor,
         Is coming down on horseback close behind me.
                                        [*Exit* TELL.
ARMGART (*with animation*).
         The viceroy comes!
              [*She goes towards the pass with her children.*
                  GESSLER *and* RUDOLPH DER HARRAS *ap-*
                  pear upon the heights on horseback.
STUSSI (*to* FRIESSHARDT). How got ye through the
              stream
         When all the bridges have been carried down?
FRIESS. We've battled with the billows; and, my friend,
         An Alpine torrent's nothing after that.
STUSSI. How! Were you out, then, in that dreadful
              storm?
FRIESS. Ay, that we were! I shall not soon forget it.
STUSSI. Stay, speak——

FRIESS.   I cannot.   I must to the castle,
    And tell them that the governor's at hand.
                 [Exit.
STUSSI.   If honest men, now, had been in the ship,
    It had gone down with every soul on board : —
    Some folks are proof 'gainst fire and water
     both.   *[Looking round.*
    Where has the huntsman gone with whom I
     spoke?   *[Exit.*

Enter GESSLER *and* RUDOLPH DER HARRAS *on horseback.*

GESSL.   Say what you please; I am the emperor's
     servant,
    And my first care must be to do his pleasure.
    He did not send me here to fawn and cringe
    And coax these boors into good humor.   No!
    Obedience he must have.   We soon shall see
    If king or peasant is to lord it here?
ARM.   Now is the moment!   Now for my petition!
GESSL.   'Twas not in sport that I set up the cap
    In Altdorf — or to try the people's hearts —
    All this I knew before.   I set it up
    That they might learn to bend those stubborn
     necks
    They carry far too proudly — and I placed
    What well I knew their eyes could never brook
    Full in the road, which they perforce must
     pass,
    That, when their eyes fell on it, they might call
    That lord to mind whom they too much forget.
HAR.   But surely, sir, the people have some rights —
GESSL.   This is no time to settle what they are.
    Great projects are at work, and hatching now;
    The imperial house seeks to extend its power.
    Those vast designs of conquests, which the sire
    Has gloriously begun, the son will end.
    This petty nation is a stumbling-block —
    One way or other it must be subjected.
      [They are about to pass on.   ARMGART
       throws herself down before GESSLER.
ARM.   Mercy, lord governor!   Oh, pardon, pardon!

GESSL. Why do you cross me on the public road?
Stand back, I say.

ARMGART. My husband lies in prison;
My wretched orphans cry for bread. Have pity,
Pity, my lord, upon our sore distress!

HAR. Who are you, woman; and who is your husband?

ARM. A poor wild-hay-man of the Rigiberg,
Kind sir, who on the brow of the abyss,
Mows down the grass from steep and craggy shelves,
To which the very cattle dare not climb.

HARRAS (*to* GESSLER).
By Heaven! a sad and miserable life!
I prithee, give the wretched man his freedom.
How great soever his offence may be,
His horrid trade is punishment enough.
                              [*To* ARMGART.
You shall have justice. To the castle bring
Your suit. This is no place to deal with it.

ARM. No, no, I will not stir from where I stand,
Until your grace restore my husband to me.
Six months already has he been in prison,
And waits the sentence of a judge in vain.

GESSL. How! would you force me, woman? Hence!
Begone!

ARM. Justice, my lord! Ay, justice! Thou art judge!
The deputy of the emperor — of Heaven!
Then do thy duty, as thou hopest for justice
From Him who rules above, show it to us!

GESSL. Hence! drive this daring rabble from my sight!

ARMGART (*seizing his horse's reins*).
No, no, by Heaven, I've nothing more to lose.
Thou stirrest not, viceroy, from this spot until
Thou dost me fullest justice. Knit thy brows,
And roll thy eyes; I fear not. Our distress
Is so extreme, so boundless, that we care
No longer for thine anger.

GESSLER. Woman, hence!
Give way, I say, or I will ride thee down.

ARM.   Well, do so; there!
                [*Throws her children and herself upon the*
                    ground before him.
                            Here on the ground I lie,
            I and my children.   Let the wretched orphans
            Be trodden by thy horse into the dust!
            It will not be the worst that thou hast done.
HAR.   Are you mad, woman?
ARMGART (*continuing with vehemence*).
                            Many a day thou hast
            Trampled the emperor's lands beneath thy feet.
            Oh, I am but a woman!   Were I man,
            I'd find some better thing to do, than here
            Lie grovelling in the dust.
                [*The music of the wedding party is again*
                    heard from the top of the pass, but more
                    softly.
GESSLER.   Where are my knaves?
            Drag her away, lest I forget myself,
            And do some deed I may repent hereafter.
HAR.   My lord, the servants cannot force a passage;
            The pass is blocked up by a marriage party.
GESSL.   Too mild a ruler am I to this people,
            Their tongues are all too bold; nor have they yet
            Been tamed to due submission, as they shall be.
            I must take order for the remedy;
            I will subdue this stubborn mood of theirs,
            And crush the soul of liberty within them.
            I'll publish a new law throughout the land;
            I will ——
                [*An arrow pierces him, — he puts his hand on*
                    his heart, and is about to sink — with a
                    feeble voice.
                        Oh God, have mercy on my soul!
HAR.   My lord! my lord!   Oh God!   What's this?
                Whence came it?
ARMGART (*starts up*).
            Dead, dead!   He reels, he falls!   'Tis in his
                heart!
HARRAS (*springs from his horse*).
            This is most horrible!   Oh Heavens! sir knight,

Address yourself to God and pray for mercy;
You are a dying man.

GESSLER. That shot was Tell's.

*[He slides from his horse into the arms of
RUDOLPH DER HARRAS, who lays him down
upon the bench. TELL appears above, upon
the rocks.*

TELL. Thou knowest the archer, seek no other hand.
Our cottages are free, and innocence
Secure from thee: thou'lt be our curse no more.

[TELL disappears. People rush in.

STUSSI. What is the matter? Tell me what has happened?

ARM. The governor is shot, — killed by an arrow!

PEOPLE *(running in).*
Who has been shot?

*[While the foremost of the marriage party are
coming on the stage, the hindmost are still
upon the heights. The music continues.*

HARRAS. He's bleeding fast to death.
Away, for help — pursue the murderer!
Unhappy man, is't thus that thou must die?
Thou wouldst not heed the warnings that I gave
thee!

STUSSI. By heaven, his cheek is pale! His life ebbs
fast.

MANY VOICES.
Who did the deed?

HARRAS. What! Are the people mad
That they make music to a murder? Silence!

*[Music breaks off suddenly. People continue
to flock in.*

Speak, if thou canst, my lord. Hast thou no
charge
To intrust me with?

*[GESSLER makes signs with his hand, which he
repeats with vehemence, when he finds they
are not understood.*

What would you have me do?
Shall I to Kussnacht? I can't guess your
meaning.

Do not give way to this impatience.   Leave
All thoughts of earth and make your peace with
    Heaven.
    [*The whole marriage party gather round the*
      dying man.

STUSSI.   See there! how pale he grows!   Death's gather-
    ing now
About his heart; his eyes grow dim and glazed.

ARMGART (*holds up a child*).
    Look, children, how a tyrant dies!

HARRAS.   Mad hag!
Have you no touch of feeling that you look
On horrors such as these without a shudder?
Help me—take hold.   What, will not one assist
To pull the torturing arrow from his breast?

WOMEN. We touch the man whom God's own hand has
    struck!

HAR.   All curses light on you!   [*Draws his sword.*

STUSSI (*seizes his arm*).   Gently, sir knight!
Your power is at an end.   'Twere best forbear.
Our country's foe is fallen.   We will brook
No further violence.   We are free men.

ALL.   The country's free!

HARRAS.   And is it come to this?
Fear and obedience at an end so soon?
    [*To the soldiers of the guard who are throng-*
      ing in.
You see, my friends, the bloody piece of work
They've acted here.   'Tis now too late for
    help,
And to pursue the murderer were vain.
New duties claim our care.   Set on to Küss-
    nacht,
And let us save that fortress for the king!
For in an hour like this all ties of order,
Fealty, and faith are scattered to the winds.
No man's fidelity is to be trusted.
    [*As he is going out with the soldiers six*
      FRATRES MISERICORDIÆ *appear.*

ARM.   Here come the brotherhood of mercy.   Room!

STUSSI.   The victim's slain, and now the ravens stoop.

BROTHERS OF MERCY (*form a semicircle round the body,
      and sing in solemn tones*).
    With hasty step death presses on,
      Nor grants to man a moment's stay,
    He falls ere half his race be run
      In manhood's pride is swept away!
    Prepared or unprepared to die,
    He stands before his Judge on high.
      [*While they are repeating the last two lines,
        the curtain falls.*

ACT V.

SCENE I.

*A common near Altdorf. In the background to the right the
keep of Uri, with the scaffold still standing, as in the third
scene of the first act. To the left the view opens upon numerous mountains, on all of which signal fires are burning.
Day is breaking, and bells are heard ringing from various
distances.*

RUODI, KUONI, WERNI, MASTER MASON, *and many other
    country people, also women and children.*

RUODI.   Look at the fiery signals on the mountains!
MASON.   Hark to the bells above the forest there!
RUODI.   The enemy's expelled.
MASON.   The forts are taken.
RUODI.   And we of Uri, do we still endure
    Upon our native soil the tyrant's keep?
    Are we the last to strike for liberty?
MASON.   Shall the yoke stand that was to bow our necks?
    Up! Tear it to the ground!
ALL.   Down, down with it!
RUODI.   Where is the Stier of Uri?
URI.   Here. What would ye?
RUODI.   Up to your tower, and wind us such a blast,
    As shall resound afar, from hill to hill;
    Rousing the echoes of each peak and glen,
    And call the mountain men in haste together!
      [*Exit* STIER OF URI — *enter* WALTER FURST.

FURST.   Stay, stay, my friends! As yet we have not learned
          What has been done in Unterwald and Schwytz.
          Let's wait till we receive intelligence!

RUODI.   Wait, wait for what? The accursed tyrant's dead,
          And the bright day of liberty has dawned!

MASON.   How! Do these flaming signals not suffice,
          That blaze on every mountain top around?

RUODI.   Come all, fall to — come, men and women, all!
          Destroy the scaffold! Tear the arches down!
          Down with the walls; let not a stone remain.

MASON.   Come, comrades, come! We built it, and we know
          How best to hurl it down.

ALL.   Come! Down with it!
                [They fall upon the building at every side.

FURST.   The floodgate's burst. They're not to be restrained.
                [Enter MELCHTHAL *and* BAUMGARTEN.

MELCH.   What! Stands the fortress still, when Sarnen lies
          In ashes, and when Rossberg is a ruin?

FURST.   You, Melchthal, here? D'ye bring us liberty?
          Say, have you freed the country of the foe?

MELCH.   We've swept them from the soil. Rejoice, my friend;
          Now, at this very moment, while we speak,
          There's not a tyrant left in Switzerland!

FURST.   How did you get the forts into your power?

MELCH.   Rudenz it was who with a gallant arm,
          And manly daring, took the keep at Sarnen.
          The Rossberg I had stormed the night before.
          But hear what chanced. Scarce had we driven the foe
          Forth from the keep, and given it to the flames,
          That now rose crackling upwards to the skies,
          When from the blaze rushed Diethelm, Gessler's page,
          Exclaiming, "Lady Bertha will be burnt!"

FURST.   Good heavens!
                [The beams of the scaffold are heard falling.

MELCH.   'Twas she herself. Here had she been
        Immured in secret by the viceroy's orders.
        Rudenz sprang up in frenzy. For we heard
        The beams and massive pillars crashing down,
        And through the volumed smoke the piteous
           shrieks
        Of the unhappy lady.

FURST.   Is she saved?

MELCH. Here was a time for promptness and decision!
        Had he been nothing but our baron, then
        We should have been most chary of our lives;
        But he was our confederate, and Bertha
        Honored the people. So without a thought,
        We risked the worst, and rushed into the flames.

FURST. But is she saved?

MELCH.   She is. Rudenz and I
        Bore her between us from the blazing pile,
        With crashing timbers toppling all around.
        And when she had revived, the danger past,
        And raised her eyes to meet the light of heaven,
        The baron fell upon my breast; and then
        A silent vow of friendship passed between us——
        A vow that, tempered in yon furnace heat,
        Will last through every shock of time and fate.

FURST. Where is the Landenberg?

MELCH.   Across the Brünig.
        No fault of mine it was, that he, who quenched
        My father's eyesight, should go hence unharmed.
        He fled — I followed — overtook and seized
           him,
        And dragged him to my father's feet. The sword
        Already quivered o'er the caitiff's head,
        When at the entreaty of the blind old man,
        I spared the life for which he basely prayed.
        He swore *Urphede,** never to return:
        He'll keep his oath, for he has felt our arm.

FURST. Thank God, our victory's unstained by blood!

---

* The Urphede was an oath of peculiar force. When a man who was at
feud with another, invaded his lands and was worsted, he often made terms
with his enemy by swearing the Urphede, by which he bound himself to
depart and never to return with a hostile intention.

CHILDREN (*running across the stage with fragments of wood*).

Liberty! Liberty! Hurrah, we're free!

FURST.   Oh! what a joyous scene! These children will,
E'en to their latest day, remember it.

[*Girls bring in the cap upon a pole. The whole stage is filled with people.*

RUODI.   Here is the cap, to which we were to bow!

BAUM.   Command us, how we shall dispose of it.

FURST.   Heavens! 'Twas beneath this cap my grandson
stood!

SEVERAL VOICES.

Destroy the emblem of the tyrant's power!
Let it burn!

FURST.   No.   Rather be preserved!
'Twas once the instrument of despots — now
'Twill be a lasting symbol of our freedom.

[*Peasants, men, women, and children, some standing, others sitting upon the beams of the shattered scaffold, all picturesquely grouped, in a large semicircle.*

MELCH.   Thus now, my friends, with light and merry
hearts,
We stand upon the wreck of tyranny ;
And gallantly have we fulfilled the oath,
Which we at Rootli swore, confederates!

FURST.   The work is but begun.   We must be firm.
For, be assured, the king will make all speed,
To avenge his viceroy's death, and reinstate,
By force of arms, the tyrant we've expelled.

MELCH.   Why, let him come, with all his armaments!
The foe within has fled before our arms;
We'll give him welcome warmly from without!

RUODI.   The passes to the country are but few ;
And these we'll boldly cover with our bodies.

BAUM.   We are bound by an indissoluble league,
And all his armies shall not make us quail.

[*Enter* ROSSELMANN *and* STAUFFACHER.

ROSSELMANN (*speaking as he enters*).

These are the awful judgments of the lord!

PEAS.   What is the matter?

Rosselmann.   In what times we live!
Furst.   Say on, what is't?   Ha, Werner, is it you?
          What tidings?
Peasant.   What's the matter?
Rosselmann.   Hear and wonder.
Stauff. We are released from one great cause of dread.
Rossel   The emperor is murdered.
Furst.   Gracious heaven!
          [Peasants *rise up and throng round* Stauf-
              facher.
All.   Murdered! the emperor? What! The emperor!
          Hear!
Melch.   Impossible! How came you by the news?
Stauff. 'Tis true! Near Bruck, by the assassin's hand,
          King Albert fell. A most trustworthy man,
          John Müller, from Schaffhausen, brought the
          news.
Furst.   Who dared commit so horrible a deed?
Stauff. The doer makes the deed more dreadful still;
          It was his nephew, his own brother's child,
          Duke John of Austria, who struck the blow.
Melch.   What drove him to so dire a parricide?
Stauff. The emperor kept his patrimony back,
          Despite his urgent importunities;
          'Twas said, indeed, he never meant to give it,
          But with a mitre to appease the duke.
          However this may be, the duke gave ear,
          To the ill counsel of his friends in arms;
          And with the noble lords, Von Eschenbach,
          Von Tegerfeld, Von Wart, and Palm, resolved,
          Since his demands for justice were despised,
          With his own hands to take revenge at least.
Furst.   But say, how compassed he the dreadful deed?
Stauff. The king was riding down from Stein to Baden,
          Upon his way to join the court at Rheinfeld, —
          With him a train of high-born gentlemen,
          And the young princes, John and Leopold.
          And when they reached the ferry of the Reuss,
          The assassins forced their way into the boat,
          To separate the emperor from his suite.
          His highness landed, and was riding on

Across a fresh-ploughed field — where once, they
    say,
A mighty city stood in Pagan times —
With Hapsburg's ancient turrets full in sight,
Where all the grandeur of his line had birth —
When Duke John plunged a dagger in his
    throat,
Palm ran him through the body with his lance,
Eschenbach cleft his skull at one fell blow,
And down he sank, all weltering in his blood,
On his own soil, by his own kinsmen slain.
Those on the opposite bank, who saw the deed,
Being parted by the stream, could only raise
An unavailing cry of loud lament.
But a poor woman, sitting by the way,
Raised him, and on her breast he bled to death.

MELCH.   Thus has he dug his own untimely grave,
Who sought insatiably to grasp at all.

STAUFF.   The country round is filled with dire alarm.
The mountain passes are blockaded all,
And sentinels on every frontier set ;
E'en ancient Zurich barricades her gates,
That for these thirty years have open stood,
Dreading the murderers, and the avengers
    more,
For cruel Agnes comes, the Hungarian queen,
To all her sex's tenderness a stranger,
Armed with the thunders of the church to
    wreak
Dire vengeance for her parent's royal blood,
On the whole race of those that murdered him, —
Upon their servants, children, children's chil-
    dren, —
Nay' on the stones that build their castle walls.
Deep has she sworn a vow to immolate
Whole generations on her father's tomb,
And bathe in blood as in the dew of May.

MELCH.   Know you which way the murderers have fled ?

STAUFF.   No sooner had they done the deed than they
Took flight, each following a different route,
And parted, ne'er to see each other more.

Duke John must still be wandering in the mountains.

FURST. And thus their crime has yielded them no fruits.
Revenge is barren. Of itself it makes
The dreadful food it feeds on; its delight
Is murder — its satiety despair.

STAUFF. The assassins reap no profit by their crime;
But we shall pluck with unpolluted hands
The teeming fruits of their most bloody deed,
For we are ransomed from our heaviest fear;
The direst foe of liberty has fallen,
And, 'tis reported, that the crown will pass
From Hapsburg's house into another line.
The empire is determined to assert
Its old prerogative of choice, I hear.

FURST *and several others.*
Has any one been named to you?

STAUFFACHER. The Count
Of Luxembourg is widely named already.

FURST. T'is well we stood so stanchly by the empire!
Now we may hope for justice, and with cause.

STAUFF. The emperor will need some valiant friends,
And he will shelter us from Austria's vengeance.
[*The peasantry embrace. Enter* SACRIST,
with imperial messenger.

SACRIST. Here are the worthy chiefs of Switzerland!

ROSSELMANN *and several others.*
Sacrist, what news?

SACRISTAN. A courier brings this letter.

ALL (*to* WALTER FURST).
Open and read it.

FURST (*reading*). " To the worthy men
Of Uri, Schwytz, and Unterwald, the Queen
Elizabeth sends grace and all good wishes!"

MANY VOICES.
What wants the queen with us? Her reign is done.

FURST (*reads*).
" In the great grief and doleful widowhood,
In which the bloody exit of her lord
Has plunged her majesty, she still remembers
The ancient faith and love of Switzerland."

MELCH.   She ne'er did that in her prosperity.

ROSSEL.   Hush, let us hear.

FURST (*reads*).   " And she is well assured,
Her people will in due abhorrence hold
The perpetrators of this damned deed.
On the three Cantons, therefore, she relies,
That they in nowise lend the murderer's aid ;
But rather, that they loyally assist
To give them up to the avenger's hand,
Remembering the love and grace which they
Of old received from Rudolph's princely house."
        [*Symptoms of dissatisfaction among the
            peasantry.*

MANY VOICES.
        The love and grace !

STAUFF. Grace from the father we, indeed, received,
But what have we to boast of from the son ?
Did he confirm the charter of our freedom,
As all preceding emperors had done ?
Did he judge righteous judgment, or afford
Shelter or stay to innocence oppressed ?
Nay, did he e'en give audience to the envoys
We sent to lay our grievances before him ?
Not one of all these things e'er did the king.
And had we not ourselves achieved our rights
By resolute valor our necessities
Had never touched him.   Gratitude to him !
Within these vales he sowed not gratitude.
He stood upon an eminence — he might
Have been a very father to his people,
But all his aim and pleasure was to raise
Himself and his own house : and now may those
Whom he has aggrandized lament for him !

FURST.   We will not triumph in his fall, nor now
Recall to mind the wrongs we have endured.
Far be't from us !   Yet, that we should avenge
The sovereign's death, who never did us good,
And hunt down those who ne'er molested us,
Becomes us not, nor is our duty.   Love
Must bring its offerings free and unconstrained ;

From all enforced duties death absolves —
And unto him we are no longer bound.

MELCH.   And if the queen laments within her bower,
Accusing heaven in sorrow's wild despair;
Here see a people from its anguish freed.
To that same heaven send up its thankful praise,
For who would reap regrets must sow affection.
[*Exit the imperial courier.*

STAUFFACHER (*to the people*).
But where is Tell? Shall he, our freedom's
founder,
Alone be absent from our festival?
He did the most — endured the worst of all.
Come — to his dwelling let us all repair,
And bid the savior of our country hail!
[*Exeunt omnes.*

SCENE II.

Interior of TELL'S *cottage. A fire burning on the hearth. The
open door shows the scene outside.*

HEDWIG, WALTER, *and* WILHELM.

HEDW.   Boys, dearest boys! your father comes to-day.
He lives, is free, and we and all are free!
The country owes its liberty to him!

WALT.   And I too, mother, bore my part in it;
I shall be named with him. My father's shaft
Went closely by my life, but yet I shook not!

HEDWIG (*embracing him*).
Yes, yes, thou art restored to me again!
Twice have I given thee birth, twice suffered all
A mother's agonies for thee, my child!
But this is past; I have you both, boys, both!
And your dear father will be back to-day.
[*A monk appears at the door.*

WILH.   See, mother, yonder stands a holy friar;
He's asking alms, no doubt.

HEDWIG.   Go lead him in,
That we may give him cheer, and make him feel
That he has come into the house of joy.
[*Exit, and returns immediately with a cup.*

WILHELM (*to the monk*).
        Come in, good man.   Mother will give you food.
WALT.   Come in, and rest, then go refreshed away!
MONK (*glancing round in terror, with unquiet looks*).
        Where am I?   In what country?
WALTER.   Have you lost
        Your way, that you are ignorant of this?
        You are at Bürglen, in the land of Uri,
        Just at the entrance of the Sheckenthal.
MONK (*to* HEDWIG).
        Are you alone?   Your husband, is he here?
HEDW.   I momently expect him.   But what ails you?
        You look as one whose soul is ill at ease.
        Whoe'er you be, you are in want; take that.
                        [*Offers him the cup.*
MONK.   Howe'er my sinking heart may yearn for food,
        I will take nothing till you've promised me ——
HEDW.   Touch not my dress, nor yet advance one step.
        Stand off, I say, if you would have me hear you.
MONK.   Oh, by this hearth's bright, hospitable blaze,
        By your dear children's heads, which I em-
            brace ——   [*Grasps the boys.*
HEDW.   Stand back, I say!   What is your purpose, man?
        Back from my boys!   You are no monk, — no, no.
        Beneath that robe content and peace should dwell,
        But neither lives within that face of thine.
MONK.   I am the veriest wretch that breathes on earth.
HEDW.   The heart is never deaf to wretchedness;
        But thy look freezes up my inmost soul.
WALTER (*springs up*).
        Mother, my father!
HEDWIG.   Oh, my God!
        [*Is about to follow, trembles and stops.*
WILHELM (*running after his brother*).   My father!
WALTER (*without*).   Thou'rt here once more!
WILHELM (*without*).   My father, my dear father!
TELL (*without*).
        Yes, here I am once more!   Where is your
          mother?   [*They enter.*
WALT.   There at the door she stands, and can no further,
        She trembles so with terror and with joy.

TELL.   Oh Hedwig, Hedwig, mother of my children!
        God has been kind and helpful in our woes.
        No tyrant's hand shall e'er divide us more.
HEDWIG (*falling on his neck*).
        Oh, Tell, what have I suffered for thy sake!
                        [*Monk becomes attentive.*
TELL.   Forget it now, and live for joy alone!
        I'm here again with you!   This is my cot!
        I stand again on mine own hearth!
WILHELM.   But, father,
        Where is your crossbow left?   I see it not.
TELL.   Nor shalt thou ever see it more, my boy.
        It is suspended in a holy place,
        And in the chase shall ne'er be used again.
HEDW.   Oh, Tell, Tell!
                        [*Steps back, dropping his hand.*
TELL.   What alarms thee, dearest wife?
HEDW.   How — how dost thou return to me?   This
                hand ——
        Dare I take hold of it?   This hand — Oh God!
TELL (*with firmness and animation*).
        Has shielded you and set my country free;
        Freely I raise it in the face of Heaven.
                [MONK *gives a sudden start — he looks at him.*
        Who is this friar here?
HEDWIG.   Ah, I forgot him.
        Speak thou with him; I shudder at his presence.
MONK (*stepping nearer*).
        Are you that Tell that slew the governor?
TELL.   Yes, I am he.   I hide the fact from no man.
MONK.   You are that Tell!   Ah! it is God's own hand
        That hath conducted me beneath your roof.
TELL (*examining him closely*).
        You are no monk.   Who are you?
MONK.   You have slain
        The governor, who did you wrong.   I too,
        Have slain a foe, who late denied me justice.
        He was no less your enemy than mine.
        I've rid the land of him.
TELL (*drawing back*).   Thou art — oh horror!
        In — children, children — in without a word.

Go, my dear wife! Go! Go! Unhappy man,
Thou shouldst be ——

HEDWIG.   Heavens, who is it?

TELL.   Do not ask.
Away! away! the children must not hear it.
Out of the house — away! Thou must not rest
'Neath the same roof with this unhappy man!

HEDW. Alas! What is it? Come!
                              [*Exit with the children.*

TELL (*to the* MONK).   Thou art the Duke
Of Austria — I know it. Thou hast slain
The emperor, thy uncle, and liege lord.

JOHN. He robbed me of my patrimony.

TELL.   How!
Slain him — thy king, thy uncle! And the earth
Still bears thee! And the sun still shines on thee!

JOHN. Tell, hear me, ere you ——

TELL.   Reeking with the blood
Of him that was thy emperor and kinsman,
Durst thou set foot within my spotless house?
Show thy fell visage to a virtuous man,
And claim the rites of hospitality?

JOHN. I hoped to find compassion at your hands.
You also took revenge upon your foe!

TELL. Unhappy man! And dar'st thou thus confound
Ambition's bloody crime with the dread act
To which a father's direful need impelled him?
Hadst thou to shield thy children's darling heads?
To guard thy fireside's sanctuary — ward off
The last, worst doom from all that thou didst love?
To heaven I raise my unpolluted hands,
To curse thine act and thee! I have avenged
That holy nature which thou hast profaned.
I have no part with thee. Thou art a murderer;
I've shielded all that was most dear to me.

JOHN. You cast me off to comfortless despair!

TELL. My blood runs cold even while I talk with thee.

Away ! Pursue thine awful course ! Nor longer
Pollute the cot where innocence abides!
> [JOHN *turns to depart.*

JOHN. I cannot live, and will no longer thus!

TELL. And yet my soul bleeds for thee — gracious
     heaven!
So young, of such a noble line, the grandson
Of Rudolph, once my lord and emperor,
An outcast — murderer — standing at my door,
The poor man's door — a suppliant, in despair!
> [*Covers his face.*

JOHN. If thou hast power to weep, oh let my fate
Move your compassion — it is horrible.
I am — say, rather was — a prince. I might
Have been most happy had I only curbed
The impatience of my passionate desires;
But envy gnawed my heart — I saw the youth
Of mine own cousin Leopold endowed
With honor, and enriched with broad domains,
The while myself, that was in years his equal,
Was kept in abject and disgraceful nonage.

TELL. Unhappy man, thy uncle knew thee well,
When he withheld both land and subjects from
     thee ;
Thou, by thy mad and desperate act hast set
A fearful seal upon his sage resolve.
Where are the bloody partners of thy crime ?

JOHN. Where'er the demon of revenge has borne them ;
I have not seen them since the luckless deed.

TELL. Know'st thou the empire's ban is out, — that
     thou
Art interdicted to thy friends, and given
An outlawed victim to thine enemies !

JOHN. Therefore I shun all public thoroughfares,
And venture not to knock at any door —
I turn my footsteps to the wilds, and through
The mountains roam, a terror to myself.
From mine own self I shrink with horror back,
Should a chance brook reflect my ill-starred form.
If thou hast pity for a fellow-mortal ——
> [*Falls down before him.*

TELL.   Stand up, stand up!
JOHN.   Not till thou shalt extend
            Thy hand in promise of assistance to me.
TELL.   Can I assist thee?   Can a sinful man?
            Yet get thee up, — how black soe'er thy crime,
            Thou art a man. I, too, am one. From Tell
            Shall no one part uncomforted. I will
            Do all that lies within my power.
DUKE JOHN (*springs up and grasps him ardently by the
            hand*).   Oh, Tell,
            You save me from the terrors of despair.
TELL.   Let go my hand! Thou must away. Thou canst
                not
            Remain here undiscovered, and discovered
            Thou canst not count on succor.   Which way,
                then,
            Wilt bend thy steps? Where dost thou hope to
                find
            A place of rest?
DUKE JOHN.   Alas! alas! I know not.
TELL.   Hear, then, what heaven suggested to my heart,
            Thou must to Italy, — to Saint Peter's city, —
            There cast thyself at the pope's feet, — confess
            Thy guilt to him, and ease thy laden soul!
JOHN.   But will he not surrender me to vengeance!
TELL.   Whate'er he does receive as God's decree.
JOHN.   But how am I to reach that unknown land?
            I have no knowledge of the way, and dare not
            Attach myself to other travellers.
TELL.   I will describe the road, and mark me well!
            You must ascend, keeping along the Reuss,
            Which from the mountains dashes wildly down.
DUKE JOHN (*in alarm*).
            What! See the Reuss? The witness of my deed!
TELL.   The road you take lies through the river's
                gorge,
            And many a cross proclaims where travellers
            Have perished 'neath the avalanche's fall.
JOHN.   I have no fear for nature's terrors, so
            I can appease the torments of my soul.
TELL.   At every cross kneel down and expiate

Your crime with burning penitential tears —
And if you 'scape the perils of the pass,
And are not whelmed beneath the drifted snows
That from the frozen peaks come sweeping down,
You'll reach the bridge that hangs in drizzling
    spray;
Then if it yield not 'neath your heavy guilt,
When you have left it safely in your rear,
Before you frowns the gloomy Gate of Rocks,
Where never sun did shine. Proceed through this,
And you will reach a bright and gladsome vale.
Yet must you hurry on with hasty steps,
For in the haunts of peace you must not linger.

JOHN. Oh, Rudolph, Rudolph, royal grandsire! thus
Thy grandson first sets foot within thy realms!

TELL. Ascending still you gain the Gotthardt's heights,
On which the everlasting lakes repose,
That from the streams of heaven itself are fed,
There to the German soil you bid farewell;
And thence, with rapid course, another stream
Leads you to Italy, your promised land.
    [*Ranz des Vaches sounded on Alp-horns is
      heard without.*
But I hear voices! Hence!

HEDWIG (*hurrying in*). Where art thou, Tell?
Our father comes, and in exulting bands
All the confederates approach.

DUKE JOHN (*covering himself*). Woe's me!
I dare not tarry 'mid this happiness!

TELL. Go, dearest wife, and give this man to eat.
Spare not your bounty. For his road is long,
And one where shelter will be hard to find.
Quick! they approach.

HEDWIG. Who is he?

TELL. Do not ask!
And when he quits thee, turn thine eyes away
That they may not behold the road he takes.
    [DUKE JOHN *advances hastily towards* TELL,
      *but he beckons him aside and exit. When
      both have left the stage, the scene changes,
      and discloses in*

Scene III.

The whole valley before Tell's *house, the heights which enclose it occupied by peasants, grouped into tableaux. Some are seen crossing a lofty bridge which crosses to the Sechen.* Walter Furst *with the two boys.* Werner *and* Stauffacher *come forward. Others throng after them. When* Tell *appears all receive him with loud cheers.*

All.   Long live brave Tell, our shield, our liberator.

        [*While those in front are crowding round* Tell *and embracing him,* Rudenz *and* Bertha *appear. The former salutes the peasantry, the latter embraces* Hedwig. *The music from the mountains continues to play. When it has stopped,* Bertha *steps into the centre of the crowd.*

Berth.   Peasants! Confederates! Into your league
          Receive me here that happily am the first
          To find protection in the land of freedom.
          To your brave hands I now intrust my rights.
          Will you protect me as your citizen?

Peas.   Ay, that we will, with life and fortune both!

Berth.   'Tis well! And to this youth I give my hand.
          A free Swiss maiden to a free Swiss man!

Rud.   And from this moment all my serfs are free!

                  [*Music and the curtain falls.*

DON CARLOS.

ACT I.

SCENE I.

The Royal Gardens in Aranjuez.

CARLOS *and* DOMINGO.

DOMINGO.

Our pleasant sojourn in Aranjuez
Is over now, and yet your highness quits
These joyous scenes no happier than before.
Our visit hath been fruitless. Oh, my prince,
Break this mysterious and gloomy silence!
Open your heart to your own father's heart!
A monarch never can too dearly buy
The peace of his own son — his only son.
[CARLOS *looks on the ground in silence.*
Is there one dearest wish that bounteous Heaven
Hath e'er withheld from her most favored child?
I stood beside, when in Toledo's walls
The lofty Charles received his vassals' homage,

117

When conquered princes thronged to kiss his hand,
And there at once six mighty kingdoms fell
In fealty at his feet: I stood and marked
The young, proud blood mount to his glowing cheek,
I saw his bosom swell with high resolves,
His eye, all radiant with triumphant pride,
Flash through the assembled throng; and that same eye
Confessed, "Now am I wholly satisfied!"
                          [CARLOS *turns away.*
This silent sorrow, which for eight long moons
Hath hung its shadows, prince, upon your brow —
The mystery of the court, the nation's grief —
Hath cost your father many a sleepless night,
And many a tear of anguish to your mother.

CARLOS (*turning hastily round*).

My mother! Grant, O heaven, I may forget
How she became my mother!

DOMINGO.

              Gracious prince!

CARLOS (*passing his hands thoughtfully over his brow*).
Alas! alas! a fruitful source of woe
Have mothers been to me. My youngest act,
When first these eyes beheld the light of day,
Destroyed a mother.

DOMINGO.

              Is it possible
That this reproach disturbs your conscience, prince

CARLOS.

And my new mother! Hath she not already
Cost me my father's heart? Scarce loved at best,
My claim to some small favor lay in this —
I was his only child! 'Tis over! She
Hath blest him with a daughter — and who knows
What slumbering ills the future hath in store?

DOMINGO.

You jest, my prince. All Spain adores its queen.
Shall it be thought that you, of all the world,

Alone should view her with the eyes of hate —
Gaze on her charms, and yet be coldly wise?
How, prince? The loveliest lady of her time,
A queen withal, and once your own betrothed?
No, no, impossible — it cannot be!
Where all men love, you surely cannot hate.
Carlos could never so belie himself.
I prithee, prince, take heed she do not learn
That she hath lost her son's regard. The news
Would pain her deeply.

CARLOS.

Ay, sir! think you so?

DOMINGO.

Your highness doubtless will remember how,
At the late tournament in Saragossa,
A lance's splinter struck our gracious sire.
The queen, attended by her ladies, sat
High in the centre gallery of the palace,
And looked upon the fight. A cry arose,
"The king! he bleeds!" Soon through the general din,
A rising murmur strikes upon her ear.
"The prince — the prince!" she cries, and forward
    rushed,
As though to leap down from the balcony,
When a voice answered, "No, the king himself!"
"Then send for his physicians!" she replied,
And straight regained her former self-composure.
                            [*After a short pause.*
But you seem wrapped in thought?

CARLOS.

In wonder, sir,
That the king's merry confessor should own
So rare a skill in the romancer's art.   [*Austerely*
Yet have I heard it said that those
Who watch men's looks and carry tales about,
Have done more mischief in this world of ours
Than the assassin's knife, or poisoned bowl.
Your labor, sir, hath been but ill-bestowed;
Would you win thanks, go seek them of the king.

DOMINGO.

This caution, prince, is wise. Be circumspect
With men — but not with every man alike.
Repel not friends and hypocrites together;
I mean you well, believe me!

CARLOS.

            Say you so?
Let not my father mark it, then, or else
Farewell your hopes forever of the purple.

DOMINGO (*starts*).

How!

CARLOS.

     Even so! Hath he not promised you
The earliest purple in the gift of Spain?

DOMINGO.

You mock me, prince!

CARLOS.

          Nay! Heaven forefend, that I
Should mock that awful man whose fateful lips
Can doom my father or to heaven or hell!

DOMINGO.

I dare not, prince, presume to penetrate
The sacred mystery of your secret grief,
Yet I implore your highness to remember
That, for a conscience ill at ease, the church
Hath opened an asylum, of which kings
Hold not the key — where even crimes are purged
Beneath the holy sacramental seal.
You know my meaning, prince — I've said enough.

CARLOS.

No! be it never said, I tempted so
The keeper of that seal.

DOMINGO.

          Prince, this mistrust ——
You wrong the most devoted of your servants.

CARLOS.

Then give me up at once without a thought
Thou art a holy man — the world knows that —
But, to speak plain, too zealous far for me.
The road to Peter's chair is long and rough,
And too much knowledge might encumber you.
Go, tell this to the king, who sent thee hither!

DOMINGO.

Who sent me hither?

CARLOS.

Ay! Those were my words.
Too well — too well, I know, that I'm betrayed,
Slandered on every hand — that at this court
A hundred eyes are hired to watch my steps.
I know, that royal Philip to his slaves
Hath sold his only son, and every wretch,
Who takes account of each half-uttered word,
Receives such princely guerdon as was ne'er
Bestowed on deeds of honor. Oh, I know ——
But hush! — no more of that! My heart will else
O'erflow and I've already said too much.

DOMINGO.

The king is minded, ere the set of sun,
To reach Madrid : I see the court is mustering.
Have I permission, prince?

CARLOS.

I'll follow straight.
[*Exit* DOMINGO.

CARLOS (*after a short silence*).

O wretched Philip! wretched as thy son!
Soon shall thy bosom bleed at every pore,
Torn by suspicion's poisonous serpent fang.
Thy fell sagacity full soon shall pierce
The fatal secret it is bent to know,
And thou wilt madden, when it breaks upon thee!

Scene II.

Carlos, Marquis of Posa.

CARLOS.

Lo! Who comes here? 'Tis he! O ye kind heavens
My Roderigo!

MARQUIS.

Carlos!

CARLOS.

Can it be?
And is it truly thou? O yes, it is!
I press thee to my bosom, and I feel
Thy throbbing heart beat wildly 'gainst mine own:
And now all's well again. In this embrace
My sick, sad heart is comforted. I hang
Upon my Roderigo's neck!

MARQUIS.

Thy heart!
Thy sick sad heart! And what is well again —
What needeth to be well? Thy words amaze me.

CARLOS.

What brings thee back so suddenly from Brussels?
Whom must I thank for this most glad surprise?
And dare I ask? Whom should I thank but thee,
Thou gracious and all bounteous Providence?
Forgive me, heaven! if joy hath crazed my brain.
Thou knewest no angel watched at Carlos' side,
And sent me this! And yet I ask who sent him.

MARQUIS.

Pardon, dear prince, if I can only meet
With wonder these tumultuous ecstacies.
Not thus I looked to find Don Philip's son.
A hectic red burns on your pallid cheek,
And your lips quiver with a feverish heat.
What must I think, dear prince? No more I see
The youth of lion heart, to whom I come
The envoy of a brave and suffering people.
For now I stand not here as Roderigo —

Not as the playmate of the stripling Carlos —
But, as the deputy of all mankind,
I clasp thee thus : — 'tis Flanders that clings here
Around thy neck, appealing with my tears
To thee for succor in her bitter need.
This land is lost, this land so dear to thee,
If Alva, bigotry's relentless tool,
Advance on Brussels with his Spanish laws.
This noble country's last faint hope depends
On thee, loved scion of imperial Charles !
And, should thy noble heart forget to beat
In human nature's cause, Flanders is lost !

CARLOS.

Then it is lost !

MARQUIS.

What do I hear ?   Alas !

CARLOS.

Thou speakest of times that long have passed away.
I, too, have had my visions of a Carlos,
Whose cheek would fire at freedom's glorious name,
But he, alas ! has long been in his grave.
He, thou seest here, no longer is that Carlos,
Who took his leave of thee in Alcala,
Who in the fervor of a youthful heart,
Resolved, at some no distant time, to wake
The golden age in Spain !   Oh, the conceit,
Though but a child's, was yet divinely fair !
Those dreams are past !

MARQUIS.

                    Said you, those dreams, my prince !
And were they only dreams ?

CARLOS.

                              Oh, let me weep,
Upon thy bosom weep these burning tears,
My only friend !   Not one have I — not one —
In the wide circuit of this earth, — not one
Far as the sceptre of my sire extends,
Far as the navies bear the flag of Spain,

There is no spot — none — none, where I dare yield
An outlet to my tears, save only this.
I charge thee, Roderigo! Oh, by all
The hopes we both do entertain of heaven,
Cast me not off from thee, my friend, my friend!
        [Posa *bends over him in silent emotion*
Look on me, Posa, as an orphan child,
Found near the throne, and nurtured by thy love.
Indeed, I know not what a father is.
I am a monarch's son.   Oh, were it so,
As my heart tells me that it surely is,
That thou from millions hast been chosen out
To comprehend my being; if it be true,
That all-creating nature has designed
In me to reproduce a Roderigo,
And on the morning of our life attuned
Our souls' soft concords to the selfsame key ;
If one poor tear, which gives my heart relief,
To thee were dearer than my father's favor ——

MARQUIS.

Oh, it is dearer far than all the world!

CARLOS.

I'm fallen so low, have grown so poor withal,
I must recall to thee our childhood's years, —
Must ask thee payment of a debt incurred
When thou and I were scarce to boyhood grown.
Dost thou remember, how we grew together,
Two daring youths, like brothers, side by side?
I had no sorrow but to see myself
Eclipsed by thy bright genius.   So I vowed,
Since I might never cope with thee in power,
That I would love thee with excess of love.
Then with a thousand shows of tenderness,
And warm affection, I besieged thy heart,
Which cold and proudly still repulsed them all.
Oft have I stood, and — yet thou sawest it never —
Hot bitter tear-drops brimming in mine eyes,
When I have marked thee, passing me unheeded,
Fold to thy bosom youths of humbler birth.
" Why only these?" in anguish, once I asked —

" Am I not kind and good to thee as they ? "
But dropping on thy knees, thine answer came,
With an unloving look of cold reserve,
" This is my duty to the monarch's son !

MARQUIS.

Oh, spare me, dearest prince, nor now recall
Those boyish acts that make me blush for shame.

CARLOS.

I did not merit such disdain from thee —
You might despise me, crush my heart, but never
Alter my love.   Three times didst thou repulse
The prince, and thrice he came to thee again,
To beg thy love, and force on thee his own.
At length chance wrought what Carlos never could.
Once we were playing, when thy shuttlecock
Glanced off and struck my aunt, Bohemia's queen,
Full in the face ! She thought 'twas with intent,
And all in tears complained unto the king.
The palace youth were summoned on the spot,
And charged to name the culprit.   High in wrath
The king vowed vengeance for the deed : " Although
It were his son, yet still should he be made
A dread example ! "   I looked around and marked
Thee stand aloof, all trembling with dismay.
Straight I stepped forth ; before the royal feet
I flung myself, and cried, " 'Twas I who did it ;
Now let thine anger fall upon thy son ! "

MARQUIS.

Ah, wherefore, prince, remind me?

CARLOS.

Hear me further !
Before the face of the assembled court,
That stood, all pale with pity, round about,
Thy Carlos was tied up, whipped like a slave ;
I looked on thee, and wept not.   Blow rained on blow ;
I gnashed my teeth with pain, yet wept I not !
My royal blood streamed 'neath the pitiless lash ;
I looked on thee, and wept not.   Then you came,

And fell half-choked with sobs before my feet:
"Carlos," you cried, "my pride is overcome;
I will repay thee when thou art a king."

MARQUIS (*stretching forth his hand to* CARLOS).

Carlos, I'll keep my word; my boyhood's vow
I now as man renew. I will repay thee.
Some day, perchance, the hour may come ——

CARLOS.

　　　　　　　　　　　Now! now!
The hour has come; thou canst repay me all.
I have sore need of love. A fearful secret
Burns in my breast; it must — it must be told.
In thy pale looks my death-doom will I read.
Listen; be petrified; but answer not.
I love — I love — my mother!

MARQUIS.

　　　　　　　O my God!

CARLOS.

Nay, no forbearance! spare me not! Speak! speak!
Proclaim aloud, that on this earth's great round
There is no misery to compare with mine.
Speak! speak! — I know all — all that thou canst say!
The son doth love his mother. All the world's
Established usages, the course of nature,
Rome's fearful laws denounce my fatal passion.
My suit conflicts with my own father's rights
I feel it all, and yet I love. This path
Leads on to madness, or the scaffold. I
Love without hope, love guiltily, love madly,
With anguish, and with peril of my life;
I see, I see it all, and yet I love.

MARQUIS.

The queen — does she know of your passion?

CARLOS.

　　　　　　　　　　　　Could I
Reveal it to her? She is Philip's wife ——
She is the queen, and this is Spanish ground,
Watched by a jealous father, hemmed around

By ceremonial forms, how, how could I
Approach her unobserved ? 'Tis now eight months,
Eight maddening months, since the king summoned me
Home from my studies, since I have been doomed
To look on her, adore her day by day,
And all the while be silent as the grave !
Eight maddening months, Roderigo ; think of this !
This fire has seethed and raged within my breast !
A thousand, thousand times, the dread confession
Has mounted to my lips, yet evermore
Shrunk, like a craven, back upon my heart.
O Roderigo ! for a few brief moments
Alone with her !

MARQUIS.

Ah ! and your father, prince !

CARLOS.

Unhappy me ! Remind me not of him.
Tell me of all the torturing pangs of conscience,
But speak not, I implore you, of my father !

MARQUIS.

Then do you hate your father ?

CARLOS.

No, oh, no !

I do not hate my father ; but the fear
That guilty creatures feel, — a shuddering dread, —
Comes o'er me ever at that terrible name.
Am I to blame, if slavish nurture crushed
Love's tender germ within my youthful heart ?
Six years I'd numbered, ere the fearful man,
They told me was my father, met mine eyes.
One morning 'twas, when with a stroke I saw him
Sign four death-warrants. After that I ne'er
Beheld him, save when, for some childish fault,
I was brought out for chastisement. O God !
I feel my heart grow bitter at the thought.
Let us away ! away !

MARQUIS.

Nay, Carlos, nay,

You must, you shall give all your sorrow vent,
Let it have words ! 'twill ease your o'erfraught heart.

CARLOS.

Oft have I struggled with myself, and oft
At midnight, when my guards were sunk in sleep,
With floods of burning tears I've sunk before
The image of the ever-blessed Virgin,
And craved a filial heart, but all in vain.
I rose with prayer unheard. O Roderigo!
Unfold this wondrous mystery of heaven,
Why of a thousand fathers only this
Should fall to me — and why to him this son,
Of many thousand better? Nature could not
In her wide orb have found two opposites
More diverse in their elements. How could
She bind the two extremes of human kind —
Myself and him — in one so holy bond?
O dreadful fate! Why was it so decreed?
Why should two men, in all things else apart,
Concur so fearfully in one desire?
Roderigo, here thou seest two hostile stars,
That in the lapse of ages, only once,
As they sweep onwards in their orbed course,
Touch with a crash that shakes them to the centre
Then rush apart forever and forever.

MARQUIS.

I feel a dire foreboding.

CARLOS.

So do I.
Like hell's grim furies, dreams of dreadful shape
Pursue me still. My better genius strives
With the fell projects of a dark despair.
My wildered subtle spirit crawls through maze
On maze of sophistries, until at length
It gains a yawning precipice's brink.
O Roderigo! should I e'er in him
Forget the father — ah! thy deathlike look
Tells me I'm understood — should I forget
The father — what were then the king to me?

MARQUIS (*after a pause*).

One thing, my Carlos, let me beg of you!

Whate'er may be your plans, do nothing, — nothing, —
Without your friend's advice. You promise this?

CARLOS.

All, all I promise that thy love can ask!
I throw myself entirely upon thee!

MARQUIS.

The king, I hear, is going to Madrid.
The time is short. If with the queen you would
Converse in private, it is only here,
Here in Aranjuez, it can be done.
The quiet of the place, the freer manners,
All favor you.

CARLOS.

   And such, too, was my hope;
But it, alas! was vain.

MARQUIS.

    Not wholly so.
I go to wait upon her. If she be
The same in Spain she was in Henry's court,
She will be frank at least. And if I can
Read any hope for Carlos in her looks —
Find her inclined to grant an interview —
Get her attendant ladies sent away ——

CARLOS.

Most of them are my friends — especially
The Countess Mondecar, whom I have gained
By service to her son, my page.

MARQUIS.

    'Tis well;
Be you at hand, and ready to appear,
Whene'er I give the signal, prince.

CARLOS.

    I will, —
Be sure I will : — and all good speed attend thee!

MARQUIS.

I will not lose a moment; so, farewell!.
      [*Exeunt severally.*

SCENE III.

*The Queen's Residence in Aranjuez. The Pleasure Grounds,
intersected by an avenue, terminated by the Queen's Palace.*

The QUEEN, DUCHESS OF OLIVAREZ, PRINCESS OF EBOLI,
and MARCHIONESS OF MONDECAR, *all advancing from
the avenue.*

QUEEN (*to the* MARCHIONESS).

I will have you beside me, Mondecar.
The princess, with these merry eyes of hers,
Has plagued me all the morning. See, she scarce
Can hide the joy she feels to leave the country.

EBOLI.

'Twere idle to conceal, my queen, that I
Shall be most glad to see Madrid once more.

MONDECAR.

And will your majesty not be so, too?
Are you so grieved to quit Aranjuez?

QUEEN.

To quit — this lovely spot at least I am.
This is my world. Its sweetness oft and oft
Has twined itself around my inmost heart.
Here, nature, simple, rustic nature greets me,
The sweet companion of my early years —
Here I indulge once more my childhood's sports,
And my dear France's gales come blowing here.
Blame not this partial fondness — all hearts yearn
For their own native land.

EBOLI.
              But then how lone,
How dull and lifeless it is here! We might
As well be in La Trappe.

QUEEN.
              I cannot see it.
To me Madrid alone is lifeless. But
What saith our duchess to it?

OLIVAREZ.

Why, methinks,
Your majesty, since kings have ruled in Spain,
It hath been still the custom for the court
To pass the summer months alternately
Here and at Pardo, — in Madrid, the winter.

QUEEN.

Well, I suppose it has! Duchess, you know
I've long resigned all argument with you.

MONDECAR.

Next month Madrid will be all life and bustle.
They're fitting up the Plaza Mayor now,
And we shall have rare bull-fights; and, besides,
A grand *auto da fé* is promised us.

QUEEN.

Promised? This from my gentle Mondecar!

MONDECAR.

Why not? 'Tis only heretics they burn!

QUEEN.

I hope my Eboli thinks otherwise!

EBOLI.

What, I? I beg your majesty may think me
As good a Christian as the marchioness.

QUEEN.

Alas! I had forgotten where I am, —
No more of this! We were speaking, I think,
About the country? And methinks this month
Has flown away with strange rapidity.
I counted on much pleasure, very much,
From our retirement here, and yet I have not
Found that which I expected. Is it thus
With all our hopes? And yet I cannot say
One wish of mine is left ungratified.

OLIVAREZ.

You have not told us, Princess Eboli,
If there be hope for Gomez, — and if we may
Expect ere long to greet you as his bride?

QUEEN.

True — thank you, duchess, for reminding me!
[*Addressing the* PRINCESS.
I have been asked to urge his suit with you.
But can I do it ?   The man whom I reward
With my sweet Eboli must be a man
Of noble stamp indeed.

OLIVAREZ.

And such he is,
A man of mark and fairest fame, — a man
Whom our dear monarch signally has graced
With his most royal favor.

QUEEN.

He's happy in
Such high good fortune ; but we fain would know,
If he can love, and win return of love.
This Eboli must answer.

EBOLI (*stands speechless and confused, her eyes bent on
the ground ; at last she falls at the* QUEEN's *feet*).

Gracious queen !
Have pity on me !   Let me — let me not, —
For heaven's sake, let me not be sacrificed.

QUEEN.

Be sacrificed !   I need no more.   Arise !
'Tis a hard fortune to be sacrificed.
I do believe you.   Rise.   And is it long
Since you rejected Gomez' suit ?

EBOLI.

Some months —
Before Prince Carlos came from Alcala.

QUEEN (*starts and looks at her with an inquisitive glance*).
Have you tried well the grounds of your refusal?

EBOLI (*with energy*).

It cannot be, my queen, no, never, never, —
For a thousand reasons, never !

QUEEN.
One's enough,
You do not love him.   That suffices me.
Now let it pass.   [*To her other ladies.*
I have not seen the Infanta
Yet this morning.   Pray bring her, marchioness.

OLIVAREZ (*looking at.the clock*).
It is not yet the hour, your majesty.

QUEEN.
Not yet the hour for me to be a mother!
That's somewhat hard.   Forget not, then, to tell me
When the right hour does come.
        [*A page enters and whispers to the first lady, who
        thereupon turns to the* QUEEN.

OLIVAREZ.
The Marquis Posa!
May it please your majesty.

QUEEN.
The Marquis Posa!

OLIVAREZ.
He comes from France, and from the Netherlands,
And craves the honor to present some letters
Intrusted to him by your royal mother.

QUEEN.
Is this allowed?

OLIVAREZ (*hesitating*).
A case so unforeseen
Is not provided for in my instructions.
When a Castilian grandee, with despatches
From foreign courts, shall in her garden find
The Queen of Spain, and tender them ——

QUEEN.
Enough!
I'll venture, then, on mine own proper peril.

OLIVAREZ.
May I, your majesty, withdraw the while?

QUEEN.

E'en as you please, good duchess!
[*Exit the* Duchess, *the* Queen *gives the* Page *a
sign, who thereupon retires.*

Scene IV.

The Queen, Princess Eboli, Marchioness of Mondecar, *and* Marquis of Posa.

QUEEN.

I bid you welcome, sir, to Spanish ground!

MARQUIS.

Ground which I never with so just a pride
Hailed for the country of my sires as now.

QUEEN (*to the two ladies*).

The Marquis Posa, ladies, who at Rheims
Coped with my father in the lists, and made
My colors thrice victorious; the first
That made me feel how proud a thing it was
To be the Queen of Spain and Spanish men.
[*Turning to the* Marquis.

When we last parted in the Louvre, sir,
You scarcely dreamed that I should ever be
Your hostess in Castile.

MARQUIS.

Most true, my liege!
For at that time I never could have dreamed
That France should lose to us the only thing
We envied her possessing.

QUEEN.

How, proud Spaniard!
The only thing! And you can venture this —
This to a daughter of the house of Valois!

MARQUIS.

I venture now to say it, gracious queen,
Since now you are our own.

QUEEN.

Your journey hither
Has led you, as I hear, through France. What news
Have you brought with you from my honored mother
And from my dearest brothers?

MARQUIS (*handing letters*).

I left your royal mother sick at heart,
Bereft of every joy save only this,
To know her daughter happy on the throne
Of our imperial Spain.

QUEEN.

Could she be aught
But happy in the dear remembrances
Of relatives so kind — in the sweet thoughts
Of the old time when —— Sir, you've visited
Full many a court in these your various travels,
And seen strange lands and customs manifold;
And now, they say, you mean to keep at home
A greater prince in your retired domain
Than is King Philip on his throne — a freer.
You're a philosopher; but much I doubt
If our Madrid will please you. We are so —
So quiet in Madrid.

MARQUIS.

And that is more
Than all the rest of Europe has to boast.

QUEEN.

I've heard as much. But all this world's concerns
Are well-nigh blotted from my memory.

[*To* PRINCESS EBOLI.

Princess, methinks I see a hyacinth
Yonder in bloom. Wilt bring it to me, sweet?

[*The* PRINCESS *goes towards the palace, the* QUEEN
softly to the MARQUIS.

I'm much mistaken, sir, or your arrival
Has made one heart more happy here at court.

MARQUIS.

I have found a sad one — one that in this world
A ray of sunshine ——

EBOLI.

As this gentleman
Has seen so many countries, he, no doubt,
Has much of note to tell us.

MARQUIS.

Doubtless, and
To seek adventures is a knight's first duty —
But his most sacred is to shield the fair.

MONDECAR.

From giants!   But there are no giants now!

MARQUIS.

Power is a giant ever to the weak.

QUEEN.

The chevalier says well.   There still are giants;
But there are knights no more.

MARQUIS.

Not long ago,
On my return from Naples, I became
The witness of a very touching story,
Which ties of friendship almost make my own
Were I not fearful its recital might
Fatigue your majesty ——

QUEEN.

Have I a choice?
The princess is not to be lightly balked.
Proceed.   I too, sir, love a story dearly.

MARQUIS.

Two noble houses in Mirandola,
Weary of jealousies and deadly feuds,
Transmitted down from Guelphs and Ghibellines
Through centuries of hate, from sire to son,
Resolved to ratify a lasting peace
By the sweet ministry of nuptial ties.
Fernando, nephew of the great Pietro,
And fair Matilda, old Colonna's child,
Were chosen to cement this holy bond.

Nature had never for each other formed
Two fairer hearts. And never had the world
Approved a wiser or a happier choice.
Still had the youth adored his lovely bride
In the dull limner's portraiture alone.
How thrilled his heart, then, in the hope to find
The truth of all that e'en his fondest dreams
Had scarcely dared to credit in her picture !
In Padua, where his studies held him bound;
Fernando panted for the joyful hour,
When he might murmur at Matilda's feet
The first pure homage of his fervent love.

> [*The* QUEEN *grows more attentive ; the* MARQUIS
> *continues, after a short pause, addressing him-
> self chiefly to* PRINCESS EBOLI.

Meanwhile the sudden death of Pietro's wife
Had left him free to wed. With the hot glow
Of youthful blood the hoary lover drinks
The fame that reached him of Matilda's charms.
He comes — he sees — he loves ! The new desire
Stifles the voice of nature in his heart.
The uncle woos his nephew's destined bride,
And at the altar consecrates his theft.

QUEEN.

And what did then Fernando ?

MARQUIS.

                     On the wings
Of love, unconscious of the fearful change,
Delirious with the promised joy, he speeds
Back to Mirandola. His flying steed
By starlight gains the gate. Tumultuous sounds
Of music, dance, and jocund revelry
Ring from the walls of the illumined palace.
With faltering stops he mounts the stair ; and now
Behold him in the crowded nuptial hall,
Unrecognized ! Amid the reeling guests
Pietro sat. An angel at his side —
An angel, whom he knows, and who to him
Even in his dreams, seemed ne'er so beautiful.

A single glance revealed what once was his —
Revealed what now was lost to him forever.

                    EBOLI.

O poor Fernando !

                    QUEEN.

                Surely, sir, your tale
Is ended ?   Nay, it must be.

                    MARQUIS.

                        No, not quite.

                    QUEEN.

Did you not say Fernando was your friend ?

                    MARQUIS.

I have no dearer in the world.

                    EBOLI.

                        But pray
Proceed, sir, with your story.

                    MARQUIS.

                    Nay, the rest
Is very sad — and to recall it sets
My sorrow fresh abroach.   Spare me the sequel.
                        [*A general silence.*

        QUEEN (*turning to the* PRINCESS EBOLI).

Surely the time is come to see my daughter,
I prithee, princess, bring her to me now !
    [*The* PRINCESS *withdraws.   The* MARQUIS *beckons a
    Page.   The* QUEEN *opens the letters, and appears
    surprised.   The* MARQUIS *talks with* MARCHIONESS
    MONDECAR.   *The* QUEEN *having read the letters,
    turns to the* MARQUIS *with a penetrating look.*

                    QUEEN.

You have not spoken of Matilda !   She
Haply was ignorant of Fernando's grief ?

                    MARQUIS.

Matilda's heart. has no one fathomed yet —
Great souls endure in silence.

QUEEN.

You look around you.   Who is it you seek?

MARQUIS.

Just then the thought came over me, how one,
Whose name I dare not mention, would rejoice
Stood he where I do now.

QUEEN.

And who's to blame,
That he does not?

MARQUIS (*interrupting her eagerly*).

My liege!   And dare I venture
To interpret thee, as fain I would?   He'd find
Forgiveness, then, if now he should appear.

QUEEN (*alarmed*).

Now, marquis, now?   What do you mean by this?

MARQUIS.

Might he, then, hope?

QUEEN.

You terrify me, marquis.
Surely he will not ——

MARQUIS.

He is here already.

SCENE V.

The QUEEN, CARLOS, MARQUIS POSA, MARCHIONESS MON-
DECAR.   *The two latter go towards the avenue.*

CARLOS (*on his knees before the* QUEEN).

At length 'tis come — the happy moment's come,
And Charles may touch this all-beloved hand.

QUEEN.

What headlong folly's this?   And dare you break
Into my presence thus?   Arise, rash man!
We are observed; my suite are close at hand.

CARLOS.

I will not rise. Here will I kneel forever,
Here will I lie enchanted at your feet,
And grow to the dear ground you tread on?

QUEEN.

Madman!

To what rude boldness my indulgence leads!
Know you, it is the queen, your mother, sir,
Whom you address in such presumptuous strain?
Know, that myself will to the king report
This bold intrusion ——

CARLOS.

And that I must die!
Let them come here, and drag me to the scaffold!
A moment spent in paradise like this
Is not too dearly purchased by a life.

QUEEN.

But then your queen?

CARLOS (*rising*).

O God, I'll go, I'll go!
Can I refuse to bend to that appeal?
I am your very plaything.   Mother, mother,
A sign, a transient glance, one broken word
From those dear lips can bid me live or die.
What would you more?   Is there beneath the sun
One thing I would not haste to sacrifice
To meet your lightest wish?

QUEEN.

Then fly!

CARLOS.

God!

QUEEN.

With tears I do conjure you, Carlos, fly!
I ask no more.   O fly! before my court,
My guards, detecting us alone together,
Bear the dread tidings to your father's ear.

CARLOS.

I bide my doom, or be it life or death.
Have I staked every hope on this one moment,
Which gives thee to me thus at length alone,
That idle fears should balk me of my purpose?
No, queen! The world may round its axis roll
A hundred thousand times, ere chance again
Yield to my prayers a moment such as this.

QUEEN.

It never shall to all eternity.
Unhappy man! What would you ask of me?

CARLOS.

Heaven is my witness, queen, how I have struggled,
Struggled as mortal never did before,
But all in vain! My manhood fails — I yield.

QUEEN.

No more of this — for my sake — for my peace.

CARLOS.

You were mine own, — in face of all the world, —
Affianced to me by two mighty crowns,
By heaven and nature plighted as my bride,
But Philip, cruel Philip, stole you from me

QUEEN.

He is your father?

CARLOS.
And he is your husband!

QUEEN.

And gives to you for an inheritance,
The mightiest monarchy in all the world

CARLOS.

And you, as mother!

QUEEN.
Mighty heavens! You rave!

CARLOS.

And is he even conscious of his treasure?
Hath he a heart to feel and value yours?

I'll not complain — no, no, I will forget,
How happy, past all utterance, I might
Have been with you, — if he were only so.
But he is not — there, there, the anguish lies!
He is not, and he never — never can be.
Oh, you have robbed me of my paradise,
Only to blast it in King Philip's arms!

QUEEN.

Horrible thought!

CARLOS.

　　　　　　　Oh, yes, right well I know
Who 'twas that knit this ill-starred marriage up.
I know how Philip loves, and how he wooed.
What are you in this kingdom — tell me, what?
Regent, belike! Oh, no! If such you were,
How could fell Alvas act their murderous deeds,
Or Flanders bleed a martyr for her faith?
Are you even Philip's wife? Impossible, —
Beyond belief. A wife doth still possess
Her husband's heart. To whom doth his belong?
If ever, perchance, in some hot feverish mood,
He yields to gentler impulse, begs he not
Forgiveness of his sceptre and gray hairs?

QUEEN.

Who told you that my lot, at Philip's side
Was one for men to pity?

CARLOS.

　　　　　　　My own heart!
Which feels, with burning pangs, how at my side
It had been to be envied.

QUEEN.

　　　　　　　Thou vain man!
What if my heart should tell me the reverse?
How, sir, if Philip's watchful tenderness,
The looks that silently proclaim his love,
Touched me more deeply than his haughty son's
Presumptuous eloquence? What, if an old man's
Matured esteem ——

CARLOS.

That makes a difference! Then,
Why then, forgiveness! — I'd no thought of this ;
I had no thought that you could love the king.

QUEEN.

To honor him's my pleasure and my wish.

CARLOS.

Then you have never loved ?

QUEEN.

Singular question!

CARLOS.

Then you have never loved ?

QUEEN.

I love no longer !

CARLOS.

Because your heart forbids it, or your oath ?

QUEEN.

Leave me ; nor never touch this theme again.

CARLOS.

Because your oath forbids it, or your heart ?

QUEEN.

Because my duty — but, alas, alas !
To what avails this scrutiny of fate,
Which we must both obey ?

CARLOS.

Must — must obey ?

QUEEN.

What means this solemn tone ?

CARLOS.

Thus much it means :
That Carlos is not one to yield to must
Where he hath power to will ! It means, besides,
That Carlos is not minded to live on.

The most unhappy man in all his realm,
When it would only cost the overthrow
Of Spanish laws to be the happiest.

QUEEN.

Do I interpret rightly? Still you hope ?.
Dare you hope on, when all is lost forever?

CARLOS.

I look on naught as lost — except the dead.

QUEEN.

For me — your mother, do you dare to hope?
　　　[*She fixes a penetrating look on him, then continues
　　　　　with dignity and earnestness.*
And yet why not ? A new elected monarch
Can do far more — make bonfires of the laws
His father left — o'erthrow his monuments —
Nay, more than this — for what shall hinder him ? —
Drag from his tomb, in the Escurial,
The sacred corpse of his departed sire,
Make it a public spectacle, and scatter
Forth to the winds his desecrated dust.
And then, at last, to fill the measure up, ——

CARLOS

Merciful heavens, finish not the picture!

QUEEN.

End all by wedding with his mother.

CARLOS.

　　　　　　　　　　　　　Oh !
Accursed son!
　　　[*He remains for some time paralyzed and speech-
　　　　　less.*
　　　　　　　Yes, now 'tis out, 'tis out !
I see it clear as day. Oh, would it had
Been veiled from me in everlasting darkness!
Yes, thou art gone from me — gone — gone forever.
The die is cast; and thou art lost to me.
Oh, in that thought lies hell ; and a hell, too,
Lies in the other thought, to call thee mine.

Oh, misery! I can bear my fate no longer,
My very heart-strings strain as they would burst.

QUEEN.

Alas, alas! dear Charles, I feel it all,
The nameless pang that rages in your breast;
Your pangs are infinite, as is your love,
And infinite as both will be the glory
Of overmastering both. Up, be a man,
Wrestle with them boldly. The prize is worthy
Of a young warrior's high, heroic heart;
Worthy of him in whom the virtues flow
Of a long ancestry of mighty kings.
Courage! my noble prince! Great Charles's grandson
Begins the contest with undaunted heart,
Where sons of meaner men would yield at once.

CARLOS.

Too late, too late! O God, it is too late!

QUEEN.

Too late to be a man! O Carlos, Carlos!
How nobly shows our virtue when the heart
Breaks in its exercise! The hand of Heaven
Has set you up on high, — far higher, prince,
Than millions of your brethren. All she took
From others she bestowed with partial hand
On thee, her favorite; and millions ask,
What was your merit, thus before your birth
To be endowed so far above mankind?
Up, then, and justify the ways of Heaven;
Deserve to take the lead of all the world,
And make a sacrifice ne'er made before.

CARLOS.

I will, I will; I have a giant's strength
To win your favor; but to lose you, none.

QUEEN.

Confess, my Carlos, I have harshly read thee;
It is but spleen, and waywardness, and pride,
Attract you thus so madly to your mother!

The heart you lavish on myself belongs
To the great empire you one day shall rule.
Look that you sport not with your sacred trust!
Love is your high vocation; until now
It hath been wrongly bent upon your mother:
Oh, lead it back upon your future realms,
And so, instead of the fell stings of conscience,
Enjoy the bliss of being more than man.
Elizabeth has been your earliest love,
Your second must be Spain.   How gladly, Carlos,
Will I give place to this more worthy choice!

CARLOS (*overpowered by emotion, throws himself at her feet.*)
    How great thou art, my angel!   Yes, I'll do
    All, all thou canst desire.   So let it be.
                                    [*He rises.*
    Here in the sight of heaven I stand and swear —
    I swear to thee, eternal — no, great Heaven! —
    Eternal silence only, — not oblivion!

                    QUEEN.
    How can I ask from you what I myself
    Am not disposed to grant?

            MARQUIS (*hastening from the alley*).
                        The king!

                QUEEN.
                                Oh God!

            MARQUIS.
    Away, away! fly from these precincts, prince!

                QUEEN.
    His jealousy is dreadful — should he see you ——

                CARLOS.
    I'll stay.

                QUEEN.
                And who will be the victim then?

        CARLOS (*seizing the* MARQUIS *by the arm*).
    Away, away!   Come, Roderigo, come!
                            [*Goes and returns*
    What may I hope to carry hence with me?

QUEEN.

Your mother's friendship.

CARLOS.

Friendship! Mother!

QUEEN.

And
These tears with it — they're from the Netherlands.
[*She gives him some letters. Exit* CARLOS *with the*
MARQUIS. *The* QUEEN *looks restlessly round in
search of her ladies, who are nowhere to be seen.
As she is about to retire up, the* KING *enters.*

SCENE VI.

The KING, *the* QUEEN, DUKE ALVA, COUNT LERMA,
DOMINGO, LADIES, GRANDEES, *who remain at a little
distance.*

KING.

How, madam, alone; not even one of all
Your ladies in attendance? Strange! Where are they?

QUEEN.

My gracious lord!

KING.

Why thus alone, I say?
[*To his attendants.*
I'll take a strict account of this neglect.
'Tis not to be forgiven. Who has the charge
Of waiting on your majesty to-day?

QUEEN.

Oh, be not angry! Good, my lord, 'tis I
Myself that am to blame — at my request
The Princess Eboli went hence but now.

KING.

At your request!

QUEEN.

To call the nurse to me,
With the Infanta, whom I longed to see.

KING.

And was your retinue dismissed for that?
This only clears the lady first in waiting.
Where was the second?

MONDECAR (*who has returned and mixed with the other
                ladies, steps forward*).

                            Your majesty, I feel
I am to blame for this.

KING.

                            You are, and so
I give you ten years to reflect upon it,
At a most tranquil distance from Madrid.
    [*The* MARCHIONESS *steps back weeping. General
        silence. The bystanders all look in confusion to-
        wards the* QUEEN.

QUEEN.

What weep you for, dear marchioness?   [*To the* KING.
                            If I
Have erred, my gracious liege, the crown I wear,
And which I never sought, should save my blushes
Is there a law in this your kingdom, sire,
To summon monarch's daughters to the bar?
Does force alone restrain your Spanish ladies?
Or need they stronger safeguard than their virtue?
Now pardon me, my liege; 'tis not my wont
To send my ladies, who have served me still
With smiling cheerfulness, away in tears.
Here, Mondecar.
    [*She takes off her girdle and presents it to the* MAR-
        CHIONESS.

                            You have displeased the king,
Not me.   Take this remembrance of my favor,
And of this hour.   I'd have you quit the kingdom.
You have only erred in Spain.   In my dear France,
All men are glad to wipe such tears away.
And must I ever be reminded thus?
In my dear France it had been otherwise.
    [*Leaning on the* MARCHIONESS *and covering her face.*

KING.

Can a reproach, that in my love had birth,
Afflict you so?   A word so trouble you,
Which the most anxious tenderness did prompt?
                    [*He turns towards the* GRANDEES.
Here stand the assembled vassals of my throne.
Did ever sleep descend upon these eyes,
Till at the close of the returning day
I've pondered, how the hearts of all my subjects
Were beating 'neath the furthest cope of heaven?
And should I feel more anxious for my throne
Than for the partner of my bosom?   No!
My sword and Alva can protect my people,
My eye alone assures thy love.

QUEEN.

                    My liege,
If that I have offended ——

KING.

                    I am called
The richest monarch in the Christian world ;
The sun in my dominions never sets.
All this another hath possessed before,
And many another will possess hereafter.
That is mine own.   All that the monarch hath
Belongs to chance — Elizabeth to Philip.
This is the point in which I feel I'm mortal.

QUEEN.

What fear you, sire ?

KING.

                    Should these gray hairs not fear?
But the same instant that my fear begins
It dies away forever.   [*To the grandees.*
                    I run over
The nobles of my court and miss the foremost.
Where is my son, Don Carlos ?   [*No one answers.*
                    He begins
To give me cause of fear.   He shuns my presence
Since he came back from school at Alcala.
His blood is hot.   Why is his look so cold?

His bearing all so stately and reserved?
Be watchful, duke, I charge you.

ALVA.

So I am:
Long as a heart against this corslet beats,
So long may Philip slumber undisturbed;
And as God's cherub guards the gates of heaven
So doth Duke Alva guard your royal throne.

LERMA.

Dare I, in all humility, presume
To oppose the judgment of earth's wisest king?
Too deeply I revere his gracious sire
To judge the son so harshly.   I fear much
From his hot blood, but nothing from his heart.

KING.

Lerma, your speech is fair to soothe the father,
But Alva here will be the monarch's shield —
No more of this.

[*Turning to his suite.*
Now speed we to Madrid,
Our royal duties summon us.   The plague
Of heresy is rife among my people;
Rebellion stalks within my Netherlands —
The times are imminent.   We must arrest
These erring spirits by some dread example.
The solemn oath which every Christian king
Hath sworn to keep I will redeem to-morrow.
'Twill be a day of doom unparalleled.
Our court is bidden to the festival.

[*He leads off the* QUEEN, *the rest follow.*

SCENE VII.

DON CARLOS (*with letters in his hand*), *and* MARQUIS
POSA *enter from opposite sides.*

CARLOS.

I am resolved — Flanders shall yet be saved:
So runs her suit, and that's enough for me!

MARQUIS.
There's not another moment to be lost:
'Tis said Duke Alva in the cabinet
Is named already as the governor.

CARLOS.
Betimes to-morrow will I see the king
And ask this office for myself. It is
The first request I ever made to him,
And he can scarce refuse. My presence here
Has long been irksome to him. He will grasp
This fair pretence my absence to secure.
And shall I confess to thee, Roderigo?
My hopes go further. Face to face with him,
'Tis possible the pleading of a son
May reinstate him in his father's favor.
He ne'er hath heard the voice of nature speak;
Then let me try for once, my Roderigo,
What power she hath when breathing from my lips.

MARQUIS.
Now do I hear my Carlos' voice once more;
Now are you all yourself again!

Scene VIII.

The preceding. COUNT LERMA.

COUNT.
Your grace,
His majesty has left Aranjuez;
And I am bidden ——

CARLOS.
Very well, my lord —
I shall overtake the king —

MARQUIS (*affecting to take leave with ceremony*).
Your highness, then,
Has nothing further to intrust to me?

CARLOS.
Nothing. A pleasant journey to Madrid!
You may, hereafter, tell me more of Flanders.
[*To* LERMA, *who is waiting for him.*
Proceed, my lord! I'll follow thee anon.

Scene IX.

Don Carlos, Marquis Posa.

CARLOS.

I understood thy hint, and thank thee for it.
A stranger's presence can alone excuse
This forced and measured tone.   Are we not brothers?
In future, let this puppet-play of rank
Be banished from our friendship.   Think that we
Had met at some gay masking festival,
Thou in the habit of a slave, and I
Robed, for a jest, in the imperial purple.
Throughout the revel we respect the cheat,
And play our parts with sportive earnestness,
Tripping it gayly with the merry throng;
But should thy Carlos beckon through his mask,
Thou'dst press his hand in silence as he passed,
And we should be as one.

MARQUIS.

                      The dream's divine!
But are you sure that it will last forever?
Is Carlos, then, so certain of himself
As to despise the charms of boundless sway?
A day will come — an all-important day —
When this heroic mind — I warn you now —
Will sink o'erwhelmed by too severe a test.
Don Philip dies; and Carlos mounts the throne,
The mightiest throne in Christendom.   How vast
The gulp that yawns betwixt mankind and him —
A god to-day, who yesterday was man!
Steeled to all human weakness — to the voice
Of heavenly duty deaf.   Humanity —
To-day a word of import in his ear —
Barters itself, and grovels 'mid the throng
Of gaping parasites; his sympathy
For human woe is turned to cold neglect,
His virtue sunk in loose voluptuous joys.
Peru supplies him riches for his folly,
His court engenders devils for his vices.
Lulled in this heaven the work of crafty slaves,

He sleeps a charmed sleep ; and while his dream
Endures his godhead lasts.   And woe to him
Who'd break in pity this lethargic trance !
What could Roderigo do ?   Friendship is true,
And bold as true.   But her bright flashing beams
Were much too fierce for sickly majesty :
You would not brook a subject's stern appeal,
Nor I a monarch's pride !

CARLOS.

Tearful and true,
Thy portraiture of monarchs.   Yes — thou'rt right,
But 'tis their lusts that thus corrupt their hearts,
And hurry them to vice.   I still am pure.
A youth scarce numbering three-and-twenty years.
What thousands waste in riotous delights,
Without remorse — the mind's more precious part —
The bloom and strength of manhood — I have kept,
Hoàrding their treasures for the future king.
What could unseat my Posa from my heart,
If woman fail to do it?

MARQUIS.

I, myself !
Say, could I love you, Carlos, warm as now,
If I must fear you ?

CARLOS.

That will never be.
What need hast thou of me ?   What cause hast thou
To stoop thy knee, a suppliant at the throne?
Does gold allure thee ?   Thou'rt a richer subject
Than I shall be a king !   Dost covet honors ?
E'en in thy youth, fame's brimming chalice stood
Full in thy grasp — thou flung'st the toy away.
Which of us, then,.must be the other's debtor,
And which the creditor ?   .Thou standest mute.
Dost tremble for the trial ?   Art thou, then,
Uncertain of thyself ?

MARQUIS.

Carlos, I yield !
Here is my hand.

CARLOS.

Is it mine own

MARQUIS.

Forever —
In the most pregnant meaning of the word!

CARLOS.

And wilt thou prove hereafter to the king
As true and warm as to the prince to-day?

MARQUIS.

I swear!

CARLOS.

And when round my unguarded heart
The serpent flattery winds its subtle coil,
Should e'er these eyes of mine forget the tears
They once were wont to shed ; or should these ears
Be closed to mercy's plea, — say, wilt thou, then,
The fearless guardian of my virtue, throw
Thine iron grasp upon me, and call up
My genius by its mighty name?

MARQUIS.

I will.

CARLOS.

And now one other favor let me beg.
Do call me *thou!*   Long have I envied this
Dear privilege of friendship to thine equals.
The brother's *thou* beguiles my ear, my heart,
With sweet suggestions of equality.
Nay, no reply : — I guess what thou wouldst say —
To thee this seems a trifle — but to me,
A monarch's son, 'tis much.   Say, wilt thou be
A brother to me?

MARQUIS.

Yes ; thy brother, yes!

CARLOS.

Now to the king — my fears are at an end.
Thus, arm-in-arm with thee, I dare defy
The universal world into the lists.   [*Exeunt*

ACT II.

Scene I.

The royal palace at Madrid.

King Philip *under a canopy;* Duke Alva *at some distance, with his head covered;* Carlos.

CARLOS.

The kingdom takes precedence — willingly
Doth Carlos to the minister give place —
He speaks for Spain ; I am but of the household.
[*Bows and steps backward.*

KING.

The duke remains — the Infanta may proceed.

CARLOS (*turning to* ALVA).

Then must I put it to your honor, sir,
To yield my father for a while to me.
A son, you know, may to a father's ear
Unbosom much, in fulness of his heart,
That not befits a stranger's ear. The king
Shall not be taken from you, sir — I seek
The father only for one little hour.

KING.

Here stands his friend.

CARLOS.

And have I e'er deserved
To think the duke should be a friend of mine ?

KING.

Or tried to make him one ? I scarce can love
Those sons who choose more wisely than their fathers.

CARLOS.

And can Duke Alva's knightly spirit brook
To look on such a scene ? Now, as I live,
I would not play the busy meddler's part,
Who thrusts himself, unasked, 'twixt sire and son,
And there intrudes without a blush, condemned
By his own conscious insignificance,
No, not, by heaven, to win a diadem !

KING (*rising, with an angry look at the Prince*).
Retire, my lord!
[ALVA *goes to the principal door, through which*
CARLOS *had entered, the* KING *points to the other.*
No, to the cabinet,
Until I call you.

SCENE II.

KING PHILIP.   DON CARLOS.

CARLOS (*as soon as the* DUKE *has left the apartment,
advances to the* KING, *throws himself at his feet, and
then, with great emotion*).
My father once again!
Thanks, endless thanks, for this unwonted favor!
Your hand, my father!   O delightful day!
The rapture of this kiss has long been strange
To your poor Carlos.   Wherefore have I been
Shut from my father's heart?   What have I done?

KING.
Carlos, thou art a novice in these arts —
Forbear, I like them not ——

CARLOS (*rising*).
And is it so?
I hear your courtiers in those words, my father!
All is not well, by heaven, all is not true,
That a priest says, and a priest's creatures plot.
I am not wicked, father; ardent blood
Is all my failing; — all my crime is youth; —
Wicked I am not — no, in truth, not wicked; —
Though many an impulse wild assails my heart,
Yet is it still untainted.

KING.
Ay, 'tis pure —
I know it — like thy prayers ——

CARLOS.
Now, then, or never!
We are, for once, alone — the barrier
Of courtly form, that severed sire and son,

Has fallen ! Now a golden ray of hope
Illumes my soul — a sweet presentment
Pervades my heart — and heaven itself inclines,
With choirs of joyous angels, to the earth,
And full of soft emotion, the thrice blest
Looks down upon this great, this glorious scene !
Pardon, my father !

[*He falls on his knees before him.*

KING.

Rise, and leave me.

CARLOS.

Father

KING (*tearing himself from him*).

This trifling grows too bold.

CARLOS.

A son's devotion

Too bold ! Alas !

KING.

And, to crown all, in tears !
Degraded boy ! Away, and quit my sight !

CARLOS.

Now, then, or never ! — pardon, O my father !

KING.

Away, and leave my sight ! Return to me
Disgraced, defeated, from the battle-field,
Thy sire shall meet thee with extended arms :
But thus in tears, I spurn thee from my feet.
A coward's guilt alone should wash its stains
In such ignoble streams.   The man who weeps
Without a blush will ne'er want cause for tears !

CARLOS.

Who is this man ? By what mistake of nature
Has he thus strayed amongst mankind ? A tear
Is man's unerring, lasting attribute.
Whose eye is dry was ne'er of woman born !
Oh, teach the eye that ne'er hath overflowed,

The timely science of a tear — thou'lt need
The moist relief in some dark hour of woe.

KING.

Think'st thou to shake thy father's strong mistrust
With specious words?

CARLOS.

Mistrust!   Then I'll remove it,
Here will I hang upon my father's breast,
Strain at his heart with vigor, till each shred
Of that mistrust, which, with a rock's endurance,
Clings firmly round it, piecemeal fall away.
And who are they who drive me from the king —
My father's favor?   What requital hath
A monk to give a father for a son ?
What compensation can the duke supply
For a deserted and a childless age?
Would'st thou be loved ?   Here in this bosom springs
A fresher, purer fountain, than e'er flowed
From those dark, stagnant, muddy reservoirs,
Which Philip's gold must first unlock.

KING.

No more,
Presuming boy!   For know the hearts thou slanderest
Are the approved, true servants of my choice.
'Tis meet that thou do honor to them.

CARLOS.

Never!
I know my worth — all that your Alva dares —
That, and much more, can Carlos.   What cares he,
A hireling! for the welfare of the realm
That never can be his ?   What careth he
If Philip's hair grow gray with hoary age?
Your Carlos would have loved you : — Oh, I dread
To think that you the royal throne must fill
Deserted and alone.

KING (*seemingly struck by this idea, stands in deep
thought ; after a pause*).

I am alone !

CARLOS (*approaching him with eagerness*).

You have been so till now.   Hate me no more,
And I will love you dearly as a son:
But hate me now no longer!   Oh, how sweet,
Divinely sweet it is to feel our being
Reflected in another's beauteous soul;
To see our joys gladden another's cheek,
Our pains bring anguish to another's bosom,
Our sorrows fill another's eye with tears!
How sweet, how glorious is it, hand in hand,
With a dear child, in inmost soul beloved,
To tread once more the rosy paths of youth,
And dream life's fond illusions o'er again!
How proud to live through endless centuries
Immortal in the virtues of a son ;
How sweet to plant what his dear hand shall reap ;
To gather what will yield him rich return,
And guess how high his thanks will one day rise!
My father of this early paradise
Your monks most wisely speak not.

KING (*not without emotion*).

Oh, my son,
Thou hast condemned thyself in painting thus
A bliss this heart hath ne'er enjoyed from thee.

CARLOS.

The Omniscient be my judge!   You till this hour
Have still debarred me from your heart, and all
Participation in your royal cares.
The heir of Spain has been a very stranger
In Spanish land — a prisoner in the realm
Where he must one day rule.   Say, was this just,
Or kind?   And often have I blushed for shame,
And stood with eyes abashed, to learn perchance
From foreign envoys, or the general rumor,
Thy courtly doings at Aranjuez.

KING.

Thy blood flows far too hotly in thy veins.
Thou would'st but ruin all.

CARLOS.
                              But try me, father.
'Tis true my blood flows hotly in my veins.
Full three-and-twenty years I now have lived,
And naught achieved for immortality.
I am aroused — I feel my inward powers —
My title to the throne arouses me
From slumber, like an angry creditor;
And all the misspent hours of early youth,
Like debts of honor, clamor in mine ears.
It comes at length, the glorious moment comes
That claims full interest on the intrusted talent
The annals of the world, ancestral fame,
And glory's echoing trumpet urge me on.
Now is the blessed hour at length arrived
That opens wide to me the list of honor.
My king, my father! dare I utter now
The suit which led me hither?

KING.
                              Still a suit?
Unfold it.

CARLOS.
                    The rebellion in Brabant
Increases to a height — the traitor's madness
By stern, but prudent, vigor must be met.
The duke, to quell the wild enthusiasm,
Invested with the sovereign's power, will lead
An army into Flanders.   Oh, how full
Of glory is such office! and how suited
To open wide the temple of renown
To me, your son!   To my hand, then, O king,
Intrust the army; in thy Flemish lands
I am well loved, and I will freely gage
My life for their fidelity and truth.

KING.
Thou speakest like a dreamer.   This high office
Demands a man — and not a stripling's arm.

CARLOS.
It but demands a human being, father:
And that is what Duke Alva ne'er hath been.

KING.

Terror alone can tie rebellion's hands :
Humanity were madness.   Thy soft soul
Is tender, son : they'll tremble at the duke.
Desist from thy request.

CARLOS.

Despatch me, sire,
To Flanders with the army — dare rely
E'en on my tender soul.   The name of prince,
The royal name emblazoned on my standard,
Conquers where Alva's butchers but dismay.
Here on my knees I crave it — this the first
Petition of my life.   Trust Flanders to me.

KING (*contemplating* CARLOS *with a piercing look*).

Trust my best army to thy thirst for rule,
And put a dagger in my murderer's hand !

CARLOS.

Great God ! and is this all — is this the fruit
Of a momentous hour so long desired !
                    [*After some thought, in a milder tone.*
Oh, speak to me more kindly — send me not
Thus comfortless away — dismiss me not
With this afflicting answer, oh, my father !
Use me more tenderly, indeed, I need it.
This is the last resource of wild despair —
It conquers every power of firm resolve
To bear it as a man — this deep contempt —
My every suit denied :   Let me away —
Unheard and foiled in all my fondest hopes,
I take my leave,   Now Alva and Domingo
May proudly sit in triumph where your son
Lies weeping in the dust.   Your crowd of courtiers,
And your long train of cringing, trembling nobles,
Your tribe of sallow monks, so deadly pale,
All witnessed how you granted me this audience.
Let me not be disgraced.   Oh, strike me not
With this most deadly wound — nor lay me bare
To sneering insolence of menial taunts !

" That strangers riot on your bounty, whilst
Carlos, your son, may supplicate in vain."
And as a pledge that you would have me honored,
Despatch me straight to Flanders with the army.

KING.

Urge thy request no farther — as thou wouldst
Avoid the king's displeasure.

CARLOS.
         I must brave
My king's displeasure, and prefer my suit
Once more, it is the last.   Trust Flanders to me!
I must away from Spain.   To linger here
Is to draw breath beneath the headsman's axe :
The air lies heavy on me in Madrid
Like murder on a guilty soul — a change,
An instant change of clime alone can cure me.
If you would save my life, despatch me straight
Without delay to Flanders.

KING (*with affected coldness*).

           Invalids,
Like thee, my son — need not be tended close,
And ever watched by the physician's eye —
Thou stayest in Spain — the duke will go to Flanders.

CARLOS (*wildly*).

Assist me, ye good angels!

KING (*starting*).

          Hold, what mean
These looks so wild?

CARLOS.

        Father, do you abide
Immovably by this determination?

KING.

It was the king's.

CARLOS.

      Then my commission's done.
          [*Exit in violent emotion*

Scene III.

King, sunk in gloomy contemplation, walks a few steps up and down; Alva approaches with embarrassment.

KING.

Hold yourself ready to depart for Brussels
Upon a moment's notice.

ALVA.

All is prepared, my liege.

KING.

And your credentials
Lie ready sealed within my cabinet, —
Meanwhile obtain an audience of the queen,
And bid the prince farewell.

ALVA.

As I came in
I met him with a look of frenzy wild
Quitting the chamber; and your majesty
Is strangely moved, methinks, and bears the marks
Of deep excitement — can it be the theme
Of your discourse——

KING.

Concerned the Duke of Alva.
[*The* KING *keeps his eye steadfastly fixed on him.*
I'm pleased that Carlos hates my councillors,
But I'm disturbed that he despises them.
[ALVA, *coloring deeply, is about to speak.*
No answer now : propitiate the prince.

ALVA.

Sire !

KING.

Tell me who it was that warned me first
Of my son's dark designs ? I listened then
To you, and not to him. I will have proof.
And for the future, mark me, Carlos stands
Nearer the throne — now duke — you may retire.
[*The* KING *retires into his cabinet. Exit* DUKE *by
another door.*

Scene IV.

The antechamber to the Queen's *apartments.* Don Carlos
enters in conversation with a Page. *The attendants retire at
his approach.*

CARLOS.

For me this letter? And a key! How's this?
And both delivered with such mystery!
Come nearer, boy : — from whom didst thou receive them?

PAGE (*mysteriously*).

It seemed to me the lady would be guessed
Rather than be described.

CARLOS (*starting*).

　　　　　　　　The lady, what!
Who art thou, boy? 　　[*Looking earnestly at the* Page.

PAGE.

　　　　　　　A page that serves the queen.

CARLOS (*affrighted, putting his hand to the* Page's *mouth*).
Hold, on your life! I know enough: no more.
　　[*He tears open the letter hastily, and retires to read
　　it; meanwhile* Duke Alva *comes, and passing the
　　Prince, goes unperceived by him into the* Queen's
　　apartment,* Carlos *trembles violently and changes
　　color; when he has read the letter he remains a long
　　time speechless, his eyes steadfastly fixed on it; at
　　last he turns to the* Page.
She gave you this herself?

PAGE.

　　　　　　　With her own hands.

CARLOS.

She gave this letter to you then herself?
Deceive me not: I ne'er have seen her writing,
And I must credit thee, if thou canst swear it;
But if thy tale be false, confess it straight,
Nor put this fraud on me.

PAGE.

　　　　　　　This fraud, on whom?

CARLOS (*looking once more at the letter, then at the* PAGE *with doubt and earnestness*).
Your parents — are they living? and your father —
Serves he the king? Is he a Spaniard born?

PAGE.
He fell a colonel on St. Quentin's field,
Served in the cavalry of Savoy's duke —
His name Alonzo, Count of Henarez.

CARLOS (*taking his hand, and looking fixedly in his eyes*).
The king gave you this letter?

PAGE (*with emotion*).
Gracious prince,
Have I deserved these doubts?
CARLOS (*reading the letter*).
"This key unlocks
The back apartments in the queen's pavilion,
The furthest room lies next a cabinet
Wherein no listener's foot dare penetrate;
Here may the voice of love without restraint
Confess those tender feelings, which till now
The heart with silent looks alone hath spoken.
The timid lover gains an audience here,
And sweet reward repays his secret sorrow."
[*As if awakening from a reverie.*
I am not in a dream, I do not rave, —
This is my right hand, this my sword — and these
Are written words. 'Tis true — it is no dream.
I am beloved, I feel I am beloved.
[*Unable to contain himself, he rushes hastily through the room, and raises his arms to heaven.*

PAGE.
Follow me, prince, and I will lead the way.

CARLOS.
Then let me first collect my scattered thoughts.
The alarm of joy still trembles in my bosom.
Did I e'er lift my fondest hopes so high,
Or trust my fancy to so bold a flight?

Show me the man can learn thus suddenly
To be a god.   I am not what I was.
I feel another heaven — another sun
That was not here before.   She loves — she loves me!

PAGE (leading him forward).

But this is not the place: prince! you forget.

CARLOS.

The king!   My father!
     [*His arms sink, he casts a timid look around, then
        collecting himself.*
                         This is dreadful!   Yes,
You're right, my friend.   I thank you: I was not
Just then myself.   To be compelled to silence,
And bury in my heart this mighty bliss,
Is terrible!
     [*Taking the* PAGE *by the hand, and leading him aside.*
                    Now here!   What thou hast seen,
And what not seen, must be within thy breast
Entombed as in the grave.   So now depart;
I shall not need thy guidance; they must not
Surprise us here!   Now go.
                    [*The* PAGE *is about to depart.*
                    Yet hold, a word!
     [*The* PAGE *returns.* CARLOS *lays his hand on his
        shoulder, and looks him steadily in the face.*
A direful secret hast thou in thy keeping,
Which, like a poison of terrific power,
Shivers the cup that holds it into atoms.
Guard every look of thine, nor let thy head
Guess at thy bosom's secret.   Be thou like
The senseless speaking-trumpet that receives
And echoes back the voice, but hears it not.
Thou art a boy!   Be ever so; continue
The pranks of youth.   My correspondent chose
Her messenger of love with prudent skill!
The king will ne'er suspect a serpent here.

PAGE.

And I, my prince, shall feel right proud to know
I am one secret richer than the king.

CARLOS.

Vain, foolish boy! 'tis this should make thee tremble.
Approach me ever with a cold respect:
Ne'er be induced by idle pride to boast
How gracious is the prince! No deadlier sin
Canst thou commit, my son, than pleasing me.
Whate'er thou hast in future for my ear,
Give not to words; intrust not to thy lips,
Ne'er on that common high road of the thoughts
Permit thy news to travel. Speak with an eye,
A finger; I will answer with a look.
The very air, the light, are Philip's creatures,
And the deaf walls around are in his pay.
Some one approaches; fly, we'll meet again.

    [*The* QUEEN'S *chamber opens, and* DUKE ALVA
      comes out.

PAGE.

Be careful, prince, to find the right apartment. [*Exit.*

CARLOS.

It is the duke! Fear not, I'll find the way.

SCENE V.

DON CARLOS. DUKE OF ALVA.

ALVA (*meeting him*).

Two words, most gracious prince.

CARLOS.

        Some other time. [*Going.*

ALVA.

The place is not the fittest, I confess;
Perhaps your royal highness may be pleased
To grant me audience in your private chamber.

CARLOS.

For what? And why not here? Only be brief.

ALVA.

The special object which has brought me hither,
Is to return your highness lowly thanks
For your good services.

CARLOS.

Thanks! thanks to me —
For what?   Duke Alva's thanks!

ALVA.

You scarce had left
His majesty, ere I received in form
Instructions to depart for Brussels.

CARLOS.

What!
For Brussels!

ALVA.

And to what, most gracious prince,
Must I ascribe this favor, but to you —
Your intercession with the king?

CARLOS.

Oh, no!
Not in the least to me; but, duke, you travel,
So Heaven be with your grace!

ALVA.

And is this all?
It seems, indeed, most strange!   And has your highness
No further orders, then, to send to Flanders?

CARLOS.

What should I have?

ALVA.

Not long ago, it seemed,
That country's fate required your presence.

CARLOS.

How?
But yes, you're right, — it was so formerly;
But now this change is better as it is.

ALVA.

I am amazed ——

CARLOS.

You are an able general,
No one doubts that — envy herself must own it.
For me, I'm but a youth — so thought the king.

The king was right, quite right. I see it now
Myself, and am content — and so no more.
God speed your journey, as you see, just now
My hands are full, and weighty business presses.
The rest to-morrow, or whene'er you will,
Or when you come from Brussels.

ALVA.

What is this?

CARLOS.

The season favors, and your route will lie
Through Milan, Lorraine. Burgundy, and on
To Germany! What, Germany? Ay, true,
In Germany it was — they know you there.
'Tis April now, May, June, — in July, then,
Just so! or, at the latest, soon in August, —
You will arrive in Brussels, and no doubt
We soon shall hear of your victorious deeds.
You know the way to win our high esteem,
And earn the crown of fame.

ALVA (*significantly*).

Indeed! condemned
By my own conscious insignificance!

CARLOS.

You're sensitive, my lord, and with some cause,
I own it was not fair to use a weapon
Against your grace you were unskilled to wield.

ALVA.

Unskilled!

CARLOS.

'Tis pity I've no leisure now
To fight this worthy battle fairly out:
But at some other time, we ——

ALVA.

Prince, we both
Miscalculate — but still in opposite ways.
You, for example, overrate your age
By twenty years, whilst on the other hand,
I, by as many, underrate it ——

CARLOS.
                                    Well
ALVA.

And this suggests the thought, how many nights
Beside this lovely Lusitanian bride —
Your mother — would the king right gladly give
To buy an arm like this, to aid his crown.
Full well he knows, far easier is the task
To make a monarch than a monarchy ;
Far easier too, to stock the world with kings
Than frame an empire for a king to rule.

CARLOS.

Most true, Duke Alva, yet ——

ALVA.
                                    And how much blood
Your subjects' dearest blood, must flow in streams
Before two drops could make a king of you.

CARLOS.

Most true, by heaven! and in two words comprised,
All that the pride of merit has to urge
Against the pride of fortune.   But the moral —
Now, Duke Alva !

ALVA.
                        Woe to the nursling babe
Of royalty that mocks the careful hand
Which fosters it !   How calmly it may sleep
On the soft cushion of our victories !
The monarch's crown is bright with sparkling gems,
But no eye sees the wounds that purchased them.
This sword has given our laws to distant realms,
Has blazed before the banner of the cross,
And in these quarters of the globe has traced
Ensanguined furrows for the seed of faith.
God was the judge in heaven, and I on earth.

CARLOS.

God, or the devil — it little matters which ;
Yours was his chosen arm — that stands confessed.
And now no more of this.   Some thoughts there are

Whereof the memory pains me.   I respect
My father's choice, — my father needs an Alva!
But that he needs him is not just the point
I envy in him : a great man you are,
This may be true, and I well nigh believe it,
Only I fear your mission is begun
Some thousand years too soon.   Alva, methinks,
Were just the man to suit the end of time.
Then when the giant insolence of vice
Shall have exhausted Heaven's enduring patience,
And the rich waving harvest of misdeeds
Stand in full ear, and asks a matchless reaper,
Then should you fill the post.   O God! my paradise!
My Flanders!   But of this I must not think.
'Tis said you carry with you a full store
Of sentences of death already signed.
This shows a prudent foresight!   No more need
To fear your foes' designs, or secret plots :
Oh, father! ill indeed I've understood thee.
Calling thee harsh, to save me from a post,
Where Alva's self alone can fitly shine!
'Twas an unerring token of your love.

ALVA.

These words deserve —

CARLOS.

What!

ALVA.

But your birth protects you.

CARLOS (*seizing his sword*).

That calls for blood!   Duke, draw your sword!

ALVA (*slightingly*).

On whom?

CARLOS (*pressing upon him*).

Draw, or I run you through.

ALVA.

Then be it so.   [*They fight.*

SCENE VI.

The QUEEN, DON CARLOS, DUKE ALVA.

QUEEN (*coming from her room alarmed*).

How! naked swords?
[*To the* PRINCE *in an indignant and commanding
tone.*

Prince Carlos!

CARLOS (*agitated at the* QUEEN'S *look, drops his arm,
stands motionless, then rushes to the* DUKE, *and
embraces him.*

Pardon, duke!
Your pardon, sir! Forget, forgive it all!
[*Throws himself in silence at the* QUEEN'S *feet, then
rising suddenly, departs in confusion.*

ALVA.

By heaven, 'tis strange!

QUEEN (*remains a few moments as if in doubt, then retiring to her apartment*).

A word with you, Duke Alva.
[*Exit, followed by the* DUKE.

SCENE VII.

The PRINCESS EBOLI'S *apartment.*

The PRINCESS *in a simple, but elegant dress, playing on the lute.
The* QUEEN'S PAGE *enters.*

PRINCESS (*starting up suddenly*)

He comes!

PAGE (*abruptly*).

Are you alone? I wonder much
He is not here already; but he must
Be here upon the instant.

PRINCESS.

Do you say must!
Then he will come, this much is certain then.

PAGE.

He's close upon my steps. You are beloved,
Adored, and with more passionate regard
Than mortal ever was, or can be loved.
Oh! what a scene I witnessed!

PRINCESS (*impatiently draws him to her*).

Quick, you spoke
With him! What said he? Tell me straight —
How did he look? what were his words? And say —
Did he appear embarrassed or confused?
And did he guess who sent the key to him?
Be quick! or did he not? He did not guess
At all, perhaps! or guessed amiss! Come, speak,
How! not a word to answer me? Oh, fie!
You never were so dull — so slow before,
'Tis past all patience.

PAGE.

Dearest lady, hear me!
Both key and note I placed within his hands,
In the queen's antechamber, and he started
And gazed with wonder when I told him that
A lady sent me!

PRINCESS.

Did he start? go on!
That's excellent. Proceed, what next ensued?

PAGE.

I would have told him more, but he grew pale,
And snatched the letter from my hand, and said
With look of deadly menace, he knew all.
He read the letter with confusion through,
And straight began to tremble.

PRINCESS.

He knew all!
He knew it all? Were those his very words?

PAGE.

He asked me, and again he asked, if you
With your own hands had given me the letter?

PRINCESS.

If I?   Then did he mention me by name?

PAGE.

By name!   no name he mentioned : there might be
Listeners, he said, about the palace, who
Might to the king disclose it.

PRINCESS (*surprised*).
                    Said he that?

PAGE.

He further said, it much concerned the king;
Deeply concerned — to know of that same letter.

PRINCESS.

The king!   Nay, are you sure you heard him right?
The king!   Was that the very word he used?

PAGE.

It was.   He called it a most perilous secret,
And warned me to be strictly on my guard,
Never with word or look to give the king
Occasion for suspicion.

PRINCESS (*after a pause, with astonishment*).
                    All agrees!
It can be nothing else — he must have heard
The tale — 'tis very strange!   Who could have told him
I wonder who?   The eagle eye of love
Alone could pierce so far.   But tell me further —
He read the letter.

PAGE.

                    Which, he said, conveyed
Such bliss as made him tremble, and till then
He had not dared to dream of.   As he spoke
The duke, by evil chance, approached the room,
And this compelled us ——

PRINCESS (*angrily*).
                    What in all the world
Could bring the duke to him at such a time?
What can detain him?   Why appears he not?

See how you've been deceived; how truly blest
Might he have been already — in the time
You've taken to describe his wishes to me!

PAGE.

The duke, I fear ——

PRINCESS.

Again, the duke! What can
The duke want here? What should a warrior want
With my soft dreams of happiness? He should
Have left him there, or sent him from his presence.
Where is the man may not be treated thus?
But Carlos seems as little versed in love
As in a woman's heart — he little knows
What minutes are. But hark! I hear a step;
Away, away! [PAGE *hastens out.*
Where have I laid my lute?
I must not seem to wait for him. My song
Shall be a signal to him.

SCENE VIII.

The PRINCESS, DON CARLOS.

The PRINCESS *has thrown herself upon an ottoman, and plays.*

CARLOS (*rushes in; he recognizes the* PRINCESS, *and stands thunderstruck*).

Gracious Heaven!

Where am I?

PRINCESS (*lets her lute fall, and meeting him*).

What? Prince Carlos! yes, in truth,

CARLOS.

Where am I? Senseless error; I have missed
The right apartment.

PRINCESS.

With what dexterous skill
Carlos contrives to hit the very room
Where ladies sit alone!

CARLOS.

Your pardon, princess!
I found — I found the antechamber open.

PRINCESS.

Can it be possible? I fastened it
Myself; at least I thought so ——

CARLOS.

Ay! you thought,
You only thought so; rest assured you did not.
You meant to lock it, that I well believe:
But most assuredly it was not locked.
A lute's sweet sounds attracted me, some hand
Touched it with skill; say, was it not a lute?

[Looking round inquiringly.

Yes, there it lies, and Heaven can bear me witness
I love the lute to madness. I became
All ear, forgot myself in the sweet strain,
And rushed into the chamber to behold
The lovely eyes of the divine musician
Who charmed me with the magic of her tones.

PRINCESS.

Innocent curiosity, no doubt!
But it was soon appeased, as I can prove.

[After a short silence, significantly.

I must respect the modesty that has,
To spare a woman's blushes, thus involved
Itself in so much fiction.

CARLOS (*with sincerity*).

Nay, I feel
I but augment my deep embarrassment,
In vain attempt to extricate myself.
Excuse me for a part I cannot play.
In this remote apartment, you perhaps
Have sought a refuge from the world, to pour
The inmost wishes of your secret heart
Remote from man's distracting eye. By me,
Unhappy that I am, your heavenly dreams
Are all disturbed, and the atonement now
Must be my speedy absence.   *[Going*

PRINCESS (*surprised and confused, but immediately
recovering herself*).

Oh! that step
Were cruel, prince, indeed!

CARLOS.
Princess, I feel
What such a look in such a place imports:
This virtuous embarrassment has claims
To which my manhood never can be deaf.
Woe to the wretch whose boldness takes new fire
From the pure blush of maiden modesty!
I am a coward when a woman trembles.

PRINCESS.
Is't possible? — such noble self-control
In one so young, and he a monarch's son!
Now, prince, indeed you shall remain with me,
It is my own request, and you must stay.
Near such high virtue, every maiden fear
Takes wing at once; but your appearance here
Disturbed me in a favorite air, and now
Your penalty shall be to hear me sing it.

CARLOS (*sits down near the* PRINCESS, *not without reluctance*).
A penalty delightful as the sin!
And sooth to say, the subject of the song
Was so divine, again and yet again
I'd gladly hear it.

PRINCESS.
What! you heard it all?
Nay, that was too bad, prince. It was, I think,
A song of love.

CARLOS.
And of successful love,
If I mistake not — dear delicious theme
From those most beauteous lips — but scarce so true,
Methinks, as beautiful.

PRINCESS.
What! not so true?
Then do you doubt the tale?

CARLOS.
I almost doubt
That Carlos and the Princess Eboli.

When they discourse on such a theme as love,
May not quite understand each other's hearts.
    [*The* PRINCESS *starts ; he observes it, and con-*
        tinues with playful gallantry.
Who would believe those rosy-tinted cheeks
Concealed a heart torn by the pangs of love.
Is it within the range of wayward chance
That the fair Princess Eboli should sigh
Unheard — unanswered ?   Love is only known
By him who hopelessly persists in love.

        PRINCESS (*with all her former vivacity*).

Hush ! what a dreadful thought! this fate indeed
Appears to follow you of all mankind,
Especially to-day.
        [*Taking his hand with insinuating interest.*
                You are not happy,
Dear prince — you're sad !   I know too well you suffer,
And wherefore, prince ?   When with such loud appeal
The world invites you to enjoy its bliss —
And nature on you pours her bounteous gifts,
And spreads around you all life's sweetest joys.
You, a great monarch's son, and more — far more —
E'en in your cradle with such gifts endowed
As far eclipsed the splendor of your rank.
You, who in those strict courts where women rule,
And pass, without appeal, unerring sentence
On manly worth and honor, even there
Find partial judges.   You, who with a·look
Can prove victorious, and whose very coldness
Kindles a flame ; and who, when warmed with passion,
Can make a paradise, and scatter round
The bliss of heaven, the rapture of the gods.
The man whom nature has adorned with gifts
To render thousands happy, gifts which she
Bestows on few — that such a man as this
Should know what misery is !   Thou, gracious Heaven,
That gavest him all those blessings, why deny
Him eyes to see the conquests he has made?

CARLOS (*who has been lost in absence of mind, suddenly recovers himself by the silence of the* PRINCESS, *and starts up*).

Charming! inimitable! Princess, sing
That passage, pray, again.

PRINCESS (*looking at him with astonishment*).
Where, Carlos, were
Your thoughts the while?

CARLOS (*jumps up*).
By heaven, you do remind me
In proper time — I must away — and quickly.

PRINCESS (*holding him back*).
Whither away?

CARLOS.
Into the open air.
Nay, do not hold me, princess, for I feel
As though the world behind me were in flames.

PRINCESS (*holding him forcibly back*).
What troubles you? Whence comes these strange, these wild,
Unnatural looks? Nay, answer me!
[CARLOS *stops to reflect, she draws him to the sofa to her.*
Dear Carlos,
You need repose, your blood is feverish.
Come, sit by me: dispel these gloomy fancies.
Ask yourself frankly can your head explain
The tumult of your heart — and if it can —
Say, can no knight be found in all the court,
No lady, generous as fair, to cure you —
Rather, I should have said, to understand you?
What, no one?

CARLOS (*hastily, without thinking*).
If the Princess Eboli ——

PRINCESS (*delighted, quickly*).
Indeed!

CARLOS.

Would write a letter for me, a few words
Of kindly intercession to my father; ——
They say your influence is great.

PRINCESS.

Who says so?
Ha! was it jealousy that held thee mute!   [*Aside.*

CARLOS.

Perchance my story is already public.
I had a sudden wish to visit Brabant
Merely to win my spurs — no more. The king,
Kind soul, is fearful the fatigues of war
Might spoil my singing!

PRINCESS.

Prince, you play me false!
Confess that by this serpent subterfuge
You would mislead me. Look me in the face,
Deceitful one! and say would he whose thoughts
Were only bent on warlike deeds — would he
E'er stoop so low as, with deceitful hand,
To steal fair ladies' ribbons when they drop,
And then — your pardon! hoard them — with such care?
    [*With light action she opens his shirt-frill, and*
        seizes a ribbon which is there concealed.

CARLOS (*drawing back with amazement*).

Nay, princess — that's too much — I am betrayed.
You're not to be deceived. You are in league
With spirits and with demons!

PRINCESS.

Are you then
Surprised at this? What will you wager, Carlos
But I recall some stories to your heart?
Nay, try it with me; ask whate'er you please,
And if the triflings of my sportive fancy —
The sound half-uttered by the air absorbed —
The smile of joy checked by returning gloom ——
If motions — looks from your own soul concealed

Have not escaped my notice — judge if I
Can err when thou wouldst have me understand thee ?

CARLOS.

Why, this is boldly ventured ; I accept
The wager, princess.   Then you undertake
To make discoveries in my secret heart
Unknown even to myself.

PRINCESS (*displeased, but earnestly*).

Unknown to thee !
Reflect a moment, prince !   Nay, look around ;
This boudoir's not the chamber of the queen,
Where small deceits are practised with full license.
You start, a sudden blush o'erspreads your face.
Who is so bold, so idle, you would ask,
As to watch Carlos when he deems himself
From scrutiny secure ?   Who was it, then,
At the last palace-ball observed you leave
The queen, your partner, standing in the dance,
And join, with eager haste, the neighboring couple,
To offer to the Princess Eboli
The hand your royal partner should have claimed ?
An error, prince, his majesty himself,
Who just then entered the apartment, noticed.

CARLOS (*with ironical smile*).

His majesty ?   And did he really so ?
Of all men he should not have seen it.

PRINCESS.

Nor yet that other scene within the chapel,
Which doubtless Carlos hath long since forgotten.
Prostrate before the holy Virgin's image,
You lay in prayer, when suddenly you heard —
'Twas not your fault — a rustling from behind
Of ladies' dresses.   Then did Philip's son,
A youth of hero courage, tremble like
A heretic before the holy office.
On his pale lips died the half-uttered prayer.
In ectasy of passion, prince — the scene
Was truly touching — for you seized the hand,

The blessed Virgin's cold and holy hand,
And showered your burning kisses on the marble.

CARLOS.

Princess, you wrong me : that was pure devotion !

PRINCESS.

Indeed ! that's quite another thing.   Perhaps
It was the fear of losing, then, at cards,
When you were seated with the queen and me,
And you with dexterous skill purloined my glove.
                    [CARLOS *starts surprised.*
That prompted you to play it for a card ?

CARLOS.

What words are these ? O Heaven, what have I done?

PRINCESS.

Nothing I hope of which you need repent !
How pleasantly was I surprised to find
Concealed within the glove a little note,
Full of the warmest tenderest romance,

CARLOS (*interrupting her suddenly*).

Mere poetry ! no more.   My fancy teems
With idle bubbles oft, which break as soon
As they arise — and this was one of them ;
So, prithee, let us talk of it no more.

PRINCESS (*leaving him with astonishment, and regarding
        him for some time at a distance.*

I am exhausted — all attempts are vain
To hold this youth.   He still eludes my grasp.
                [*Remains silent a few moments.*
But stay !   Perchance 'tis man's unbounded pride,
That thus to add a zest to my delight.
Assumes a mask of timid diffidence.
'Tis so.
        [*She approaches the* PRINCE *again, and looks at
        him doubtingly.*
        Explain yourself, prince, I entreat you.
For here I stand before a magic casket,
Which all my keys are powerless to unlock.

CARLOS.

As I before you stand.

PRINCESS (*leaves him suddenly, walks a few steps up and down in silence, apparently lost in deep thought. After a pause, gravely and solemnly*).

Then thus at last —
I must resolve to speak, and Carlos, you
Shall be my judge. Yours is a noble nature,
You are a prince — a knight — a man of honor.
I throw myself upon your heart — protect me:
Or if I'm lost beyond redemption's power,
Give me your tears in pity for my fate.

[*The* PRINCE *draws nearer.*

A daring favorite of the king demands
My hand — his name Ruy Gomez, Count of Silva,
The king consents — the bargain has been struck,
And I am sold already to his creature.

CARLOS (*with evident emotion*).

Sold ! you sold ! Another bargain, then,
Concluded by this royal southern trader !

PRINCESS.

No; but hear all — 'tis not enough that I
Am sacrificed to cold state policy,
A snare is laid to entrap my innocence.
Here is a letter will unmask the saint !

[CARLOS *takes the paper, and without reading it listens with impatience to her recital.*

Where shall I find protection, prince ? Till now
My virtue was defended by my pride,
At length ——

CARLOS.

At length you yielded ! Yielded ? No.
For God's sake say not so !

PRINCESS.

Yielded ! to whom ?
Poor piteous reasoning. Weak beyond contempt
Your haughty minds, who hold a woman's favor,
And love's pure joys, as wares to traffic for !

Love is the only treasure on the face
Of this wide earth that knows no purchaser
Besides itself — love has no price but love.
It is the costly gem, beyond all price,
Which I must freely give away, or — bury
For ever unenjoyed — like that proud merchant
Whom not the wealth of all the rich Rialto
Could tempt — a great rebuke to kings! to save
From the deep ocean waves his matchless pearl,
Too proud to barter it beneath its worth!

CARLOS (*aside*).

Now, by great heaven, this woman's beautiful.

PRINCESS.

Call it caprice or pride, I ne'er will make
Division of my joys. To him, alone,
I choose as mine, I give up all forever.
One only sacrifice I make; but that
Shall be eternal. One true heart alone
My love shall render happy: but that one
I'll elevate to God. The keen delight
Of mingling souls — the kiss — the swimming joys
Of that delicious hour when lovers meet,
The magic power of heavenly beauty — all
Are sister colors of a single ray —
Leaves of one single blossom. Shall I tear
One petal from this sweet, this lovely flower,
With reckless hand, and mar its beauteous chalice?
Shall I degrade the dignity of woman,
The masterpiece of the Almighty's hand,
To charm the evening of a reveller?

CARLOS.

Incredible! that in Madrid should dwell
This matchless creature! and unknown to me
Until this day.

PRINCESS.

Long since had I forsaken
This court — the world — and in some blest retreat
Immured myself; but one tie binds me still
Too firmly to existence. Perhaps — alas!

'Tis but a phantom — but 'tis dear to me.
I love — but am not loved in turn.

CARLOS (*full of ardor, going towards her*).

You are!
As true as God is throned in heaven! I swear
You are — you are unspeakably beloved.

PRINCESS.

You swear it, you! — sure 'twas an angel's voice.
Oh, if you swear it, Carlos, I'll believe it.
Then I am truly loved!

CARLOS (*embracing her with tenderness*).

Bewitching maid,
Thou creature worthy of idolatry!
I stand before thee now all eye, all ear,
All rapture and delight. What eye hath seen thee —
Under yon heaven what eye could e'er have seen thee,
And boast he never loved? What dost thou here
In Philip's royal court! Thou beauteous angel!
Here amid monks and all their princely train.
This is no clime for such a lovely flower —
They fain would rifle all thy sweets — full well
I know their hearts. But it shall never be —
Not whilst I draw life's breath. I fold thee thus
Within my arms, and in these hands I'll bear thee
E'en through a hell replete with mocking fiends.
Let me thy guardian angel prove.

PRINCESS (*with a countenance full of love*).

O Carlos!
How little have I known thee! and how richly
With measureless reward thy heart repays
The weighty task of — comprehending thee!

[*She takes his hand and is about to kiss it.*

CARLOS (*drawing it back*).

Princess! What mean you?

PRINCESS (*with tendernesss and grace, looking at his hand attentively*).

Oh, this beauteous hand!
How lovely 'tis, and rich! This hand has yet

Two costly presents to bestow! — a crown —
And Carlos' heart : — and both these gifts perchance
Upon one mortal! — both on one — Oh, great
And godlike gift — almost too much for one!
How if you share the treasure, prince! A queen
Knows naught of love — and she who truly loves
Cares little for a crown! 'Twere better, prince,
Then to divide the treasure — and at once —
What says my prince? Have you done so already?
Have you in truth? And do I know the blest one?

CARLOS.

Thou shalt. I will unfold myself to thee,
To thy unspotted innocence, dear maid,
Thy pure, unblemished nature. In this court
Thou art the worthiest — first — the only one
To whom this soul has stood revealed. Then, yes!
I will not now conceal it — yes, I love!

PRINCESS.

Oh, cruel heart! Does this avowal prove
So painful to thee? Must I first deserve
Thy pity — ere I hope to win thy love?

CARLOS (*starting*).

What say'st thou?

PRINCESS.

So to trifle with me, prince!
Indeed it was not well — and to deny
The key!

CARLOS.

The key! the key! Oh yes, 'tis so!
[*After a dead silence.*
I see it all too plainly! Gracious heaven!
[*His knees totter, he leans against a chair, and covers
his face with his hands. A long silence on both
sides. The* PRINCESS *screams and falls.*

PRINCESS.

Oh, horrible! What have I done!

CARLOS.

Hurled down
So far from all my heavenly joys! 'Tis dreadful!

PRINCESS (*hiding her face in the cushion*).
Oh, God! What have I said?

CARLOS (*kneeling before her*).

I am not guilty.
My passion — an unfortunate mistake —
By heaven, I am not guilty ——

PRINCESS (*pushing him from her*).

Out of my sight,
For heaven's sake!

CARLOS.

No, I will not leave thee thus.
In this dread anguish leave thee ——

PRINCESS (*pushing him forcibly away*).

Oh, in pity —
For mercy's sake, away — out of my sight!
Wouldst thou destroy me? How I hate thy presence!
[CARLOS *going.*
Give, give me back the letter and the key.
Where is the other letter?

CARLOS.

The other letter?
What other?

PRINCESS.

That from the king, to me ——

CARLOS (*terrified*).

From whom?

PRINCESS.

The one I just now gave you.

CARLOS.

From the king!
To you!

PRINCESS.

Oh, heavens, how dreadfully have I
Involved myself!   The letter, sir!   I must
Have it again.

CARLOS.

The letter from the king!
To you!

PRINCESS.

The letter! give it, I implore you
By all that's sacred! give it.

CARLOS.

What, the letter
That will unmask the saint!   Is this the letter?

PRINCESS.

Now I'm undone!   Quick, give it me ——

CARLOS.

The letter ——

PRINCESS (*wringing her hands in despair*).
What have I done?   O dreadful, dire imprudence!

CARLOS.

This letter comes, then, from the king!   Princess,
That changes all indeed, and quickly, too.
This letter is beyond all value — priceless!
All Philip's crowns are worthless, and too poor
To win it from my hands.   I'll keep this letter.

PRINCESS (*throwing herself prostrate before him as
he is going*).
Almighty Heaven! then I am lost forever.

[*Exit* CARLOS.

SCENE IX.

The PRINCESS *alone.*

*She seems overcome with surprise, and is confounded.
After* CARLOS' *departure she hastens to call him back.*

PRINCESS.

Prince, but one word!   Prince, hear me.   He is gone.
And this, too, I am doomed to bear — his scorn!

And I am left in lonely wretchedness,
Rejected and despised!

> [*Sinks down upon a chair. After a pause* —

And yet not so;
I'm but displaced — supplanted by some wanton.
He loves! of that no longer doubt is left;
He has himself confessed it — but my rival —
Who can she be? Happy, thrice happy one!
This much stands clear: he loves where he should not.
He dreads discovery, and from the king
He hides his guilty passion! Why from him
Who would so gladly hail it? Or, is it not
The father that he dreads so in the parent?
When the king's wanton purpose was disclosed,
His features glowed with triumph, boundless joy
Flashed in his eyes, his rigid virtue fled;
Why was it mute in such a cause as this?
Why should he triumph? What hath he to gain
If Philip to his queen ——

> [*She stops suddenly, as if struck by a thought,
> then drawing hastily from her bosom the rib-
> bon which she had taken from* CARLOS, *she
> seems to recognize it.*

> Fool that I am!

At length 'tis plain. Where have my senses been?
My eyes are opened now. They loved each other
Long before Philip wooed her, and the prince
Ne'er saw me but with her! She, she alone
Was in his thoughts when I believed myself
The object of his true and boundless love.
O matchless error! and have I betrayed
My weakness to her?

> [*Pauses.*

> Should his love prove hopeless?

Who can believe it? Would a hopeless love
Persist in such a struggle? Called to revel
In joys for which a monarch sighs in vain!
A hopeless love makes no such sacrifice.
What fire was in his kiss! How tenderly
He pressed my bosom to his beating heart!
Well nigh the trial had proved dangerous
To his romantic, unrequited passion!

With joy he seized the key he fondly thought
The queen had sent : — in this gigantic stride
Of love he puts full credence — and he comes —
In very truth comes here — and so imputes
To Philip's wife a deed so madly rash.
And would he so, had love not made him bold ?
'Tis clear as day — his suit is heard — she loves!
By heaven, this saintly creature burns with passion ;
How subtle, too, she is ! With fear I trembled
Before this lofty paragon of virtue !
She towered beside me, an exalted being,
And in her beams I felt myself eclipsed ;
I envied her the lovely, cloudless calm,
That kept her soul from earthly tumults free.
And was this soft serenity but show ?
Would she at both feasts revel, holding up
Her virtue's godlike splendor to our gaze,
And riot in the secret joys of vice ?
And shall the false dissembler cozen thus,
And win a safe immunity from this ——
That no avenger comes ? By heavens she shall not!
I once adored her, — that demands revenge : —
The king shall know her treachery — the king !
                              [*After a pause*
'Tis the sure way to win the monarch's ear !   [*Exit*

Scene X.

A chamber in the royal palace.

Duke of Alva, Father Domingo.

DOMINGO.

Something to tell me !

ALVA.

                        Ay ! a thing of moment,
Of which I made discovery to-day,
And I would have your judgment on it.

DOMINGO.

                                    How !

Discovery ! To what do you allude ?

ALVA.

Prince Carlos and myself this morning met
In the queen's antechamber. I received
An insult from him — we were both in heat —
The strife grew loud — and we had drawn our swords.
Alarmed, from her apartments rushed the queen.
She stepped between us, — with commanding eye
Of conscious power, she looked upon the prince.
'Twas but a single glance, — but his arm dropped,
He fell upon my bosom — gave me then
A warm embrace, and vanished.

DOMINGO (*after a pause*).

This seems strange.
It brings a something to my mind, my lord!
And thoughts like these I own have often sprung
Within my breast; but I avoid such fancies —
To no one have I e'er confided them.
There are such things as double-edged swords
And untrue friends, — I fear them both. 'Tis hard
To judge among mankind, but still more hard
To know them thoroughly. Words slipped at random
Are confidants offended — therefore I
Buried my secret in my breast, till time
Should drag it forth to light. 'Tis dangerous
To render certain services to kings.
They are the bolts, which if they miss the mark,
Recoil upon the archer! I could swear
Upon the sacrament to what I saw.
Yet one eye-witness — one word overheard —
A scrap of paper — would weigh heavier far
Than my most strong conviction! Cursed fate
That we are here in Spain!

ALVA.

And why in Spain?

DOMINGO.

There is a chance in every court but this
For passion to forget itself, and fall.
Here it is warned by ever-wakeful laws.
Our Spanish queens would find it hard to sin —

And only there do they meet obstacles,
Where best 'twould serve our purpose to surprise them.

ALVA.

But listen further: Carlos had to-day
An audience of the king; the interview
Lasted an hour, and earnestly he sought
The government of Flanders for himself.
Loudly he begged, and fervently. I heard him
In the adjoining cabinet. His eyes
Were red with tears when I encountered him.
At noon he wore a look of lofty triumph,
And vowed his joy at the king's choice of me.
He thanked the king. "Matters are changed," he said
"And things go better now." He's no dissembler:
How shall I reconcile such contradictions?
The prince exults to see himself rejected,
And I receive a favor from the king
With marks of anger! What must I believe?
In truth this new-born dignity doth sound
Much more like banishment than royal favor!

DOMINGO.

And is it come to this at last? to this?
And has one moment crumbled into dust
What cost us years to build? And you so calm,
So perfectly at ease! Know you this youth?
Do you foresee the fate we may expect
Should he attain to power? The prince! No foe
Am I of his. Far other cares than these
Gnaw at my rest — cares for the throne — for God,
And for his holy church! The royal prince —
(I know him, I can penetrate his soul),
Has formed a horrible design, Toledo!
The wild design — to make himself the regent,
And set aside our pure and sacred faith.
His bosom glows with some new-fangled virtue,
Which, proud and self-sufficient, scorns to rest
For strength on any creed. He dares to think!
His brain is all on fire with wild chimeras;
He reverences the people! And is this
A man to be our king?

ALVA.

Fantastic dreams !
No more.   A boy's ambition, too, perchance
To play some lofty part !   What can he less ?
These thoughts will vanish when he's called to rule.

DOMINGO.

I doubt it !   Of his freedom he is proud,
And scorns those strict restraints all men must bear
Who hope to govern others.   Would he suit
Our throne ?   His bold gigantic mind
Would burst the barriers of our policy.
In vain I sought to enervate his soul
In the loose joys of this voluptuous age.
He stood the trial.   Fearful is the spirit
That rules this youth ; and Philip soon will see
His sixtieth year.

ALVA.

Your vision stretches far !

DOMINGO.

He and the queen are both alike in this.
Already works, concealed in either breast,
The poisonous wish for change and innovation.
Give it but way, 'twill quickly reach the throne.
I know this Valois !   We may tremble for
The secret vengeance of this quiet foe
If Philip's weakness hearken to her voice !
Fortune so far hath smiled upon us.   Now
We must anticipate the foe, and both
Shall fall together in one fatal snare.
Let but a hint of such a thing be dropped
Before the king, proved or unproved, it recks not !
Our point is gained if he but waver.   We
Ourselves have not a doubt ; and once convinced,
'Tis easy to convince another's mind.
Be sure we shall discover more if we
Start with the faith that more remains concealed.

ALVA.

But soft !   A vital question !   Who is he
Will undertake the task to tell the king ?

DOMINGO.

Nor you, nor I! Now shall you learn, what long
My busy spirit, full of its design,
Has been at work with, to achieve its ends.
Still is there wanting to complete our league
A third important personage. The king
Loves the young Princess Eboli — and I
Foster this passion for my own designs.
I am his go-between. She shall be schooled
Into our plot. If my plan fail me not,
In this young lady shall a close ally —
A very queen, bloom for us. She herself
Asked me, but now, to meet her in this chamber.
I'm full of hope. And in one little night
A Spanish maid may blast this Valois lily.

ALVA.

What do you say! Can I have heard aright?
By Heaven! I'm all amazement. Compass this,
And I'll bow down to thee, Dominican!
The day's our own.

DOMINGO.

Soft! Some one comes: 'tis she —
'Tis she herself!

ALVA.

I'm in the adjoining room
If you should ——

DOMINGO.

Be it so: I'll call you in. [*Exit* ALVA.

SCENE XI.

PRINCESS, DOMINGO.

DOMINGO.

At your command, princess.

PRINCESS.

We are perhaps
Not quite alone? [*Looking inquisitively after the* DUKE.
You have, as I observe,
A witness still by you.

DOMINGO.

How ?

PRINCESS.

Who was he,

That left your side but now ?

DOMINGO.

It was Duke Alva.

Most gracious princess, he requests you will
Admit him to an audience after me.

PRINCESS.

Duke Alva! How ? What can he want with me?
You can, perhaps, inform me?

DOMINGO.

I ? — and that

Before I learn to what important chance
I owe the favor, long denied, to stand
Before the Princess Eboli once more ?

[*Pauses awaiting her answer.*

Has any circumstance occured at last
To favor the king's wishes ? Have my hopes
Been not in vain, that more deliberate thought
Would reconcile you to an offer which
Caprice alone and waywardness could spurn?
I seek your presence full of expectation ——

PRINCESS.

Was my last answer to the king conveyed?

DOMINGO.

I have delayed to inflict this mortal wound.
There still is time, it rests with you, princess,
To mitigate its rigor.

PRINCESS.

Tell the king

That I expect him.

DOMINGO.

May I, lovely princess,

Indeed accept this as your true reply?

PRINCESS.

I do not jest. By heaven, you make me tremble!
What have I done to make e'en you grow pale?

DOMINGO.

Nay, lady, this surprise — so sudden — I
Can scarcely comprehend it.

PRINCESS.

                    Reverend sir!
You shall not comprehend it. Not for all
The world would I you comprehended it.
Enough for you it is so — spare yourself
The trouble to investigate in thought,
Whose eloquence hath wrought this wondrous change
But for your comfort let me add, you have
No hand in this misdeed, — nor has the church.
Although you've proved that cases might arise
Wherein the church, to gain some noble end,
Might use the persons of her youthful daughters!
Such reasonings move not me; such motives, pure,
Right reverend sir, are far too high for me.

DOMINGO.

When they become superfluous, your grace,
I willingly retract them.

PRINCESS.

                    Seek the king,
And ask him as from me, that he will not
Mistake me in this business. What I have been
That am I still. 'Tis but the course of things
Has changed. When I in anger spurned his suit,
I deemed him truly happy in possessing
Earth's fairest queen. I thought his faithful wife
Deserved my sacrifice. I thought so then,
But now I'm undeceived.

DOMINGO.

                    Princess, go on!
I hear it all — we understand each other.

PRINCESS.

Enough. She is found out. I will not spare her.
The hypocrite's unmasked ! She has deceived
The king, all Spain, and me. She loves, I know
She loves ! I can bring proofs that will make you tremble.
The king has been deceived — but he shall not,
By heaven, go unrevenged ! The saintly mask
Of pure and superhuman self-denial
I'll tear from her deceitful brow, that all
May see the forehead of the shameless sinner.
'Twill cost me dear, but here my triumph lies,
That it will cost her infinitely more.

DOMINGO.

Now all is ripe, let me call in the duke.
         [*Goes out.*
   PRINCESS (*astonished*).

What means all this ?

SCENE XII.

The PRINCESS, DUKE ALVA, DOMINGO.

DOMINGO (*leading the* DUKE *in*).
      Our tidings, good my lord,
Come somewhat late. The Princess Eboli
Reveals to us a secret we had meant
Ourselves to impart to her.

ALVA.
      My visit, then,
Will not so much surprise her, but I never
Trust my own eyes in these discoveries.
They need a woman's more discerning glance.

PRINCESS.

Discoveries ! How mean you ?

DOMINGO.
      Would we knew
What place and fitter season you ——

PRINCESS.
                              Just so!
To-morrow noon I will expect you both.
Reasons I have why this clandestine guilt
Should from the king no longer be concealed.

ALVA.

'Tis this that brings us here.   The king must know it
And he shall hear the news from you, princess,
From you alone : — for to what tongue would he
Afford such ready credence as to yours,
Friend and companion ever of his spouse?

DOMINGO.

As yours, who more than any one at will
Can o'er him exercise supreme command.

ALVA.

I am the prince's open enemy.

DOMINGO.

And that is what the world believes of me.
The Princess Eboli's above suspicion.
We are compelled to silence, but your duty,
The duty of your office, calls on you
To speak.   The king shall not escape our hands.
Let your hints rouse him, we'll complete the work.

ALVA.

It must be done at once, without delay;
Each moment now is precious.   In an hour
The order may arrive for my departure.

DOMINGO (*after a short pause, turns to the* PRINCESS).

Cannot some letters be discovered ?   Truly,
An intercepted letter from the prince
Would work with rare effect.   Ay! let me see ——
Is it not so ?   You sleep, princess, I think,
In the same chamber with her majesty?

PRINCESS.

The next to hers.   But of what use is that?

DOMINGO.

Oh, for some skill in locks! Have you observed
Where she is wont to keep her casket key?

PRINCESS (*in thought*).

Yes, that might lead to something; yes, I think
The key is to be found.

DOMINGO.

Letters, you know,
Need messengers. Her retinue is large;
Who do you think could put us on the scent?
Gold can do much.

ALVA.

Can no one tell us whether
The prince has any trusty confidant?

DOMINGO.

Not one; in all Madrid not one.

ALVA.

That's strange!

DOMINGO.

Rely on me in this. He holds in scorn
The universal court. I have my proofs.

ALVA.

Stay! It occurs to me, as I was leaving
The queen's apartments, I beheld the prince
In private conference with a page of hers.

PRINCESS (*suddenly interrupting*).

O no! that must have been of something else.

DOMINGO.

Could we not ascertain the fact? It seems
Suspicious.   [*To the* DUKE.
Did you know the page, my lord!

PRINCESS.

Some trifle; what else could it be? Enough,
I'm sure of that. So we shall meet again
Before I see the king; and by that time
We may discover much.

DOMINGO (*leading her aside*).

What of the king?

Say, may he hope? May I assure him so?
And the entrancing hour which shall fulfil
His fond desires, what shall I say of that?

PRINCESS.

In a few days I will feign sickness, and
Shall be excused from waiting on the queen.
Such is, you know, the custom of the court,
And I may then remain in my apartment.

DOMINGO.

'Tis well devised! Now the great game is won,
And we may bid defiance to all queens!

PRINCESS.

Hark! I am called. I must attend the queen,
So fare you well.   [*Exit*

Scene XIII.

Alva *and* Domingo.

DOMINGO (*after a pause, during which he has watched
        the* PRINCESS).

My lord! these roses, and ——
Your battles ——

ALVA.

And your God — why, even so!
Thus we'll await the lightning that shall scathe us!

[*Exeunt.*

Scene XIV.

A Carthusian Convent.

Don Carlos *and the* Prior.

CARLOS (*to the* PRIOR, *as he comes in*).

Been here already? I am sorry for it.

PRIOR.

Yes, thrice since morning. 'Tis about an hour
Since he went hence.

CARLOS.

But he will sure return.
Has he not left some message?

PRIOR.

Yes; he promised
To come again at noon.

CARLOS (*going to a window, and looking round the country*).

Your convent lies
Far from the public road.   Yonder are seen
The turrets of Madrid — just so — and there
The Mansanares flows.   The scenery is
Exactly to my wish, and all around
Is calm and still as secrecy itself.

PRIOR.

Or as the entrance to another world.

CARLOS.

Most worthy sir, to your fidelity
And honor, have I now intrusted all
I hold most dear and sacred in the world.
No mortal man must know, or even suspect,
With whom I here hold secret assignation.
Most weighty reasons prompt me to deny,
To all the world, the friend whom I expect,
Therefore I choose this convent.   Are we safe
From traitors and surprise?   You recollect
What you have sworn.

PRIOR.

Good sir, rely on us.
A king's suspicion cannot pierce the grave,
And curious ears haunts only those resorts
Where wealth and passion dwell — but from these walls
The world's forever banished.

CARLOS.

You may think,
Perhaps, beneath this seeming fear and caution
There lies a guilty conscience?

PRIOR.
                              I think nothing.
CARLOS.

If you imagine this, most holy father,
You err — indeed you err.   My secret shuns
The sight of man — but not the eye of God.

PRIOR.

Such things concern us little.   This retreat
To guilt, and innocence alike, is open,
And whether thy designs be good or ill,
Thy purpose criminal or virtuous, — that
We leave to thee to settle with thy heart.

CARLOS (*with warmth*).

Our purpose never can disgrace your God.
'Tis his own noblest work.   To you indeed,
I may reveal it.

PRIOR.

              To what end, I pray ?
Forego, dear prince, this needless explanation.
The world and all its troubles have been long
Shut from my thoughts — in preparation for
My last long journey.   Why recall them to me
For the brief space that must precede my death ?
'Tis little for salvation that we need —
But the bell rings, and summons me to prayer.
                                    [*Exit* PRIOR

SCENE XV.

DON CARLOS ; *the* MARQUIS POSA *enters.*

CARLOS.

At length once more, — at length ——

MARQUIS.

                              Oh, what a trial
For the impatience of a friend !   The sun
Has risen twice — twice set — since Carlos' fate
Has been resolved, and am I only now
To learn it : speak, — you're reconciled !

CARLOS.

With whom?

MARQUIS.

The king! And Flanders, too, — its fate is settled!

CARLOS.

The duke sets out to-morrow. That is fixed

MARQUIS.

That cannot be — it is not surely so.
Can all Madrid be so deceived? 'Tis said
You had a private audience, and the king ——

CARLOS.

Remained inflexible, and we are now
Divided more than ever.

MARQUIS.

Do you go

To Flanders?

CARLOS.

No!

MARQUIS.

Alas! my blighted hopes!

CARLOS.

Of this hereafter. Oh, Roderigo! since
We parted last, what have I not endured?
But first thy counsel? I must speak with her!

MARQUIS.

Your mother? No! But wherefore?

CARLOS.

I have hopes ——
But you turn pale! Be calm — I should be happy.
And I shall be so: but of this anon —
Advise me now, how I may speak with her.

MARQUIS.

What mean you? What new feverish dream is this?

CARLOS.

By the great God of wonders 'tis no dream!
'Tis truth, reality ——
    [*Taking out the* KING's *letter to the* PRINCESS EBOLI
                Contained in this
Important paper —yes, the queen is free, —
Free before men and in the eyes of heaven;
There read, and cease to wonder at my words.

MARQUIS (*opening the letter*).

What do I here behold? The king's own hand!
                       [*After he has read it*
To whom addressed?

CARLOS.

        To Princess Eboli.
Two days ago, a page who serves the queen,
Brought me, from unknown hands, a key and letter,
Which said that in the left wing of the palace,
Where the queen lodges, lay a cabinet, —
That there a lady whom I long had loved
Awaited me. I straight obeyed the summons.

MARQUIS.

Fool! madman! you obeyed it ——

CARLOS.

                  Not that I
The writing knew; but there was only one
Such woman, who could think herself adored
By Carlos. With delight intoxicate
I hastened to the spot. A heavenly song,
Re-echoing from the innermost apartment,
Served me for guide. I reached the cabinet —
I entered and beheld — conceive my wonder!

MARQUIS.

I guess it all ——

CARLOS.

             I had been lost forever,
But that I fell into an angel's hands!
She, hapless chance, by my imprudent looks,
Deceived, had yielded to the sweet delusion

And deemed herself the idol of my soul.
Moved by the silent anguish of my breast,
With thoughtless generosity, her heart
Nobly determined to return my love;
Deeming respectful fear had caused my silence,
She dared to speak, and all her lovely soul
Laid bare before me.

MARQUIS.

And with calm composure,
You tell this tale! The Princess Eboli
Saw through your heart; and doubtless she has pierced
The inmost secret of your hidden love.
You've wronged her deeply, and she rules the king.

CARLOS (*confidently*).

But she is virtuous!

MARQUIS.

She may be so
From love's mere selfishness. But much I fear
Such virtue — well I know it: know how little
It hath the power to soar to that ideal,
Which, first conceived in sweet and stately grace,
From the pure soul's maternal soil, puts forth
Spontaneous shoots, nor asks the gardener's aid
To nurse its lavish blossoms into life.
'Tis but a foreign plant, with labor reared,
And warmth that poorly imitates the south,
In a cold soil and an unfriendly clime.
Call it what name you will — or education,
Or principle, or artificial virtue ——
Won from the heat of youth by art and cunning,
In conflicts manifold — all noted down
With scrupulous reckoning to that heaven's account,
Which is its aim, and will requite its pains.
Ask your own heart! Can she forgive the queen
That you should scorn her dearly-purchased virtue,
To pine in hopeless love for Philip's wife.

CARLOS.

Knowest thou the princess, then, so well?

MARQUIS.

Not I —

I've scarcely seen her twice.   And yet thus much
I may remark.   To me she still appears
To shun alone the nakedness of vice,
Too weakly proud of her imagined virtue.
And then I mark the queen.   How different, Carlos,
Is everything that I behold in her!
In native dignity, serene and calm,
Wearing a careless cheerfulness — unschooled
In all the trained restraints of conduct, far
Removed from boldness and timidity,
With firm, heroic step, she walks along
The narrow middle path of rectitude,
Unconscious of the worship she compels,
Where she of self-approval never dreamed.
Say, does my Carlos in this mirror trace
The features of his Eboli?   The princess
Was constant while she loved; love was the price,
The understood condition of her virtue.
You failed to pay that price — 'twill therefore fall.

CARLOS (*with warmth*).

No, no!   [*Hastily pacing the apartment*
          I tell thee, no!   And, Roderigo,
Ill it becomes thee thus to rob thy Carlos
Of his high trust in human excellence,
His chief, his dearest joy!

MARQUIS.

Deserve I this?
Friend of my soul, this would I never do —
By heaven I would not.   Oh, this Eboli!
She were an angel to me, and before
Her glory would I bend me prostrate down,
In reverence deep as thine, if she were not
The mistress of thy secret.

CARLOS.

See how vain,
How idle are thy fears!   What proofs has she
That will not stamp her maiden brow with shame?

Say, will she purchase with her own dishonor
The wretched satisfaction of revenge?

MARQUIS.

Ay! to recall a blush, full many a one
Has doomed herself to infamy.

CARLOS (*with increased vehemence*).

Nay, that
Is far too harsh — and cruel! She is proud
And noble; well I know her, and fear nothing.
Vain are your efforts to alarm my hopes.
I must speak to my mother.

MARQUIS.

Now? for what?

CARLOS.

Because I've nothing more to care for now.
And I must know my fate. Only contrive
That I may speak with her.

MARQUIS.

And wilt thou show
This letter to her?

CARLOS.

Question me no more,
But quickly find the means that I may see her.

MARQUIS (*significantly*).

Didst thou not tell me that thou lov'st thy mother?
And wouldst thou really show this letter to her?
[CARLOS *fixes his eyes on the ground, and remains
    silent.*
I read a something, Carlos, in thy looks
Unknown to me before. Thou turn'st thine eyes
Away from me. Then it is true, and have I
Judged thee aright? Here, let me see that paper.
[CARLOS *gives him the letter, and the* MARQUIS *tears it.*

CARLOS.

What! art thou mad? [*Moderating his warmth.*
In truth — I must confess it, —
That letter was of deepest moment to me.

MARQUIS.

So it appeared : on that account I tore it.
> [*The* MARQUIS *casts a penetrating look on the* PRINCE,
> *who surveys him with doubt and surprise. A long
> silence.*

Now speak to me with candor, Carlos.   What
Have desecrations of the royal bed
To do with thee — thy love?   Dost thou fear Philip ?
How are a husband's violated duties
Allied with thee and thy audacious hopes ?
Has he sinned there, where thou hast placed thy love ?
Now then, in truth, I learn to comprehend thee —
How ill till now I've understood thy love !

CARLOS.

What dost thou think, Roderigo ?

MARQUIS.

Oh, I feel
From what it is that I must wean myself.
Once it was otherwise !   Yes, once thy soul
Was bounteous, rich, and warm, and there was room
For a whole world in thy expanded heart.
Those feelings are extinct — all swallowed up
In one poor, petty, selfish passion.   Now
Thy heart is withered, dead !   No tears hast thou
For the unhappy fate of wretched Flanders —
No, not another tear.   Oh, Carlos ! see
How poor, how beggarly, thou hast become,
Since all thy love has centered in thyself !

CARLOS (*flings himself into a chair.   After a pause, with
scarcely suppressed tears*).

Too well I know thou lovest me no more !

MARQUIS.

Not so, my Carlos.   Well I understand
This fiery passion : 'tis the misdirection
Of feelings pure and noble in themselves.
The queen belonged to thee : the king, thy father,
Despoiled thee of her — yet till now thou hast
Been modestly distrustful of thy claims.

Philip, perhaps, was worthy of her! **Thou**
Scarce dared to breathe his sentence in a whisper —
This letter has resolved thy doubts, and proved
Thou art the worthier man. With haughty joy
Thou saw'st before thee rise the doom that waits
On tyranny convicted of a theft,
But thou wert proud to be the injured one:
Wrongs undeserved great souls can calmly suffer,
Yet here thy fancy played thee false: thy pride
Was touched with satisfaction, and thy heart
Allowed itself to hope: I plainly saw
This time, at least, thou didst not know thyself.

CARLOS (*with emotion*).

Thou'rt wrong, Roderigo; for my thoughts were far
Less noble than thy goodness would persuade me.

MARQUIS.

And am I then e'en here so little known?
See, Carlos, when thou errest, 'tis my way,
Amid a hundred virtues, still to find
That one to which I may impute thy fall.
Now, then, we understand each other better,
And thou shalt have an audience of the queen.

CARLOS (*falling on his neck*).

Oh, how I blush beside thee!

MARQUIS.

Take my word,
And leave the rest to me. A wild, bold thought,
A happy thought is dawning in my mind;
And thou shalt hear it from a fairer mouth,
I hasten to the queen. Perhaps to-morrow
Thy wish may be achieved. Till then, my Carlos,
Forget not this — " That a design conceived
Of lofty reason, which involves the fate,
The sufferings of mankind, though it be baffled
Ten thousand times, should never be abandoned."
Dost hear? Remember Flanders.

CARLOS.

Yes! all, all
That thou and virtue bid me not forget.

MARQUIS (*going to a window*).

The time is up — I hear thy suite approaching.

[*They embrace.*

Crown prince again, and vassal.

CARLOS.

Dost thou go

Straight to Madrid?

MARQUIS.

Yes, straight.

CARLOS.

Hold! one word more.

How nearly it escaped me! Yet 'twas news
Of deep importance. " Every letter now
Sent to Brabant is opened by the king! "
So be upon thy guard. The royal post
Has secret orders.

MARQUIS.

How have you learned this?

CARLOS.

Don Raymond Taxis is my trusty friend.

MARQUIS (*after a pause*).

Well! then they may be sent through Germany.

[*Exeunt on different sides.*

ACT III.

SCENE I.

*The king's bedchamber. On the toilet two burning lights. In the
background several pages asleep resting on their knees. The
KING, in half undress, stands before the table, with one arm
bent over the chair, in a reflecting posture. Before him is a
medallion and papers.*

KING.

Of a warm fancy she has ever been!
Who can deny it? I could never love her,
Yet has she never seemed to miss my love.
And so 'tis plain — she's false!

[*Makes a movement which brings him to himself.
He looks round with surprise.*

Where have I been?
Is no one watching here, then, save the king?
The light's burnt out, and yet it is not day.
I must forego my slumbers for to-night.
Take it, kind nature, for enjoyed! No time
Have monarchs to retrieve the nights they lose.
I'm now awake, and day it shall be.

   [*He puts out the candles, and draws aside the win-
      dow-curtain. He observes the sleeping pages —
      remains for some time standing before them —
      then rings a bell.*

                    All
Asleep within the antechamber, too?

SCENE II.

The KING, COUNT LERMA.

LERMA (*surprised at seeing the* KING).
Does not your majesty feel well?

KING.
               The left
Pavilion of the palace was in flames:
Did you not hear the alarum?

LERMA.
              No, my liege.

KING.
No! What? And did I only dream it then?
'Twas surely real! Does not the queen sleep there?

LERMA.
She does, your majesty.

KING.
          This dream affrights me!
In future let the guards be doubled there
As soon as it grows dark. Dost hear? And yet
Let it be done in secret. I would not ——
Why do you gaze on me?

LERMA.
          Your bloodshot eyes,
I mark, that beg repose. Dare I remind

My liege of an inestimable life,
And of your subjects, who with pale dismay
Would in such features read of restless nights?
But two brief hours of morning sleep would——

KING (with troubled look).

Sleep!

Shall I find sleep within the Escurial?
Let the king sleep, and he may lose his crown,
The husband, his wife's heart. But no! not so;
This is but slander. Was it not a woman
Whispered the crime to me? Woman, thy name
Is calumny? The deed I'll hold unproved,
Until a man confirms the fatal truth!
   [*To the pages, who in the meanwhile have awaked.*
Summon Duke Alva!   [*Pages go.*
Count, come nearer to me.
[*Fixes a searching look on the* COUNT.
Is all this true? Oh for omniscience now,
Though but so long as a man's pulse might beat.
Is it true? Upon your oath! Am I deceived?

LERMA.

My great, my best of kings!

KING (drawing back).

King! naught but king!

And king again! No better answer than
Mere hollow echo! When I strike this rock
For water, to assuage my burning thirst,
It gives me molten gold.

LERMA.

What true, my liege?

KING.

Oh, nothing, nothing! Leave me! Get thee gone!
   [*The* COUNT *going, the* KING *calls him back again.*
Say, are you married? and are you a father?

LERMA.

I am, your majesty.

KING.

What! married — yet
You dare to watch a night here with your king!
Your hair is gray, and yet you do not blush
To think your wife is honest. Get thee home;
You'll find her locked, this moment, in your son's
Incestuous embrace. Believe your king.
Now go; you stand amazed; you stare at me
With searching eye, because of my gray hairs.
Unhappy man, reflect. Queens never taint
Their virtue thus: doubt it, and you shall die!

LERMA (*with warmth*).

Who dare do so? In all my monarch's realms
Who has the daring hardihood to breathe
Suspicion on her angel purity?
To slander thus the best of queens ——

KING.

The best!
The best, from you, too! She has ardent friends,
I find, around. It must have cost her much —
More than methinks she could afford to give.
You are dismissed; now send the duke to me.

LERMA.

I hear him in the antechamber.   [*Going.*

KING (*with a milder tone*).

Count,
What you observed is very true. My head
Burns with the fever of this sleepless night!
What I have uttered in this waking dream,
Mark you, forget! I am your gracious king!
    [*Presents his hand to kiss. Exit* LERMA, *opening
    the door at the same time to* DUKE ALVA.

SCENE III.

The KING *and* DUKE ALVA.

ALVA (*approaching the* KING *with an air of doubt*).
This unexpected order, at so strange

An hour!   [*Starts on looking closer at the* KING.
And then those looks!

KING (*has seated himself, and taken hold of the medallion
on the table. Looks at the* DUKE *for some time in
silence.*

                                    And is it true
I have no faithful servant!

ALVA.
How?

KING.

                                    A blow
Aimed at my life in its most vital part!
Full well 'twas known, yet no one warned me of it.

ALVA (*with a look of astonishment*).
A blow aimed at your majesty! and yet
Escape your Alva's eye?

KING (*showing him letters*).
                          Know you this writing?

ALVA.
It is the prince's hand.

KING (*a pause — watches the* DUKE *closely*).
                          Do you suspect
Then nothing? Often have you cautioned me
'Gainst his ambition.   Was there nothing more
Than his ambition should have made me tremble?

ALVA.
Ambition is a word of largest import,
And much it may comprise.

KING.
                          And had you naught
Of special purport to disclose ?

ALVA (*after a pause, mysteriously*).
                                    Your majesty
Hath given the kingdom's welfare to my charge:
On this my inmost, secret thoughts are bent,

And my best vigilance.   Beyond this charge
What I may think, suspect, or know belongs
To me alone.   These are the sacred treasures
Which not the vassal only, but the slave,
The very slave, may from a king withhold.
Not all that to my mind seems plain is yet
Mature enough to meet the monarch's ear.
Would he be answered — then must I implore
He will not question as a king.

KING (*handing the letters*).
Read these.

ALVA (*reads them, and turns to the* KING *with a look
of terror*).
Who was the madman placed these fatal papers
In my king's hands ?

KING.
You know, then, who is meant ?
No name you see is mentioned in the paper.

ALVA (*stepping back confused*).
I was too hasty !

KING.
But you know !

ALVA (*after some consideration*).
'Tis spoken !
The king commands, — I dare not now conceal.
I'll not deny it — I do know the person.

KING (*starting up in violent emotion*).
God of revenge ! inspire me to invent
Some new, unheard-of torture !   Is their crime
So clear, so plain, so public to the world,
That without e'en the trouble of inquiry
The veriest hint suffices to reveal it ?
This is too much !   I did not dream of this !
I am the last of all, then, to discern it —
The last in all my realm ?

ALVA (*throwing himself at the* KING's *feet*).
                              Yes, I confess
My guilt, most gracious monarch. I'm ashamed
A coward prudence should have tied my tongue
When truth, and justice, and my sovereign's honor
Urged me to speak. But since all else are silent
And since the magic spell of beauty binds
All other tongues, I dare to give it voice;
Though well I know a son's warm protestations,
A wife's seductive charms and winning tears ——

          KING (*suddenly with warmth*).
Rise, Alva! thou hast now my royal promise;
Rise, and speak fearlessly!

               ALVA (*rising*).
                              Your majesty,
Perchance, may bear in your remembrance still
What happened in the garden at Aranjuez.
You found the queen deserted by her ladies,
With looks confused — alone, within a bower, ——

               KING.
Proceed.   What further have I yet to hear?

               ALVA.
The Marchioness of Mondecar was banished
Because she boldly sacrificed herself
To save the queen! It has been since discovered
She did no more than she had been commanded.
Prince Carlos had been there.

          KING (*starting*).
                    The prince!   What more?
               ALVA.
Upon the ground the footsteps of a man
Were traced, till finally they disappeared
Close to a grotto, leftward of the bower,
Where lay a handkerchief the prince had dropped.
This wakened our suspicions.   But besides,
The gardener met the prince upon the spot, —
Just at the time, as near as we can guess,
Your majesty appeared within the walk.

KING (*recovering from gloomy thought*).

And yet she wept when I but seemed to doubt!
She made me blush before the assembled court,
Blush to my very self! By heaven! I stood
In presence of her virtue, like a culprit.
[*A long and deep silence. He sits down and hides
his face.*
Yes, Alva, you are right! All this may lead
To something dreadful — leave me for a moment ——

ALVA.

But, gracious sire, all this is not enough ——

KING (*snatching up the papers*).

Nor this, nor this ? — nor all the harmony
Of these most damning proofs? 'Tis clear as day —
I knew it long ago — their heinous guilt
Began when first I took her from your hands,
Here in Madrid. I think I see her now,
With look of horror, pale as midnight ghost,
Fixing her eyes upon my hoary hair!
'Twas then the treacherous game began!

ALVA.

The prince,
In welcoming a mother — lost his bride!
Long had they nursed a mutual passion, long
Each other's ardent feelings understood,
Which her new state forbade her to indulge.
The fear which still attends love's first avowal
Was long subdued. Seduction, bolder grown,
Spoke in those forms of easy confidence
Which recollections of the past allowed.
Allied by harmony of souls and years,
And now by similar restraints provoked,
They readily obeyed their wild desires.
Reasons of state opposed their early union —
But can it, sire, be thought she ever gave
To the state council such authority?
That she subdued the passion of her soul
To scrutinize with more attentive eye

The election of the cabinet.   Her heart
Was bent on love, and won a diadem.

       KING (*offended, and with bitterness*).

You are a nice observer, duke, and I
Admire your eloquence.   I thank you truly.
                   [*Rising coldly and haughtily.*
But you are right.   The queen has deeply erred
In keeping from me letters of such import,
And in concealing the intrusive visit
The prince paid in the garden : — from a false
Mistaken honor she has deeply erred
And I shall question further.   [*Ringing the bell.*
                  Who waits now
Within the antechamber ?   You, Duke Alva,
I need no longer.   Go.

           ALVA.

           And has my zeal
A second time displeased your majesty ?

       KING (*to a page who enters*).

Summon Domingo.   Duke, I pardon you
For having made me tremble for a moment,
With secret apprehension, lest yourself
Might fall a victim to a foul misdeed.   [*Exit* ALVA.

          SCENE IV.

       The KING, DOMINGO.

KING *walks up and down the room to collect his thoughts.*

    DOMINGO (*after contemplating the* KING *for some time
            with a respectful silence*).
How joyfully surprised I am to find
Your majesty so tranquil and collected.

          KING.

Surprised !

         DOMINGO.

     And heaven be thanked my fears were groundless !
Now may I hope the best.

KING.

Your fears! What feared you?

DOMINGO.

I dare not hide it from your majesty
That I had learned a secret ——

KING (*gloomily*).

And have I
Expressed a wish to share your secret with you?
Who ventures to anticipate me thus?
Too forward, by mine honor!

DOMINGO.

Gracious monarch!
The place, the occasion, seal of secrecy
'Neath which I learned it — free me from this charge.
It was intrusted to me at the seat
Of penitence — intrusted as a crime
That deeply weighed upon the tender soul
Of the fair sinner who confessed her guilt,
And sought the pardon of offended heaven.
Too late the princess weeps a foul misdeed
That may involve the queen herself in ruin.

KING.

Indeed! Kind soul! You have correctly guessed
The occasion of your summons. You must guide me
Through this dark labyrinth wherein blind zeal
Has tangled me. From you I hope for truth.
Be candid with me; what must I believe,
And what determine? From your sacred office
I look for strictest truth.

DOMINGO.

And if, my liege,
The mildness ever incident to this
My holy calling, did not such restraint
Impose upon me, still I would entreat
Your majesty, for your own peace of mind,
To urge no further this discovery,
And cease forever to pursue a secret
Which never can be happily explained.

All that is yet discovered may be pardoned.
Let the king say the word — and then the queen
Has never sinned. The monarch's will bestows
Virtue and fortune, both with equal ease.
And the king's undisturbed tranquillity
Is, in itself, sufficient to destroy
The rumors set on foot by calumny.

KING.

What! Rumors! and of me! among my subjects!

DOMINGO.

All falsehood, sire! Naught but the vilest falsehood!
I'll swear 'tis false! Yet what's believed by all,
Groundless and unconfirmed although it be,
Works its effect, as sure as truth itself.

KING.

Not in this case, by heaven!

DOMINGO.

                    A virtuous name
Is, after all, my liege, the only prize
Which queens and peasants' wives contest together.

KING.

For which I surely have no need to tremble.
    [*He looks doubtingly at* DOMINGO. *After a pause*
Priest, thou hast something fearful to impart.
Delay it not. I read it plainly stamped
In thy ill-boding looks. Then out with it,
Whate'er it be. Let me no longer tremble
Upon the rack. What do the people say?

DOMINGO.

The people, sire, are liable to err,
Nay err assuredly. What people think
Should not alarm the king. Yet that they should
Presume so far as to indulge such thoughts ——

KING.

Why must I beg this poisonous draught so long?

DOMINGO.

The people often muse upon that month
Which brought your majesty so near the grave,
From that time, thirty weeks had scarce elapsed,
Before the queen's delivery was announced.

[*The* KING *rises and rings the bell.* DUKE ALVA
enters. DOMINGO *alarmed.*

I am amazed, your majesty !

KING (*going towards* ALVA).

Toledo !
You are a man — defend me from this priest !

DOMINGO (*he and* DUKE ALVA *exchange embarrassed looks.
After a pause*).

Could we have but foreseen that this occurrence
Would be avenged upon its mere relater.

KING.

Said you a bastard ?   I had scarce, you say,
Escaped the pangs of death when first she felt
She should, in nature's time, become a mother.
Explain how this occurred !   'Twas then, if I
Remember right, that you, in every church,
Ordered devotions to St. Dominick,
For the especial wonder he vouchsafed.
On one side or the other, then, you lie !
What would you have me credit ?   Oh, I see
Full plainly through you now !   If this dark plot
Had then been ripe your saint had lost his fame.

ALVA.

This plot ?

KING.

How can you with a harmony
So unexampled in your very thoughts
Concur, and not have first conspired together ?
Would you persuade me thus ?   Think you that I
Perceived not with what eagerness you pounced
Upon your prey ?   With what delight you fed
Upon my pain, — my agony of grief ?
Full well I marked the ardent, burning zeal

With which the duke forestalled the mark of grace
I destined for my son.   And how this priest
Presumed to fortify his petty spleen
With my wrath's giant arm!   I am, forsooth,
A bow which each of you may bend at pleasure
But I have yet a will.   And if I needs
Must doubt — perhaps I may begin with you.

ALVA.

Reward like this our truth did ne'er expect.

KING.

Your truth!   Truth warns of apprehended danger.
'Tis malice that speaks only of the past.
What can I gain by your officiousness?
Should your suspicion ripen to full truth,
What follows but the pangs of separation,
The melancholy triumphs of revenge?
But no: you only fear — you feed me with
Conjectures vague.   To hell's profound abyss
You lead me on, then flee yourself away.

DOMINGO.

What other proofs than these are possible,
When our own eyes can scarcely trust themselves?

KING (*after a long pause, turning earnestly and solemnly
towards* DOMINGO).

The grandees of the realm shall be convened,
And I will sit in judgment.   Then step forth
In front of all, if you have courage for it,
And charge her as a strumpet.   She shall die —
Die without mercy — and the prince, too, with her!
But mark me well: if she but clear herself
That doom shall fall on you.   Now, dare you show
Honor to truth by such a sacrifice?
Determine.   No, you dare not.   You are silent.
Such is the zeal of liars!

ALVA (*who has stood at a distance, answers coldly and
calmly*).

                    I will do it.

KING (*turns round with astonishment and looks at the
DUKE for a long time without moving*).

That's boldly said! But thou hast risked thy life
In stubborn conflicts for far less a prize.
Has risked it with a gamester's recklessness —
For honor's empty bubble. What is life
To thee? I'll not expose the royal blood
To such a madman's power, whose highest hope
Must be to yield his wretched being up
With some renown. I spurn your offer. Go;
And wait my orders in the audience chamber.

[*Exeunt.*

Scene V.

The KING alone.

Now give me, gracious Providence! a man.
Thou'st given me much already. Now vouchsafe me
A man! for thou alone canst grant the boon.
Thine eye doth penetrate all hidden things
Oh! give me but a friend: for I am not
Omniscient like to thee. The ministers
Whom thou hast chosen for me thou dost know —
And their deserts: and as their merits claim,
I value them. Their subjugated vices,
Coerced by rein severe, serve all my ends,
As thy storms purify this nether world.
I thirst for truth. To reach its tranquil spring,
Through the dark heaps of thick surrounding error,
Is not the lot of kings. Give me the man,
So rarely found, of pure and open heart,
Of judgment clear, and eye unprejudiced,
To aid me in the search. I cast the lots.
And may I find that man, among the thousands
Who flutter in the sunshine of a court.

[*He opens an escritoire and takes out a portfolio.
After turning over the leaves a long time.*
Nothing but names, mere names are here: — no note
E'en of the services to which they owe
Their place upon the roll! Oh, what can be
Of shorter memory than gratitude!

Here, in this other list, I read each fault
Most accurately marked. That is not well!
Can vengeance stand in need of such a help?

       [He reads further.

Count Egmont! What doth he here? Long ago
The victory of St. Quentin is forgotten.
I place him with the dead.

    [He effaces this name and writes it on the other
     roll after he has read further.

       The Marquis Posa!

The Marquis Posa! I can scarce recall
This person to mind. And doubly marked!
A proof I destined him for some great purpose.
How is it possible? This man, till now,
Has ever shunned my presence — still has fled
His royal debtor's eye? The only man,
By heaven, within the compass of my realm,
Who does not court my favor. Did he burn
With avarice, or ambition, long ago
He had appeared before my throne. I'll try
This wondrous man. He who can thus dispense
With royalty will doubtless speak the truth.

Scene VI.

The Audience Chamber.

Don Carlos *in conversation with the* Prince of Parma.
Dukes Alva, Feria, *and* Medina Sidonia, Count
Lerma, *and other* Grandees, *with papers in their
hands, awaiting the* King.

Medina Sidonia (*seems to be shunned by all the* Grandees,
turns towards Duke Alva, *who, alone and absorbed in
himself, walks up and down*).

Duke, you have had an audience of the king?
How did you find him minded?

      ALVA.

        Somewhat ill
For you, and for the news you bring.

MEDINA SIDONIA.

My heart
Was lighter 'mid the roar of English cannon
Than here on Spanish ground.

[CARLOS, *who had regarded him with silent sympathy, now approaches him and presses his hand.*

My warmest thanks,
Prince, for this generous tear. You may perceive
How all avoid me. Now my fate is sealed.

CARLOS.

Still hope the best both from my father's favor,
And your own innocence.

MEDINA SIDONIA.

Prince, I have lost
A fleet more mighty than e'er ploughed the waves.
And what is such a head as mine to set
'Gainst seventy sunken galleons? And therewith
Five hopeful sons! Alas! that breaks my heart.

SCENE VII.

The KING *enters from his chamber, attired. The former all uncover and make room on both sides, while they form a semicircle round him. Silence.*

KING (*rapidly surveying the whole circle*).

Be covered, all.

[DON CARLOS *and the* PRINCE OF PARMA *approach first and kiss the* KING'S *hand: he turns with friendly mien to the latter, taking no notice of his son.*

Your mother, nephew, fain
Would be informed what favor you have won
Here in Madrid.

PARMA.

That question let her ask
When I have fought my maiden battle, sire.

KING.

Be satisfied; your turn will come at last,
When these old props decay.

[*To the* DUKE OF FERIA.
What brings you here?

FERIA (*kneeling to the* KING).

The master, sire, of Calatrava's order
This morning died.   I here return his cross.
KING (*takes the order and looks round the whole circle*).
And who is worthiest after him to wear it?

> [*He beckons to* DUKE ALVA, *who approaches and
> bends on one knee.   The* KING *hangs the order
> on his neck.*

You are my ablest general!   Ne'er aspire
To more, and, duke, my favors shall not fail you.

> [*He perceives the* DUKE *of* MEDINA SIDONIA.

My admiral!

MEDINA SIDONIA.

And here you see, great king,
All that remains of the Armada's might,
And of the flower of Spain.

KING (*after a pause*).

God rules above us!
I sent you to contend with men, and not
With rocks and storms.   You're welcome to Madrid.

> [*Extending his hand to him to kiss.*

I thank you for preserving in yourself
A faithful servant to me.   For as such
I value him, my lords; and 'tis my will
That you should honor him.

> [*He motions him to rise and cover himself, then
> turns to the others.*

What more remains?

> [*To* DON CARLOS *and the* PRINCE OF PARMA.

Princes, I thank you.

> [*They retire; the other* GRANDEES *approach, and
> kneeling, hand their papers to the* KING.   *He
> looks over them rapidly, and hands them to*
> DUKE ALVA.

Duke, let these be laid
Before me in the council.   Who waits further?

> [*No one answers.*

How comes it that amidst my train of nobles
The Marquis Posa ne'er appears?   I know

This Marquis Posa served me with distinction.
Does he still live? Why is he not among you?

LERMA.

The chevalier is just returned from travel,
Completed through all Europe. He is now
Here in Madrid, and waits a public day
To cast himself before his sovereign's feet.

ALVA.

The Marquis Posa? Right, he is the same
Bold Knight of Malta, sire, of whom renown
Proclaims this gallant deed. Upon a summons
Of the Grand Master, all the valiant knights
Assembled in their island, at that time
Besieged by Soliman. This noble youth,
Scarce numbering eighteen summers, straightway fled
From Alcala, where he pursued his studies,
And suddenly arrived at La Valette.
"This Cross," he said, "was bought for me; and now
To prove I'm worthy of it." He was one
Of forty knights who held St. Elmo's Castle,
At midday, 'gainst Piali, Ulucciali,
And Mustapha, and Hassem; the assault
Being thrice repeated. When the castle fell,
And all the valiant knights were killed around him,
He plunged into the ocean, and alone
Reached La Valette in safety. Two months after
The foe deserts the island, and the knight
Returned to end his interrupted studies.

FERIA.

It was the Marquis Posa, too, who crushed
The dread conspiracy in Catalonia;
And by his marked activity preserved
That powerful province to the Spanish crown.

KING.

I am amazed! What sort of man is this
Who can deserve so highly, yet awake
No pang of envy in the breasts of three
Who speak his praise? The character he owns

Must be of noble stamp indeed, or else
A very blank.   I'm curious to behold
This wondrous man.   [*To* Duke Alva
                    Conduct him to the council
When mass is over.
                    [*Exit* Duke.   *The* King *calls* Feria
                        And do you preside
Here in my place.   [*Exit*

FERIA.

The king is kind to-day.

MEDINA SIDONIA.

Call him a god!   So he has proved to me!

FERIA.

You well deserve your fortune, admiral!
You have my warmest wishes.

ONE OF THE GRANDEES.

                        Sir, and mine.
A SECOND.

And also mine!

A THIRD.

                My heart exults with joy —
So excellent a general!

THE FIRST.

                The king
Showed you no kindness, 'twas your strict desert.

LERMA (*to* MEDINA SIDONIA, *taking leave*).

Oh, how two little words have made your fortune!
                                    [*Exeunt all.*

SCENE VIII.

The King's *Cabinet.*

MARQUIS POSA *and* DUKE ALVA.

MARQUIS (*as he enters*).

Does he want me?   What, me?   Impossible!
You must mistake the name.   What can he want
With me?

ALVA.

To know you.

MARQUIS.

Curiosity!
No more; and I regret the precious minutes
That I must lose: time passes swiftly by.

ALVA.

I now commend you to your lucky stars.
The king is in your hands. Employ this moment
To your own best advantage; for, remember,
If it is lost, you are alone to blame.

SCENE IX.

The MARQUIS *alone.*

MARQUIS.

Duke, 'tis well spoken! Turn to good account
The moment which presents itself but once!
Truly this courtier reads a useful lesson:
If not in his sense good, at least in mine.
    [*Walks a few steps backwards and forwards.*
How came I here? Is it caprice or chance
That shows me now my image in this mirror?
Why, out of millions, should it picture me —
The most unlikely — and present my form
To the king's memory? Was this but chance?
Perhaps 'twas something more! — what else is chance
But the rude stone which from the sculptor's hand
Receives its life? Chance comes from Providence,
And man must mould it to his own designs.
What the king wants with me but little matters;
I know the business I shall have with him.
Were but one spark of truth with boldness flung
Into the despot's soul, how fruitful 'twere
In the kind hand of Providence; and so
What first appeared capricious act of chance,
May be designed for some momentous end.
Whate'er it be, I'll act on this belief.
   [*He takes a few turns in the room, and stands* **at last**
    in tranquil contemplation before a painting. ***The***

KING *appears in the neighboring room, where he gives some orders. He then enters and stands motionless at the door, and contemplates the* MARQUIS *for some time without being observed.*

SCENE X.

The KING, *and* MARQUIS POSA.

The MARQUIS, *as soon as he observes the* KING, *comes forward and sinks on one knee; then rises and remains standing before him without any sign of confusion.*

KING (*looks at him with surprise*).

We've met before then?

MARQUIS.

No.

KING.

You did my crown
Some service?   Why then do you shun my thanks?
My memory is thronged with suitor's claims.
One only is omniscient.   'Twas your duty
To seek your monarch's eye!   Why did you not?

MARQUIS.

Two days have scarce elapsed since my return
From foreign travel, sire.

KING.

I would not stand
Indebted to a subject; ask some favor ——

MARQUIS.

I enjoy the laws.

KING.

So does the murderer!

MARQUIS.

Then how much more the honest citizen!
My lot contents me, sire.

KING (*aside*).

By heavens! a proud
And dauntless mind! That was to be expected.
Proud I would have my Spaniards. Better far
The cup should overflow than not be full.
They say you've left my service?

MARQUIS.

To make way
For some one worthier, I withdrew.

KING.

·'Tis pity.
When spirits such as yours make holiday,
The state must suffer. But perchance you feared
To miss the post best suited to your merits.

MARQUIS.

Oh, no! I doubt not the experienced judge,
In human nature skilled — his proper study, —
Will have discovered at a glance wherein
I may be useful to him, wherein not.
With deepest gratitude, I feel the favor
Wherewith, by so exalted an opinion,
Your majesty is loading me; and yet —— [*He pauses.*

KING.

You hesitate?

MARQUIS.

I am, I must confess,
Sire, at this moment, unprepared to clothe
My thoughts, as the world's citizen, in phrase
Beseeming to your subject. When I left
The court forever, sire, I deemed myself
Released from the necessity to give
My reasons for this step.

KING.

Are they so weak?
What do you fear to risk by their disclosure?

MARQUIS.

My life at farthest, sire, — were time allowed
For me to weary you — but this denied —

Then truth itself must suffer.   I must choose
'Twixt your displeasure and contempt.   And if
I must decide, I rather would appear
Worthy of punishment than pity.

KING (*with a look of expectation*).

Well?

MARQUIS.

I cannot be the servant of a prince.
[*The* KING *looks at him with astonishment*
I will not cheat the buyer.   Should you deem
Me worthy of your service, you prescribe
A course of duty for me ; you command
My arm in battle and my head in council.
Then, not my actions, but the applause they meet
At court becomes their object.   But for me
Virtue possesses an intrinsic worth.
I would, myself, create that happiness
A monarch, with my hand, would seek to plant,
And duty's task would prove an inward joy,
And be my willing choice.   Say, like you this ?
And in your own creation could you bear
A new creator ?   For I ne'er could stoop
To be the chisel where I fain would be
The sculptor's self.   I dearly love mankind,
My gracious liege, but in a monarchy
I dare not love another than myself.

KING.

This ardor is most laudable.   You wish
To do good deeds to others ; how you do them
Is but of small account to patriots,
Or to the wise.   Choose then within these realms
The office where you best may satisfy
This noble impulse.

MARQUIS.

'Tis not to be found.

KING.

How !

MARQUIS.

What your majesty would spread abroad,
Through these my hands — is it the good of men?
Is it the happiness that my pure love
Would to mankind impart? Before such bliss
Monarchs would tremble. No! Court policy
Has raised up new enjoyments for mankind.
Which she is always rich enough to grant;
And wakened, in the hearts of men, new wishes
Which such enjoyments only can content.
In her own mint she coins the truth — such truth!
As she herself can tolerate: all forms
Unlike her own are broken. But is that
Which can content the court enough for me?
Must my affection for my brother pledge
Itself to work my brother injury?
To call him happy when he dare not think?
Sire, choose not me to spread the happiness
Which you have stamped for us. I must decline
To circulate such coin. I cannot be
The servant of a prince.

KING (*suddenly*).

You are, perhaps,

A Protestant?

MARQUIS (*after some reflection*).

Our creeds, my liege, are one.

[*A pause.*

I am misunderstood. I feared as much.
You see the veil torn by my hand aside
From all the mysteries of majesty.
Who can assure you I shall still regard
As sacred that which ceases to alarm me?
I may seem dangerous, because I think
Above myself. I am not so, my liege;
My wishes lie corroding here. The rage

[*Laying his hand on his breast.*

For innovation, which but serves to increase
The heavy weight of chains it cannot break,
Shall never fire my blood! The world is yet

Unripe for my ideal; and I live
A citizen of ages yet to come.
But does a fancied picture break your rest?
A breach of yours destroys it.

KING.

Say, am I
The first to whom your views are known?

MARQUIS.

You are.

KING (*rises, walks a few paces and then stops opposite the*
MARQUIS — *aside*).
This tone, at least, is new ; but flattery
Exhausts itself.   And men of talent still
Disdain to imitate.   So let us test
Its opposite for once.   Why should I not?
There is a charm in novelty.   Should we
Be so agreed, I will bethink me now
Of some new state employment, in whose duties
Your powerful mind ——

MARQUIS.

Sire, I perceive how small,
How mean, your notions are of manly worth.
Suspecting, in an honest man's discourse,
Naught but a flatterer's artifice — methinks
I can explain the cause of this your error.
Mankind compel you to it.   With free choice
They have disclaimed their true nobility,
Lowered themselves to their degraded state.
Before man's inward worth, as from a phantom,
They fly in terror — and contented with
Their poverty, they ornament their chains
With slavish prudence; and they call it virtue
To bear them with a show of resignation.
Thus did you find the world, and thus it was
By your great father handed o'er to you.
In this debased conection — how could you
Respect mankind ?

KING.

Your words contain some truth.

MARQUIS.

Alas! that when from the Creator's hand
You took mankind, and moulded him to suit
Your own ideas, making yourself the god
Of this new creature, you should overlook
That you yourself remained a human being —
A very man, as from God's hands you came.
Still did you feel a mortal's wants and pains.
You needed sympathy ; but to a God
One can but sacrifice, and pray, and tremble —
Wretched exchange ! Perversion most unblest
Of sacred nature ! Once degrade mankind,
And make him but a thing to play upon,
Who then can share the harmony with you?

KING (*aside*).

By heaven, he moves me!

MARQUIS.

But this sacrifice
To you is valueless. You thus become
A thing apart, a species of your own.
This is the price you pay for being a god ;
'Twere dreadful were it not so, and if you
Gained nothing by the misery of millions!
And if the very freedom you destroyed
Were the sole blessing that could make you happy.
Dismiss me, sire, I pray you ; for my theme
Bears me too far; my heart is full; too strong
The charm, to stand before the only man
To whom I may reveal it.

[*The* COUNT LERMA *enters, and whispers a few
words to the* KING, *who signs him to withdraw,
and continues sitting in his former posture.*

KING (*to the* MARQUIS, *after* LERMA *is gone*).

Nay, continue.

MARQUIS (*after a pause*).

I feel, sire — all the worth ——

KING.

Proceed ; you had
Yet more to say to me.

MARQUIS.

Your majesty,
I lately passed through Flanders and Brabant,
So many rich and blooming provinces,
Filled with a valiant, great, and honest people.
To be the father of a race like this
I thought must be divine indeed; and then
I stumbled on a heap of burnt men's bones.
    [*He stops, he fixes a penetrating look on the* KING,
        *who endeavors to return his glance ; but he looks
        on the ground, embarrassed and confused.*
True, you are forced to act so; but that you
Could dare fulfil your task — this fills my soul
With shuddering horror! Oh, 'tis pity that
The victim, weltering in his blood, must cease
To chant the praises of his sacrificer!
And that mere men — not beings loftier far —
Should write the history of the world. But soon
A milder age will follow that of Philip,
An age of truer wisdom; hand in hand,
The subjects' welfare and the sovereign's greatness
Will walk in union. Then the careful state
Will spare her children, and necessity
No longer glory to be thus inhuman.

KING.

When, think you, would that blessed age arrive,
If I had shrunk before the curse of this?
Behold my Spain, see here the burgher's good
Blooms in eternal and unclouded peace.
A peace like this will I bestow on Flanders.

MARQUIS (*hastily*).

The churchyard's peace! And do you hope to end
What you have now begun? Say, do you hope
To check the ripening change of Christendom,
The universal spring, that shall renew
The earth's fair form? Would you alone, in Europe,
Fling yourself down before the rapid wheel
Of destiny, which rolls its ceaseless course,
And seize its spokes with human arm. Vain thought!

Already thousands have your kingdom fled
In joyful poverty : the honest burgher
For his faith exiled, was your noblest subject !
See ! with a mother's arms, Elizabeth
Welcomes the fugitives, and Britain blooms
In rich luxuriance, from our country's arts.
Bereft of the new Christian's industry,
Granada lies forsaken, and all Europe
Exulting, sees his foe oppressed with wounds,
By its own hands inflicted !
    [*The* KING *is moved ; the* MARQUIS *observe*
     and advances a step nearer.
        You would plant
For all eternity, and yet the seeds
You sow around you are the seeds of death !
This hopeless task, with nature's laws at strife,
Will ne'er survive the spirit of its founder.
You labor for ingratitude ; in vain,
With nature you engage in desperate struggle —
In vain you waste your high and royal life
In projects of destruction. Man is greater
Than you esteem him. He will burst the chains
Of a long slumber, and reclaim once more
His just and hallowed rights. With Nero's name,
And fell Busiris', will he couple yours ;
And — ah ! you once deserved a better fate.

KING.

How know you that ?

MARQUIS.

     In very truth you did —
Yes, I repeat it — by the Almighty power !
Restore us all you have deprived us of,
And, generous as strong, let happiness
Flow from your horn of plenty — let man's mind
Ripen in your vast empire — give us back
All you have taken from us — and become,
Amidst a thousand kings, a king indeed !
    [*He advances boldly, and fixes on him a look of*
     earnestness and enthusiasm.
Oh, that the eloquence of all those myriads,

Whose fate depends on this momentous hour,
Could hover on my lips, and fan the spark
That lights thine eye into a glorious flame!
Renounce the mimicry of godlike powers
Which level us to nothing. Be, in truth,
An image of the Deity himself!
Never did mortal man possess so much
For purpose so divine. The kings of Europe
Pay homage to the name of Spain. Be you
The leader of these kings. One pen-stroke now,
One motion of your hand, can new create
The earth! but grant us liberty of thought.

[Casts himself at his feet

KING (*surprised, turns away his face, then again
looks towards the* MARQUIS).

Enthusiast most strange! arise; but I ——

MARQUIS.

Look round on all the glorious face of nature,
On freedom it is founded — see how rich,
Through freedom it has grown. The great **Creator**
Bestows upon the worm its drop of dew,
And gives free-will a triumph in abodes
Where lone corruption reigns. See your creation,
How small, how poor! The rustling of a leaf
Alarms the mighty lord of Christendom.
Each virtue makes you quake with fear. While he,
Not to disturb fair freedom's blest appearance,
Permits the frightful ravages of evil
To waste his fair domains. The great Creator
We see not — he conceals himself within
His own eternal laws. The sceptic sees
Their operation, but beholds not Him.
" Wherefore a God!" he cries, " the world itself
Suffices for itself!" And Christian prayer
Ne'er praised him more than doth this blasphemy.

KING.

And will you undertake to raise up this
Exalted standard of weak human nature
In my dominions?

MARQUIS.

You can do it, sire.
Who else? Devote to your own people's bliss
The kingly power, which has too long enriched
The greatness of the throne alone. Restore
The prostrate dignity of human nature,
And let the subject be, what once he was,
The end and object of the monarch's care,
Bound by no duty, save a brother's love.
And when mankind is to itself restored,
Roused to a sense of its own innate worth,
When freedom's lofty virtues proudly flourish —
Then, sire, when you have made your own wide realms
The happiest in the world, it then may be
Your duty to subdue the universe.

KING (*after a long pause*).

I've heard you to the end. Far differently
I find, than in the minds of other men,
The world exists in yours. And you shall not
By foreign laws be judged. I am the first
To whom you have your secret self disclosed;
I know it — so believe it — for the sake
Of this forbearance — that you have till now
Concealed these sentiments, although embraced
With so much ardor, — for this cautious prudence.
I will forget, young man, that I have learned them,
And how I learned them. Rise! I will confute
Your youthful dreams by my matured experience,
Not by my power as king. Such is my will,
And therefore act I thus. Poison itself
May, in a worthy nature, be transformed
To some benignant use. But, sir, beware
My Inquisition! 'Twould afflict me much ——

MARQUIS.

Indeed!

KING (*lost in surprise*).

Ne'er met I such a man as that!
No, marquis, no! you wrong me! Not to you
Will I become a Nero — not to you! —

All happiness shall not be blasted round me,
And you at least, beneath my very eyes,
May dare continue to remain a man.

MARQUIS (*quickly*).

And, sire, my fellow-subjects? Not for me,
Nor my own cause, I pleaded. Sire! your subjects ——

KING.

Nay, if you know so well how future times
Will judge me, let them learn at least from you,
That when I found a man, I could respect him.

MARQUIS.

Oh, let not the most just of kings at once
Be the most unjust! In your realm of Flanders
There are a thousand better men than I.
But you — sire! may I dare to say so much —
For the first time, perhaps, see liberty
In milder form portrayed.

KING (*with gentle severity*).

No more of this,
Young man! You would, I know, think otherwise
Had you but learned to understand mankind
As I. But truly — I would not this meeting
Should prove our last. How can I hope to win you?

MARQUIS.

Pray leave me as I am. What value, sire,
Should I be to you were you to corrupt me?

KING.

This pride I will not bear. From this day forth
I hold you in my service. No remonstrance —
For I will have it so. [*After a pause.*
But how is this?
What would I now? Was it not truth I wished?
But here is something more. Marquis, so far
You've learned to know me as a king; but yet
You know me not as man —
[*The* MARQUIS *seems to meditate.*

I understand you —
Were I the most unfortunate of fathers,
Yet as a husband may I not be blest?

MARQUIS.

If the possession of a hopeful son,
And a most lovely spouse, confer a claim
On mortal to assume that title, sire,
In both respects, you are supremely blest.

KING (*with a serious look*).

That am I not — and never, till this hour,
Have I so deeply felt that I am not so.
      [*Contemplating the* MARQUIS *with a look of
        melancholy.*

MARQUIS.

The prince possesses a right noble mind.
I ne'er have known him otherwise.

KING.

                I have!
The treasure he has robbed me of, no crown
Can e'er requite. So virtuous a queen!

MARQUIS.

Who dare assert it, sire?

KING.

           The world! and scandal!
And I myself! Here lie the damning proofs
Of doubtless guilt — and others, too, exist,
From which I fear the worst. But still 'tis hard
To trust one proof alone. Who brings the charge?
And oh! if this were possible — that she,
The queen, so foully could pollute her honor,
Then how much easier were it to believe
An Eboli may be a slanderer!
Does not that priest detest my son and her?
And can I doubt that Alva broods revenge?
My wife has higher worth than all together.

MARQUIS.

And there exists besides in woman's soul
A treasure, sire, beyond all outward show,
Above the reach of slander — female virtue!

KING.

Marquis! those thoughts are mine. It costs too much
To sink so low as they accuse the queen.
The sacred ties of honor are not broken
With so much ease, as some would fain persuade me.
Marquis, you know mankind. Just such a man
As you I long have wished for — you are kind —
Cheerful — and deeply versed in human nature —
Therefore I've chosen you ——

MARQUIS (*surprised and alarmed*).

Me, sire!

KING.

You stand
Before your king and ask no special favor —
For yourself nothing! — that is new to me —
You will be just — ne'er weakly swayed by passion.
Watch my son close — search the queen's inmost heart.
You shall have power to speak with her in private.
Retire.   [*He rings a bell.*

MARQUIS.

And if with but one hope fulfilled
I now depart, then is this day indeed
The happiest of my life.

KING (*holds out his hand to him to kiss*).

I hold it not
Amongst my days a lost one.
      [*The* MARQUIS *rises and goes.* COUNT LERMA
         enters.

Count, in future,
The marquis is to enter, unannounced.

ACT IV.

Scene I.

The Queen's Apartment.

Queen, Duchess Olivarez, Princess Eboli, Countess
Fuentes.

QUEEN (*to the first lady as she rises*).

And so the key has not been found! My casket
Must be forced open then — and that at once.
   [*She observes* Princess Eboli, *who approaches and
    kisses her hand.*
Welcome, dear princess! I rejoice to see you
So near recovered. But you still look pale.

FUENTES (*with malice*).

The fault of that vile fever which affects
The nerves so painfully. Is't not, princess?

QUEEN.

I wished to visit you, dear Eboli,
But dared not.

OLIVAREZ.

        Oh! the Princess Eboli
Was not in want of company.

QUEEN.

            Why, that
I readily believe, but what's the matter?
You tremble ——

PRINCESS.

        Nothing — nothing, gracious queen.
Permit me to retire.

QUEEN.

        You hide it from us —
And are far worse than you would have us think.
Standing must weary you. Assist her, countess,
And let her rest awhile upon that seat.

PRINCESS (*going*).

I shall be better in the open air.

QUEEN.

Attend her, countess.   What a sudden illness!
   [*A* PAGE *enters and speaks to the* DUCHESS, *who then
      addresses the* QUEEN.

OLIVAREZ.

The Marquis Posa waits, your majesty,
With orders from the king.

QUEEN.

         Admit him then.
    [PAGE *admits the* MARQUIS *and exit.*

SCENE II.

MARQUIS POSA.   *The former.*

The MARQUIS *falls on one knee before the* QUEEN, *who
signs to him to rise.*

QUEEN.

What are my lord's commands?   And may I dare
Thus publicly to hear ——

MARQUIS.

        My business is
In private with your royal majesty.
    [*The ladies retire on a signal from the* QUEEN.

SCENE III.

The QUEEN, MARQUIS POSA.

QUEEN (*full of astonishment*).

How!   Marquis, dare I trust my eyes?   Are you
Commissioned to me from the king?

MARQUIS.

               Does this
Seem such a wonder to your majesty?
To me 'tis otherwise.

QUEEN.

The world must sure
Have wandered from its course! That you and he —
I must confess ——

MARQUIS.

It does sound somewhat strange —
But be it so. The present times abound
In prodigies.

QUEEN.

But none can equal this.

MARQUIS.

Suppose I had at last allowed myself
To be converted, and had weary grown
Of playing the eccentric at the court
Of Philip. The eccentric! What is that?
He who would be of service to mankind
Must first endeavor to resemble them.
What end is gained by the vain-glorious garb
Of the sectarian? Then suppose — for who
From vanity is so completely free
As for his creed to seek no proselytes?
Suppose, I say, I had it in my mind
To place my own opinions on the throne!

QUEEN.

No, marquis! no! Not even in jest could I
Suspect you of so wild a scheme as this;
No visionary you! to undertake
What you can ne'er accomplish.

MARQUIS.

But that seems
To be the very point at issue.

QUEEN.

What
I chiefly blame you, marquis, for, and what
Could well estrange me from you — is ——

MARQUIS.

Perhaps
Duplicity!

QUEEN.

At least — a want of candor.
Perhaps the king himself has no desire
You should impart what now you mean to tell me.

MARQUIS.

No.

QUEEN.

And can evil means be justified
By honest ends? And — pardon me the doubt —
Can your high bearing stoop to such an office ?
I scarce can think it.

MARQUIS.

Nor, indeed, could I,
Were my sole purpose to deceive the king.
'Tis not my wish — I mean to serve him now
More honestly than he himself commands.

QUEEN.

'Tis spoken like yourself. Enough of this —
What would the king ?

MARQUIS.   .

The king? I can, it seems,
Retaliate quickly on my rigid judge :
And what I have deferred so long to tell,
Your majesty, perhaps, would willingly
Longer defer to hear. But still it must
Be heard. The king requests your majesty
Will grant no audience to the ambassador
Of France to-day. Such were my high commands —
They're executed.

QUEEN.

Marquis, is that all
You have to tell me from him ?

MARQUIS.

Nearly all
That justifies me thus to seek your presence.

QUEEN.

Well, marquis, I'm contented not to hear
What should, perhaps, remain a secret from me.

MARQUIS.

True, queen! though were you other than yourself,
I should inform you straight of certain things —
Warn you of certain men — but this to you
Were a vain office. Danger may arise
And disappear around you, unperceived.
You will not know it — of too little weight
To chase the slumber from your angel brow.
But 'twas not this, in sooth, that brought me hither,
Prince Carlos ——

QUEEN.

What of him? How have you left him?

MARQUIS.

E'en as the only wise man of his time,
In whom it is a crime to worship truth —
And ready, for his love to risk his life,
As the wise sage for his. I bring few words —
But here he is himself.

[Giving the QUEEN *a letter.*

QUEEN (*after she has read it*).

He says he must

Speak with me ——

MARQUIS.

So do I.

QUEEN.

And will he thus
Be happy — when he sees with his own eyes,
That I am wretched?

MARQUIS.

No; but more resolved,

More active.

QUEEN.

How?

MARQUIS.

Duke Alva is appointed

To Flanders.

QUEEN.

Yes, appointed — so I hear.

MARQUIS.

The king cannot retract : — we know the king.
This much is clear, the prince must not remain
Here in Madrid, nor Flanders be abandoned.

QUEEN.

And can you hinder it ?

MARQUIS.

Perhaps I can,
But then the means are dangerous as the evil —
Rash as despair — and yet I know no other.

QUEEN.

Name them.

MARQUIS.

To you, and you alone, my queen,
Will I reveal them ; for from you alone,
Carlos will hear them named without a shudder.
The name they bear is somewhat harsh.

QUEEN.

Rebellion !

MARQUIS.

He must prove faithless to the king, and fly
With secrecy to Brussels, where the Flemings
Wait him with open arms.   The Netherlands
Will rise at his command.   Our glorious cause
From the king's son will gather matchless strength,
The Spanish throne shall tremble at his arms,
And what his sire denied him in Madrid,
That will he willingly concede in Brussels.

QUEEN.

You've spoken with the king to-day — and yet
Maintain all this.

MARQUIS.

Yes, I maintain it all,
Because I spoke with him.

QUEEN (*after a pause*).
                    The daring plan
Alarms and pleases me.   You may be right—
The thought is bold, and that perhaps enchants me.
Let it but ripen.   Does Prince Carlos know it?

MARQUIS.
It was my wish that he should hear it first
From your own lips.

QUEEN.
                    The plan is doubtless good,
But then the prince's youth ——

MARQUIS.
                    No disadvantage!
He there will find the bravest generals
Of the Emperor Charles — an Egmont and an Orange —
In battle daring, and in council wise.

QUEEN (*with vivacity*).
True — the design is grand and beautiful!
The prince must act; I feel it sensibly.
The part he's doomed to play here in Madrid
Has bowed me to the dust on his account.
I promise him the aid of France and Savoy;
I think with you, lord marquis — he must act —
But this design needs money ——

MARQUIS.
                    It is ready.

QUEEN.
I, too, know means.

MARQUIS.
                    May I then give him hopes
Of seeing you?

QUEEN.
                I will consider it.

MARQUIS.
The prince, my queen, is urgent for an answer.
I promised to procure it.
            [*Presenting his writing tablet to the* QUEEN.
                    Two short lines
Will be enough.

QUEEN (*after she has written*).
      When do we meet again?

MARQUIS.
Whene'er you wish.

QUEEN.
      Whene'er I wish it, marquis!
How can I understand this privilege?

MARQUIS.
As innocently, queen, as e'er you may.
But we enjoy it — that is sure enough.

QUEEN (*interrupting*).
How will my heart rejoice should this become
A refuge for the liberties of Europe,
And this through him!   Count on my silent aid!

MARQUIS (*with animation*).
Right well I knew your heart would understand me.
              [*The* DUCHESS OLIVAREZ *enters*

QUEEN (*coldly to the* MARQUIS).
My lord! the king's commands I shall respect
As law.   Assure him of the queen's submission.
              [*She makes a sign to him.   Exit* MARQUIS

SCENE IV.

A Gallery.

DON CARLOS, COUNT LERMA.

CARLOS.
Here we are undisturbed.   What would you now
Impart to me?

LERMA.
      Your highness has a friend
Here at the court.

CARLOS (*starting*).
      A friend!   I knew it not!
But what's your meaning?

LERMA.

I must sue for pardon
That I am learned in more than I should know.
But for your highness' comfort I've received it
From one I may depend upon — in short,
I have it from myself.

CARLOS.

Whom speak you of?

LERMA.

The Marquis Posa.

CARLOS.

What!

LERMA.

And if your highness
Has trusted to him more of what concerns you
Than every one should know, as I am led
To fear ——

CARLOS.

You fear!

LERMA.

He has been with the king.

CARLOS.

Indeed!

LERMA.

Two hours in secret converse too.

CARLOS.

Indeed!

LERMA.

The subject was no trifling matter.

CARLOS.

That I can well believe.

LERMA.

And several times
I heard your name.

CARLOS.

That's no bad sign, I hope.

LERMA.

And then, this morning, in the king's apartment,
The queen was spoken of mysteriously.

CARLOS (*starts back astonished*).
Count Lerma!

LERMA.

When the marquis had retired
I was commanded to admit his lordship
In future unannounced.

CARLOS.

Astonishing!

LERMA.

And without precedent do I believe,
Long as I served the king ——

CARLOS.

'Tis strange, indeed!
How did you say the queen was spoken of?

LERMA (*steps back*).
No, no, my prince! that were against my duty.

CARLOS.

'Tis somewhat strange!   One secret you impart.
The other you withhold.

LERMA.

The first was due
To you, the other to the king.

CARLOS.

You're right.

LERMA.

And still I've thought you, prince, a man of honor.

CARLOS.

Then you have judged me truly.

LERMA.

But all virtue
Is spotless till it's tried.

CARLOS.
Some stand the trial.

LERMA.

A powerful monarch's favor is a prize
Worth seeking for; and this alluring bait
Has ruined many a virtue.

CARLOS.
Truly said!

LERMA.

And oftentimes 'tis prudent to discover
What scarce can longer be concealed.

CARLOS.

Yes, prudent
It may be, but you say you've ever known
The marquis prove himself a man of honor.

LERMA.

And if he be so still my fears are harmless,
And you become a double gainer, prince.   [*Going.*

CARLOS (*follows him with emotion, and presses his hand*).

Trebly I gain, upright and worthy man,
I gain another friend, nor lose the one
Whom I before possessed.   [*Exit* LERMA.

SCENE V.

MARQUIS POSA *comes through the gallery.* CARLOS.

MARQUIS.

Carlos! My Carlos!

CARLOS.

Who calls me? Ah! 'tis thou — I was in haste
To gain the convent! You will not delay.   [*Going.*

MARQUIS.

Hold! for a moment.

CARLOS.

We may be observed.

MARQUIS.

No chance of that. 'Tis over now.   The queen ——

CARLOS.

You've seen my father.

MARQUIS.

Yes! he sent for me.

CARLOS (*full of expectation*).

Well!

MARQUIS.

'Tis all settled — you may see the queen.

CARLOS.

Yes! but the king!   What said the king to you?

MARQUIS.

Not much.   Mere curiosity to learn
My history.   The zeal of unknown friends —
I know not what.   He offered me employment.

CARLOS.

Which you, of course, rejected?

MARQUIS.

Yes, of course!

CARLOS.

How did you separate?

MARQUIS.

Oh, well enough!

CARLOS.

And was I mentioned?

MARQUIS.

Yes ; in general terms.
[*Taking out a pocketbook and giving it to the* PRINCE
See here are two lines written by the queen,
To-morrow I will settle where and how.

CARLOS (*reads it carelessly, puts the tablet in his pocket
and is going.*)

You'll meet me at the prior's ?

MARQUIS.

Yes! But stay ——
Why in such haste? No one is coming hither.

CARLOS (*with a forced smile*).

Have we in truth changed characters? To-day
You seem so bold and confident.

MARQUIS.

To-day, —

Wherefore to-day?

CARLOS.

What writes the queen to me?

MARQUIS.

Have you not read this instant?

CARLOS.

I? Oh yes.

MARQUIS.

What is't disturbs you now?

CARLOS (*reads the tablet again, delighted and fervently*).

Angel of Heaven!
I will be so, — I will be worthy of thee.
Love elevates great minds. So come what may,
Whatever thou commandest, I'll perform.
She writes that I must hold myself prepared
For a great enterprise! What can she mean?
Dost thou not know?

MARQUIS.

And, Carlos, if I knew,
Say, art thou now prepared to hear it from me?

CARLOS.

Have I offended thee? I was distracted.
Roderigo, pardon me.

MARQUIS.

Distracted! How?

CARLOS.

I scarcely know! But may I keep this tablet?

MARQUIS.

Not so! I came to ask thee for thine own.

CARLOS.

My tablet! Why?

MARQUIS.

And whatsoever writings
You have, unfit to meet a stranger's eye —
Letters or memorandums, and in short,
Your whole portfolio.

CARLOS.

Why?

MARQUIS.

That we may be
Prepared for accidents. Who can prevent
Surprise? They'll never seek them in my keeping.
Here, give them to me ——

CARLOS (*uneasy*).

Strange! What can it mean?

MARQUIS.

Be not alarmed! 'Tis nothing of importance!
A mere precaution to prevent surprise.
You need not be alarmed!

CARLOS (*gives him the portfolio*).

Be careful of it.

MARQUIS.

Be sure I will.

CARLOS (*looks at him significantly*).

I give thee much, Roderigo!

MARQUIS.

Not more than I have often had from thee.
The rest we'll talk of yonder. Now farewell. [*Going.*

CARLOS (*struggling with himself, then calls him back*).

Give me my letters back; there's one amongst them
The queen addressed to me at Alcala,
When I was sick to death. Still next my heart

I carry it; to take this letter from me
Goes to my very soul.   But leave me that,
And take the rest.
> [*He takes it out, and returns the portfolio.*

MARQUIS.

> I yield unwillingly ——
For 'twas that letter which I most required.

CARLOS.

Farewell !
> [*He goes away slowly, stops a moment at the door, turns*
> *back again, and brings him the letter.*
> You have it there.
> [*His hand trembles, tears start from his eyes, he falls*
> *on the neck of the* MARQUIS, *and presses his face to*
> *his bosom.*

> Oh, not my father,
Could do so much, Roderigo !   Not my father !
> [*Exit hastily.*

SCENE VI.

MARQUIS (*looks after him with astonishment*).

And is this possible !   And to this hour
Have I not known him fully ?   In his heart
This blemish has escaped my eye.   Distrust
Of me — his friend !   But no, 'tis calumny !
What hath he done that I accuse him thus
Of weakest weakness.   I myself commit
The fault I charge on him.   What have I done
Might well surprise him !   When hath he displayed
To his best friend such absolute reserve ?
Carlos, I must afflict thee — there's no help —
And longer still distress thy noble soul.
In me the king hath placed his confidence,
His holiest trust reposed — as in a casket,
And this reliance calls for gratitude.
How can disclosure serve thee when my silence
Brings thee no harm — serves thee, perhaps ?   Ah ! why
Point to the traveller the impending storm ?

Enough, if I direct its anger past thee!
And when thou wakest the sky's again serene.   [*Exit.*

SCENE VII.

The KING'S *Cabinet.*

The KING *seated, near him the* INFANTA CLARA EUGENIA.

KING (*after a deep silence*).

No — she is sure my daughter — or can nature
Thus lie like truth! Yes, that blue eye is mine!
And I am pictured in thy every feature.
Child of my love! for such thou art — I fold thee
Thus to my heart; thou art my blood. [*Starts and pauses.*
                                My blood —
What's worse to fear? Are not my features his?
    [*Takes the miniature in his hand and looks first at
        the portrait, then at the mirror opposite; at last he
        throws it on the ground, rises hastily, and pushes
        the* INFANTA *from him.*
Away, away! I'm lost in this abyss.

SCENE VIII.

COUNT LERMA *and the* KING.

LERMA.

Her majesty is in the antechamber.

KING.

What! Now?

LERMA.

                And begs the favor of an audience.

KING.

Now! At this unaccustomed hour! Not now —
I cannot see her yet.

LERMA.

                Here comes the queen.
                        [*Exit* LERMA.

Scene IX.

The KING, *the* QUEEN *enters, and the* INFANTA.

The INFANTA *runs to meet the* QUEEN *and clings to her; the* QUEEN *falls at the* KING's *feet, who is silent, and appears confused and embarrassed.*

QUEEN.

My lord! My husband! I'm constrained to seek
Justice before the throne!

KING.
What? Justice!

QUEEN.
Yes!
I'm treated with dishonor at the court!
My casket has been rifled.

KING.
What! Your casket?

QUEEN.
And things I highly value have been plundered.

KING.
Things that you highly value.

QUEEN.
From the meaning
Which ignorant men's officiousness, perhaps,
Might give to them ——

KING.
What's this? Officiousness,
And meaning! How? But rise.

QUEEN.
Oh no, my husband!
Not till you bind yourself by sacred promise,
By virtue of your own authority,
To find the offender out, and grant redress,
Or else dismiss my suite, which hides a thief.

KING.
But rise! In such a posture! Pray you, rise.

QUEEN (*rises*).

'Tis some one of distinction — I know well ;
My casket held both diamonds and pearls
Of matchless value, but he only took
My letters.

KING.

May I ask ——

QUEEN.

Undoubtedly,
My husband.   They were letters from the prince :
His miniature as well.

KING.

From whom ?

QUEEN.

The prince,

Your son.

KING.

To you ?

QUEEN.

Sent by the prince to me.

KING.

What !   From Prince Carlos !   Do you tell me that ?

QUEEN.

Why not tell you, my husband ?

KING.

And not blush.

QUEEN.

What mean you ?   You must surely recollect
The letters Carlos sent me to St. Germains,
With both courts' full consent.   Whether that leave
Extended to the portrait, or alone
His hasty hope dictated such a step,
I cannot now pretend to answer ; but
If even rash, it may at least be pardoned
For thus much I may be his pledge — that then
He never thought the gift was for his mother.
                    [*Observes the agitation of the* KING
What moves you ?   What's the matter ?

INFANTA (*who has found the miniature on the ground, and has been playing with it, brings it to the* QUEEN.

Look, dear mother!
See what a pretty picture!

QUEEN.

What then my ——
[*She recognizes the miniature, and remains in speechless astonishment. They both gaze at each other. After a long pause.*
In truth, this mode of trying a wife's heart
Is great and royal, sire! But I should wish
To ask one question?

KING.

'Tis for me to question.

QUEEN.

Let my suspicions spare the innocent.
And if by your command this theft was done ——

KING.

It was so done!

QUEEN.

Then I have none to blame,
And none to pity — other than yourself —
Since you possess a wife on whom such schemes
Are thrown away.

KING.

This language is not new —
Nor shall you, madam, now again deceive me
As in the gardens of Aranjuez —
My queen of angel purity, who then
So haughtily my accusation spurned —
I know her better now.

QUEEN.

What mean you, sire?

KING.

Madam! thus briefly and without reserve —
Say is it true? still true, that you conversed
With no one there? Is really that the truth?

QUEEN.

I spoke there with the prince.

KING.

              Then it is clear
As day! So daring! heedless of mine honor!

QUEEN.

Your honor, sire! If that be now the question,
A greater honor is, methinks, at stake
Than Castile ever brought me as a dowry.

KING.

Why did you then deny the prince's presence?

QUEEN.

Because I'm not accustomed to be questioned
Like a delinquent before all your courtiers;
I never shall deny the truth when asked
With kindness and respect. Was that the tone
Your majesty used towards me in Aranjuez?
Are your assembled grandees the tribunal
Queens must account to for their private conduct?
I gave the prince the interview he sought
With earnest prayer, because, my liege and lord,
I — the queen — wished and willed it, and because
I never can admit that formal custom
Should sit as judge on actions that are guiltless;
And I concealed it from your majesty
Because I chose not to contend with you
About this right in presence of your courtiers.

KING.

You speak with boldness, madam!

QUEEN.

              I may add,
Because the prince, in his own father's heart,
Scarce finds that kindness he so well deserves.

KING.

So well deserves!

QUEEN.

Why, sire! should I conceal it!
Highly do I esteem him — yes! and love him
As a most dear relation, who was once
Deemed worthy of a dearer — tenderer — title.
I've yet to learn that he, on this account,
Should be estranged from me beyond all others, —
Because he once was better loved than they.
Though your state policy may knit together
What bands it pleases — 'tis a harder task
To burst such ties! I will not hate another
For any one's command — and since I must
So speak — such dictates I will not endure.

KING.

Elizabeth! you've seen me in weak moments —
And their remembrance now emboldens you.
On that strong influence you now depend,
Which you have often, with so much success,
Against my firmness tried. But fear the more!
The power which has seduced me to be weak
May yet inflame me to some act of madness.

QUEEN.

What have I done?

KING (*takes her hand*).

If it should prove but so —
And is it not already? If the full
Accumulated measure of your guilt
Become but one breath heavier — should I be
Deceived —— [*Lets her hand go.*
I can subdue these last remains
Of weakness — can and will — then woe betide
Myself and you, Elizabeth!

QUEEN.

What crime
Have I committed?

KING.

On my own account then
Shall blood be shed.

QUEEN.

And has it come to this?

Oh, Heaven!

KING.

I shall forget myself — I shall
Regard no usage and no voice of nature —
Not e'en the law of nations.

QUEEN.

Oh, how much

I pity you!

KING.

The pity of a harlot!

INFANTA (*clinging to her mother in terror*).
The king is angry, and my mother weeps.
    [KING *pushes the child violently from the* QUEEN.

QUEEN (*with mildness and dignity, but with faltering
voice*).
This child I must protect from cruelty —
Come with me, daughter.   [*Takes her in her arms.*
              If the king no more
Acknowledge thee — beyond the Pyrenees
I'll call protectors to defend our cause.   [*Going.*

KING (*embarrassed*).

Queen!

QUEEN.

I can bear no more — it is too much!
    [*Hastening to the door, she falls with her child on
the threshold.*

KING (*running to her assistance*).
Heavens! What is that?

INFANTA (*cries out with terror*).

She bleeds! My mother bleeds!
                   [*Runs out.*

KING (*anxiously assisting her*).
Oh, what a fearful accident! You bleed;
Do I deserve this cruel punishment?
Rise and collect yourself — rise, they are coming!

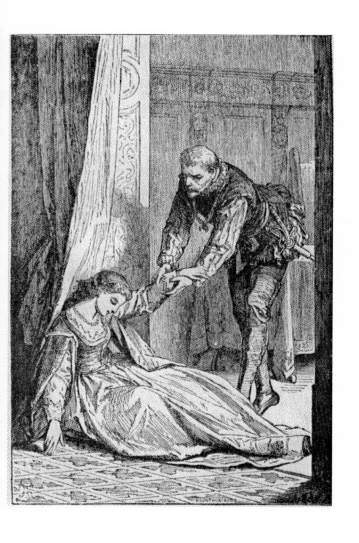

They will surprise us! Shall the assembled court
Divert themselves with such a spectacle?
Must I entreat you? Rise.

> [*She rises, supported by the* KING.

SCENE X.

The former, ALVA, DOMINGO *entering, alarmed, ladies
follow.*

KING.

Now let the queen
Be led to her apartment; she's unwell.

> [*Exit the* QUEEN, *attended by her ladies.* ALVA *and*
> DOMINGO *come forward.*

ALVA.

The queen in tears, and blood upon her face!

KING.

Does that surprise the devils who've misled me?

ALVA *and* DOMINGO.

We?

KING.

You have said enough to drive me mad.
But nothing to convince me.

ALVA.

We gave you
What we ourselves possessed.

KING.

May hell reward you!
I've done what I repent of! Ah! was hers
The language of a conscience dark with guilt?

MARQUIS POSA (*from without*).

Say, can I see the king?

SCENE XI.

The former, MARQUIS POSA.

KING (*starts up at the sound of his voice, and advances
some paces to meet him*).

Ah! here he comes.

Right welcome, marquis! Duke! I need you now
No longer. Leave us.

> [ALVA *and* DOMINGO *look at each other with silent
> astonishment and retire.*

SCENE XII.

The KING, *and* MARQUIS POSA.

MARQUIS.

    That old soldier, sire,
Who has faced death, in twenty battles, for you,
Must hold it thankless to be so dismissed.

KING.

'Tis thus for you to think — for me to act;
In a few hours you have been more to me
Than that man in a lifetime. Nor shall I
Keep my content a secret. On your brow
The lustre of my high and royal favor
Shall shine resplendent — I will make that man
A mark for envy whom I choose my friend.

MARQUIS.

What if the veil of dark obscurity
Were his sole claim to merit such a title?

KING.

What come you now to tell me?

MARQUIS.

      As I passed
Along the antechamber a dread rumor
Fell on my ear, — it seemed incredible, —
Of a most angry quarrel — blood — the queen ——

KING.

Come you from her?

MARQUIS.

     I should be horrified
Were not the rumor false: or should perhaps
Your majesty meantime have done some act —
Discoveries of importance I have made,
Which wholly change the aspect of affairs.

KING.

How now?

MARQUIS.

I found an opportunity
To seize your son's portfolio, with his letters,
Which, as I hope, may throw some light——

[*He gives the* PRINCE's *portfolio to the* KING.

KING (*looks through it eagerly*).

A letter
From the emperor, my father. How! a letter
Of which I ne'er remember to have heard.

[*He reads it through, puts it aside, and goes to the
other papers.*

A drawing of some fortress — detached thoughts
From Tacitus — and what is here? The hand
I surely recognize — it is a lady's.

[*He reads it attentively, partly to himself, and partly
aloud.*

"This key — the farthest chamber of the queen's
Pavilion!" Ha! what's this? "The voice of love, —
The timid lover — may — a rich reward."
Satanic treachery! I see it now.
'Tis she — 'tis her own writing!

MARQUIS.

The queen's writing!

Impossible?

KING.

The Princess Eboli's.

MARQUIS.

Then, it was true, what the queen's page confessed,
Not long since — that he brought this key and letter.

KING (*grasping the* MARQUIS' *hand in great emotion*).

Marquis! I see that I'm in dreadful hands.
This woman — I confess it — 'twas this woman
Forced the queen's casket : and my first suspicions
Were breathed by her. Who knows how deep the priest
May be engaged in this? I am deceived
By cursed villany.

MARQUIS.

Then it was lucky ——

KING.

Marquis! O marquis! I begin to fear
I've wronged my wife.

MARQUIS.

If there exist between
The prince and queen some secret understandings,
They are of other import, rest assured,
Than those they charge her with. I know, for certain
The prince's prayer to be despatched to Flanders
Was by the queen suggested.

KING.

I have thought so.

MARQUIS.

The queen's ambitious. Dare I speak more fully?
She sees, with some resentment, her high hopes
All disappointed, and herself shut out
From share of empire. Your son's youthful ardor
Offers itself to her far-reaching views,
Her heart! I doubt if she can love.

KING.

Her schemes
Of policy can never make me tremble.

MARQUIS.

Whether the Infant loves her — whether we
Have something worse to fear from him,— are things
Worthy our deep attention. To these points
Our strictest vigilance must be directed.

KING.

You must be pledge for him.

MARQUIS.

And if the king
Esteem me capable of such a task,
I must entreat it be intrusted to me
Wholly without conditions.

KING.

So it shall.

MARQUIS.

That in the steps which I may think required,
I may be thwarted by no coadjutors,
Whatever name they bear.

KING.

I pledge my word
You shall not. You have proved my guardian angel.
How many thanks I owe you for this service!
                    [LERMA *enters — the* KING *to him.*
How did you leave the queen?

LERMA.

But scarce recovered
From her deep swoon.
                    [*He looks at the* MARQUIS *doubtfully, and exit.*

MARQUIS (*to the* KING, *after a pause*).

One caution yet seems needful.
The prince may be advised of our design,
For he has many faithful friends in Ghent,
And may have partisans among the rebels.
Fear may incite to desperate resolves;
Therefore I counsel that some speedy means
Be taken to prevent this fatal chance.

KING.

You are quite right — but how?

MARQUIS.

Your majesty
May sign a secret warrant of arrest
And place it in my hands, to be employed,
As may seem needful, in the hour of danger.
                    [*The* KING *appears thoughtful.*
This step must be a most profound state secret
Until ——

KING (*going to his desk and writing the warrant of arrest*).

The kingdom is at stake, and now
The pressing danger sanctions urgent measures.
Here marquis! I need scarcely say — use prudence.

MARQUIS (*taking the warrant*).
'Tis only for the last extremity.

KING (*laying his hand on the shoulder of the* MARQUIS).
Go! Go, dear marquis! Give this bosom peace,
And bring back slumber to my sleepless pillow.
                    [*Exeunt at different sides.*

SCENE XIII.

A Gallery.

CARLOS *entering in extreme agitation,* COUNT LERMA
                    meeting him.

CARLOS.
I have been seeking you.
                    LERMA.

                    And I your highness.

CARLOS.
For heaven's sake is it true?

                    LERMA.
                    What do you mean?
                    CARLOS.

That the king drew his dagger, and that she
Was borne, all bathed in blood, from the apartment?
Now answer me, by all that's sacred; say,
What am I to believe? What truth is in it?

                    LERMA.
She fainted, and so grazed her skin in falling:
That is the whole.
                    CARLOS.

                    Is there no further danger?
Count, answer on your honor.

                    LERMA.
                    For the queen
No further danger; for yourself there's much!

CARLOS.

None for my mother.   Then, kind Heaven, I thank thee.
A dreadful rumor reached me that the king
Raved against child and mother, and that some
Dire secret was discovered.

LERMA.

And the last

May possibly be true.

CARLOS.

Be true !   What mean you ?

LERMA.

One warning have I given you, prince, already,
And that to-day, but you despised it ; now
Perhaps you'll profit better by a second.

CARLOS.

Explain yourself.

LERMA.

If I mistake not, prince,
A few days since I noticed in your hands
An azure-blue portfolio, worked in velvet
And chased with gold.

CARLOS (*with anxiety*).

Yes, I had such a one.

LERMA.

And on the cover, if I recollect,
A portrait set in pearls ?

CARLOS.

'Tis right; go on.

LERMA.

I entered the king's chamber on a sudden,
And in his hands I marked that same portfolio,
The Marquis Posa standing by his side.

CARLOS (*after a short silence of astonishment, hastily*).
'Tis false !

LERMA (*warmly*).
Then I'm a traitor !

CARLOS (*looking steadfastly at him*).

         That you are!

LERMA.

Well, I forgive you.

CARLOS (*paces the apartment in extreme agitation, at
   length stands still before him*).

        Has he injured thee?
What have our guiltless ties of friendship done,
That with a demon's zeal thou triest to rend them?

LERMA.

Prince, I respect the grief which renders you
So far unjust.

CARLOS.

     Heaven shield me from suspicion!

LERMA.

And I remember, too, the king's own words.
Just as I entered he addressed the marquis:
"How many thanks I owe you for this news."

CARLOS.

Oh, say no more!

LERMA.

     Duke Alva is disgraced!
The great seal taken from the Prince Ruy Gomez,
And given to the marquis.

CARLOS (*lost in deep thought*).

         And from me
Has he concealed all this?   And why from me?

LERMA.

As minister all-powerful, the court
Looks on him now — as favorite unrivalled!

CARLOS.

He loved me — loved me greatly: I was dear
As his own soul is to him.   That I know —
Of that I've had a thousand proofs.   But should
The happiness of millions yield to one?
Must not his country dearer to him prove

Than Carlos ?   One friend only is too few
For his capacious heart.   And not enough
Is Carlos' happiness to engross his love.
He offers me a sacrifice to virtue ;
And shall I murmur at him ?   Now 'tis certain
I have forever lost him.

> [*He steps aside and covers his face.*

LERMA.

Dearest prince !
How can I serve you ?

CARLOS (*without looking at him*).

Get you to the king ;
Go and betray me.   I have naught to give.

LERMA.

Will you then stay and brave the ill that follows ?

CARLOS (*leans on a balustrade and looks forward with a vacant gaze*).

I've lost him now, and I am destitute !

LERMA (*approaching him with sympathizing emotion*).
And will you not consult your safety, prince ?

CARLOS.

My safety !   Generous man !

LERMA.

And is there, then,
No other person you should tremble for ?

CARLOS (*starts up*).

Heavens ! you remind me now.   Alas !   My mother !
The letter that I gave him — first refused —
Then after gave him !

> [*He paces backwards and forwards with agitation, wringing his hands.*

Has she then deserved
This blow from him ?   He should have spared her, Lerma.

> [*In a hasty, determined tone.*

But I must see her — warn her of her danger —
I must prepare her, Lerma, dearest Lerma !

Whom shall I send ?   Have I no friend remaining ?
Yes ! Heaven be praised !   I still have one ; and now
The worst is over.   [*Exit quickly*

LERMA (*follows, and calls after him*).
                   Whither, whither, prince ?

SCENE IV.

The QUEEN, ALVA, DOMINGO.

ALVA.

If we may be permitted, gracious queen ——

QUEEN.

What are your wishes?

DOMINGO.

                                        A most true regard
For your high majesty forbids us now
To watch in careless silence an event
Pregnant with danger to your royal safety.

ALVA.

We hasten, by a kind and timely warning,
To counteract a plot that's laid against you.

DOMINGO.

And our warm zeal, and our best services,
To lay before your feet, most gracious queen !

QUEEN (*looking at them with astonishment*).

Most reverend sir, and you, my noble duke,
You much surprise me.   Such sincere attachment,
In truth, I had not hoped for from Domingo,
Nor from Duke Alva.   Much I value it.
A plot you mention, menacing my safety —
Dare I inquire by whom ——

ALVA.

                                        We must entreat
You will beware a certain Marquis Posa.
He has of late been secretly employed
In the king's service.

QUEEN.

With delight I hear
The king has made so excellent a choice.
Report, long since, has spoken of the marquis
As a deserving, great, and virtuous man —
The royal grace was ne'er so well bestowed!

DOMINGO.

So well bestowed! We think far otherwise.

ALVA.

It is no secret now, for what designs
This man has been employed.

QUEEN.

How! What designs?
You put my expectation on the rack.

DOMINGO.

How long is it since last your majesty
Opened your casket?

QUEEN.

Why do you inquire?

DOMINGO.

Did you not miss some articles of value?

QUEEN.

Why these suspicions? What I missed was then
Known to the court! But what of Marquis Posa?
Say, what connection has all this with him?

ALVA.

The closest, please your majesty — the prince
Has lost some papers of importance;
And they were seen this morning with the king
After the marquis had an audience of him.

QUEEN (*after some consideration*).

This news is strange indeed — inexplicable —
To find a foe where I could ne'er have dreamed it,
And two warm friends I knew not I possessed!
[*Fixing her eyes steadfastly upon them.*

And, to speak truth, I had well nigh imputed
To you the wicked turn my husband served me.

ALVA.

To us!

QUEEN.

To you yourselves!

DOMINGO.

To us! Duke Alva!

QUEEN (*her eyes still fastened on them*).

I am glad to be so timely made aware
Of my rash judgment — else had I resolved
This very day to beg his majesty
Would bring me face to face with my accusers.
But I'm contented now.   I can appeal
To the Duke Alva for his testimony.

ALVA.

For mine?   You would not sure do that!

QUEEN.

Why not?

ALVA.

'Twould counteract the services we might
Render in secret to you.

QUEEN.

How! in secret?
[*With stern dignity.*
I fain would know what secret projects, duke,
Your sovereign's spouse can have to form with you,
Or, priest! with you — her husband should not know?
Think you that I am innocent or guilty?

DOMINGO.

Strange question!

ALVA.

Should the monarch prove unjust —
And at this time ——

QUEEN.

Then I must wait for justice
Until it come — and they are happiest far
Whose consciences may calmly wait their right.
[*Bows to them and exit.* DOMINGO *and* ALVA
exeunt on the opposite side.

SCENE XV.

Chamber of PRINCESS EBOLI.

PRINCESS EBOLI. CARLOS *immediately after.*

EBOLI.

Is it then true — the strange intelligence,
That fills the court with wonder?

CARLOS (*enters*).

Do not fear
Princess! I shall be gentle as a child.

EBOLI.

Prince, this intrusion!

CARLOS.

Are you angry still?
Offended still with me ——

EBOLI.

Prince!

CARLOS (*earnestly*).

Are you angry?
I pray you answer me.

EBOLI.

What can this mean?
You seem, prince, to forget—what would you with me?

CARLOS (*seizing her hand with warmth*).
Dear maiden! Can you hate eternally?
Can injured love ne'er pardon?

EBOLI (*disengaging herself*).
Prince! of what
Would you remind me?

CARLOS.

Of your kindness, dearest!
And of my deep ingratitude. Alas,
Too well I know it! deeply have I wronged thee —
Wounded thy tender heart, and from thine eyes,
Thine angel eyes, wrung precious tears, sweet maid!
But ah! 'tis not repentance leads me hither.

EBOLI.

Prince! leave me — I ——

CARLOS.

I come to thee, because
Thou art a maid of gentle soul — because
I trust thy heart — thy kind and tender heart.
Think, dearest maiden! think, I have no friend,
No friend but thee, in all this wretched world —
Thou who wert once so kind wilt not forever
Hate me, nor will thy anger prove eternal.

EBOLI (*turning away her face*).

O cease! No more! for heaven's sake! leave me, prince.

CARLOS.

Let me remind thee of those golden hours —
Let me remind thee of thy love, sweet maid —
That love which I so basely have offended!
Oh, let me now appear to thee again
As once I was — and as thy heart portrayed me.
Yet once again, once only, place my image,
As in days past, before thy tender soul,
And to that idol make a sacrifice
Thou canst not make to me.

EBOLI.

Oh, Carlos, cease!
Too cruelly thou sportest with my feelings!

CARLOS.

Be nobler than thy sex! Forgive an insult!
Do what no woman e'er has done before thee,
And what no woman, after thee, can equal.
I ask of thee an unexampled favor.

Grant me — upon my knees I ask of thee —
Grant me two moments with the queen, my mother!
                    [*He casts himself at her feet.*

SCENE XVI.

The former. MARQUIS POSA *rushes in ; behind him two officers of the Queen's Guard.*

MARQUIS (*breathless and agitated, rushing between* CARLOS *and the* PRINCESS).
Say, what has he confessed? Believe him not!

              CARLOS (*still on his knees, with loud voice*).
By all that's holy ——

              MARQUIS (*interrupting him with vehemence*).
                    He is mad! He raves!
Oh, listen to him not!

              CARLOS (*louder and more urgent*).
                    It is a question
Of life and death; conduct me to her straight.

MARQUIS (*dragging the* PRINCESS *from him by force*).
You die, if you but listen.
              [*To one of the officers, showing an order.*
                    Count of Cordova!
In the king's name, Prince Carlos is your prisoner.
    [CARLOS *stands bewildered. The* PRINCESS *utters a
    cry of horror, and tries to escape. The officers are
    astounded. A long and deep pause ensues. The*
    MARQUIS *trembles violently, and with difficulty
    preserves his composure.*   [*To the* PRINCE.
I beg your sword — The Princess Eboli
Remains ——   [*To the officers.*
              And you, on peril of your lives,
Let no one with his highness speak — no person —
Not e'en yourselves.
    [*He whispers a few words to one officer, then turns
    to the other.*
                    I hasten, instantly,

To cast myself before our monarch's feet,
And justify this step ——   [*To the* PRINCE.
          And prince! for you —

Expect me in an hour.
    [CARLOS *permits himself to be led away without any*
      signs of consciousness, except that in passing he
      casts a languid, dying look on the MARQUIS. *The*
      PRINCESS *endeavors again to escape ; the* MAR-
      QUIS *pulls her back by the arm.*

SCENE XVII.

PRINCESS EBOLI, MARQUIS POSA.

EBOLI.

For Heaven's sake let me leave this place ——

MARQUIS (*leads her forward with dreadful earnestness*).
                      Thou wretch!
    What has he said to thee?

EBOLI.

                  Oh, leave me! Nothing.

MARQUIS (*with earnestness ; holding her back by force*).
How much has he imparted to thee?   Here
No way is left thee to escape.   To none
In this world shalt thou ever tell it.

      EBOLI (*looking at him with terror*).
                      Heavens!
What would you do?   Would you then murder me?

      MARQUIS (*drawing a dagger*).
Yes, that is my resolve.   Be speedy!

EBOLI.

                    Mercy!
What have I then committed ?

MARQUIS (*looking towards heaven, points the dagger to*
      her breast).
                Still there's time —
The poison has not issued from these lips.

Dash but the bowl to atoms, all remains
Still as before! The destinies of Spain
Against a woman's life!
> [*Remains doubtingly in this position.*

EBOLI (*having sunk down beside him, looks in his face*).
> Do not delay —
Why do you hesitate? I beg no mercy —
I have deserved to die, and I am ready.

MARQUIS (*letting his hand drop slowly — after some
reflection*).
It were as cowardly as barbarous.
No! God be praised! another way is left.
> [*He lets the dagger fall and hurries out. The*
> PRINCESS *hastens out through another door.*

SCENE XVIII.

A Chamber of the Queen.

The QUEEN *to the* COUNTESS FUENTES.

What means this noisy tumult in the palace?
Each breath to-day alarms me! Countess! see
What it portends, and hasten back with speed.
> [*Exit* COUNTESS FUENTES — *the* PRINCESS EBOLI
> *rushes in.*

SCENE XIX.

The QUEEN, PRINCESS EBOLI.

EBOLI (*breathless, pale, and wild, falls before the* QUEEN).
Help! Help! O Queen! he's seized!

QUEEN.
> Who?

EBOLI.
> He's arrested
By the king's orders given to Marquis Posa.

QUEEN.
Who is arrested? Who?

EBOLI.
> The prince!

QUEEN.

Thou ravest!

EBOLI.

This moment they are leading him away.

QUEEN.

And who arrested him?

EBOLI.

The Marquis Posa.

QUEEN.

Then heaven be praised! it was the marquis seized him!

EBOLI.

Can you speak thus, and with such tranquil mien?
Oh, heavens! you do not know — you cannot think —

QUEEN.

The cause of his arrest! some trifling error,
Doubtless arising from his headlong youth!

EBOLI.

No! no! I know far better. No, my queen!
Remorseless treachery! There's no help for him.
He dies!

QUEEN.

He dies!

EBOLI.

And I'm his murderer!

QUEEN.

What! Dies? Thou ravest! Think what thou art
saying?

EBOLI.

And wherefore — wherefore dies he? Had I known
That it would come to this!

QUEEN (*takes her affectionately by the hand*).

Oh, dearest princess,
Your senses are distracted, but collect
Your wandering spirits, and relate to me
More calmly, not in images of horror

That fright my inmost soul, whate'er you know!
Say, what has happened?

EBOLI.

Oh, display not, queen,
Such heavenly condescension! Like hot flames
This kindness sears my conscience. I'm not worthy
To view thy purity with eyes profane.
Oh, crush the wretch, who, agonized by shame,
Remorse, and self-reproach writhes at thy feet!

QUEEN.

Unhappy woman! Say, what is thy guilt?

EBOLI.

Angel of light! Sweet saint! thou little knowest
The demon who has won thy loving smiles.
Know her to-day; I was the wretched thief
Who plundered thee.

QUEEN.

What! Thou?

EBOLI.

And gave thy letters

Up to the king?

QUEEN.

What! Thou?

EBOLI.

And dared accuse thee!

QUEEN.

Thou! Couldst thou this?

EBOLI.

Revenge and madness — love —
I hated thee, and loved the prince!

QUEEN.

And did

His love so prompt thee?

EBOLI.

I had owned my love,
But met with no return.

QUEEN (*after a pause*).

Now all's explained !
Rise up ! — you loved him — I have pardoned you !
I have forgotten all.   Now, princess, rise.
                    [*Holding out her hand to the* PRINCESS.

EBOLI.

No, no; a foul confession still remains.
I will not rise, great queen, till I ——

QUEEN.

Then speak !
What have I yet to hear ?

EBOLI.

The king !   Seduction !
Oh, now you turn away.   And in your eyes
I read abhorrence.   Yes ; of that foul crime
I charged you with, I have myself been guilty.
    [*She presses her burning face to the ground.   Exit*
    QUEEN.   *A long pause.   The* COUNTESS OLIVA-
    REZ, *after some minutes, comes out of the cabinet,
    into which the* QUEEN *entered, and finds the* PRIN-
    CESS *still lying in the above posture.   She ap-
    proaches in silence.   On hearing a noise, the latter
    looks up and becomes like a mad person when she
    misses the* QUEEN.

SCENE XX.

PRINCESS EBOLI, COUNTESS OLIVAREZ.

EBOLI.

Heavens ! she has left me.   I am now undone !

OLIVAREZ (*approaching her*).

My princess — Eboli !

EBOLI.

I know your business,
Duchess, and you come hither from the queen,
To speak my sentence to me ; do it quickly.

OLIVAREZ.

I am commanded by your majesty
To take your cross and key.

EBOLI (*takes from her breast a golden cross, and gives it to the* DUCHESS).

And but once more

May I not kiss my gracious sovereign's hand

OLIVAREZ.

In holy Mary's convent shall you learn
Your fate, princess.

EBOLI (*with a flood of tears*).

Alas! then I no more

Shall ever see the queen.

OLIVAREZ (*embraces her with her face turned away*).

Princess, farewell.

[*She goes hastily away. The* PRINCESS *follows her as far as the door of the cabinet, which is immediately locked after the* DUCHESS. *She remains a few minutes silent and motionless on her knees before it. She then rises and hastens away, covering her face.*

SCENE XXI.

QUEEN, MARQUIS POSA.

QUEEN.

Ah, marquis, I am glad you're come at last!

MARQUIS (*pale, with a disturbed countenance and trembling voice, in solemn, deep agitation, during the whole scene*).

And is your majesty alone? Can none
Within the adjoining chamber overhear us?

QUEEN.

No one! But why? What news would you impart?
[*Looking at him closely, and drawing back alarmed.*
And what has wrought this change in you? Speak,
marquis,

You make me tremble — all your features seem
So marked with death!

MARQUIS.

You know, perhaps, already.

QUEEN.

That Carlos is arrested — and they add,
By you! Is it then true? From no one else
Would I believe it but yourself.

MARQUIS.

'Tis true.

QUEEN.

By you?

MARQUIS.

By me?

QUEEN (*looks at him for some time doubtingly*).

I still respect your actions
E'en when I comprehend them not. In this
Pardon a timid woman! I much fear
You play a dangerous game.

MARQUIS.

And I have lost it.

QUEEN.

Merciful heaven!

MARQUIS.

Queen, fear not! He is safe,
But I am lost myself.

QUEEN.

What do I hear?

MARQUIS.

Who bade me hazard all on one chance throw?
All? And with rash, foolhardy confidence,
Sport with the power of heaven? Of bounded mind,
Man, who is not omniscient, must not dare
To guide the helm of destiny. 'Tis just!
But why these thoughts of self. This hour is precious
As life can be to man: and who can tell

Whether the parsimonious hand of fate
May not have measured my last drops of life?

QUEEN.

The hand of fate! What means this solemn tone?
I understand these words not — but I shudder.

MARQUIS.

He's saved! no matter at what price — he's saved!
But only for to-day — a few short hours
Are his. Oh, let him husband them! This night
The prince must leave Madrid.

QUEEN.

This very night?

MARQUIS.

All measures are prepared. The post will meet him
At the Carthusian convent, which has served
So long as an asylum to our friendship.
Here will he find, in letters of exchange,
All in the world that fortune gifts me with.
Should more be wanting, you must e'en supply it.
In truth, I have within my heart full much
To unburden to my Carlos — it may chance
I shall want leisure now to tell him all
In person — but this evening you will see him,
And therefore I address myself to you.

QUEEN.

Oh, for my peace of mind, dear marquis, speak!
Explain yourself more clearly! Do not use
This dark, and fearful, and mysterious language!
Say, what has happened?

MARQUIS.

I have yet one thing,
A matter of importance on my mind:
In your hands I deposit it. My lot
Was such as few indeed have e'er enjoyed —
I loved a prince's son. My heart to one —
To that one object given — embraced the world!
I have created in my Carlos' soul,
A paradise for millions! Oh, my dream

Was lovely! But the will of Providence
Has summoned me away, before my hour,
From this my beauteous work. His Roderigo
Soon shall be his no more, and friendship's claim
Will be transferred to love. Here, therefore, here,
Upon this sacred altar — on the heart
Of his loved queen — I lay my last bequest
A precious legacy — he'll find it here,
When I shall be no more.

        [*He turns away, his voice choked with grief.*

QUEEN.

                 This is the language
Of a dying man — it surely emanates
But from your blood's excitement — or does sense
Lie hidden in your language?

MARQUIS (*has endeavored to collect himself, and continues*
              in a solemn voice).

                Tell the prince,
That he must ever bear in mind the oath
We swore, in past enthusiastic days,
Upon the sacred host. I have kept mine —
I'm true to him till death — 'tis now his turn ——

QUEEN.

Till death?

MARQUIS.

        Oh, bid him realize the dream,
The glowing vision which our friendship painted,
Of a new — perfect realm! And let him lay
The first hand on the rude, unshapened stone.
Whether he fail or prosper — all alike —
Let him commence the work. When centuries
Have rolled away shall Providence again
Raise to the throne a princely youth like him,
And animate again a favorite son
Whose breast shall burn with like enthusiasm.
Tell him, in manhood, he must still revere
The dreams of early youth, nor ope the heart
Of heaven's all-tender flower to canker-worms
Of boasted reason, — nor be led astray

When, by the wisdom of the dust, he hears
Enthusiasm, heavenly-born, blasphemed.
I have already told him.

QUEEN.

Whither, marquis ?
Whither does all this tend ?

MARQUIS.

And tell him further,
I lay upon his soul the happiness
Of man — that with my dying breath I claim,
Demand it of him — and with justest title.
I had designed a new, a glorious morn,
To waken in these kingdoms : for to me
Philip had opened all his inmost heart —
Called me his son — bestowed his seals upon me —
And Alva was no more his counsellor.
[*He pauses, and looks at the* QUEEN *for a few
moments in silence.*
You weep ! I know those tears, beloved soul !
Oh, they are tears of joy ! — but it is past —
Forever past ! Carlos or I ? The choice
Was prompt and fearful. One of us must perish !
And I will be that one. Oh, ask no more !

QUEEN.

Now, now, at last, I comprehend your meaning,
Unhappy man ! What have you done ?

MARQUIS.

Cut off
Two transient hours of evening to secure
A long, bright summer-day ! I now give up
The king forever. What were I to the king?
In such cold soil no rose of mine could bloom ;
In my great friend must Europe's fortune ripen.
Spain I bequeath to him, still bathed in blood
From Philip's iron hand. But woe to him,
Woe to us both, if I have chosen wrong !
But no — oh, no ! I know my Carlos better —

'Twill never come to pass ! — for this, my queen,
You stand my surety.   [*After a silence*
                    Yes ! I saw his love
In its first blossom — saw his fatal passion
Take root in his young heart.   I had full power
To check it ; but I did not.   The attachment
Which seemed to me not guilty, I still nourished.
The world may censure me, but I repent not,
Nor does my heart accuse me.   I saw life
Where death appeared to others.   In a flame
So hopeless I discerned hope's golden beam.
I wished to lead him to the excellent —
To exalt him to the highest point of beauty.
Mortality denied a model to me,
And language, words.   Then did I bend his views
To this point only — and my whole endeavor
Was to explain to him his love.

                    QUEEN.
                    Your friend,
Marquis ! so wholly occupied your mind,
That for his cause you quite forgot my own —
Could you suppose that I had thrown aside
All woman's weaknesses, that you could dare
Make me his angel, and confide alone
In virtue for his armor ?   You forget
What risks this heart must run, when we ennoble
Passion with such a beauteous name as this.

                    MARQUIS.
Yes, in all other women — but in one,
One only, 'tis not so.   For you, I swear it.
And should you blush to indulge the pure desire
To call heroic virtue into life ?
Can it affect King Philip, that his works
Of noblest art, in the Escurial, raise
Immortal longings in the painter's soul,
Who stands entranced before them ?   Do the sounds
That slumber in the lute, belong alone
To him who buys the chords ?   With ear unmoved
He may preserve his treasure : — he has bought
The wretched right to shiver it to atoms,

But not the power to wake its silver tones,
Or, in the magic of its sounds, dissolve.
Truth is created for the sage, as beauty
Is for the feeling heart. They own each other.
And this belief, no coward prejudice
Shall make me e'er disclaim. Then promise, queen,
That you will ever love him. That false shame,
Or fancied dignity, shall never make you
Yield to the voice of base dissimulation : —
That you will love him still, unchanged, forever.
Promise me this, oh, queen! Here solemnly
Say, do you promise?

QUEEN.

That my heart alone
Shall ever vindicate my love, I promise ——

MARQUIS (*drawing his hand back*).

Now I die satisified — my work is done.
[*He bows to the* QUEEN, *and is about to go.*

QUEEN (*follows him with her eyes in silence*).

You are then going, marquis, and have not
Told me how soon — and when — we meet again?

MARQUIS (*comes back once more, his face turned away*).

Yes, we shall surely meet again !

QUEEN.

Now, Posa,
I understand you. Why have you done this?

MARQUIS.

Carlos or I myself!

QUEEN.

No ! no ! you rush
Headlong into a deed you deem sublime.
Do not deceive yourself : I know you well :
Long have you thirsted for it. If your pride
But have its fill, what matters it to you
Though thousand hearts should break. Oh! now, at
    length,
I comprehend your feelings — 'tis the love
Of admiration which has won your heart ——

MARQUIS (*surprised, aside*).
No! I was not prepared for this ——

QUEEN (*after a pause*).

Oh, marquis!
Is there no hope of preservation?

MARQUIS.

None.

QUEEN.

None?   Oh, consider well!   None possible!
Not e'en by me?

MARQUIS.

Not even, queen, by thee.

QUEEN.

You but half know me — I have courage, marquis ——

MARQUIS.

I know it ——

QUEEN.

And no means of safety?

MARQUIS.

None!

QUEEN (*turning away and covering her face*).
Go!   Never more shall I respect a man ——

MARQUIS (*casts himself on his knees before her in evident
emotion*).

O queen! O heaven! how lovely still is life!
[*He starts up and rushes out.   The* QUEEN *retires
into her cabinet.*

SCENE XXII.

DUKE ALVA *and* DOMINGO *walking up and down in silence and
separately.* COUNT LERMA *comes out of the* KING'S *cabinet,
and afterwards* DON RAYMOND OF TAXIS, *the Postmaster-
General.*

LERMA.

Has not the marquis yet appeared?

ALVA.

Not yet.

[LERMA *about to re-enter the cabinet.*

TAXIS *(enters).*

Count Lerma! Pray announce me to the king?

LERMA.

His majesty cannot be seen.

TAXIS.

But say
That I must see him; that my business is
Of urgent import to his majesty.
Make haste — it will admit of no delay.

[LERMA *enters the cabinet.*

ALVA.

Dear Taxis, you must learn a little patience —
You cannot see the king.

TAXIS.

Not see him! Why?

ALVA.

You should have been considerate, and procured
Permission from the Marquis Posa first —
Who keeps both son and father in confinement.

TAXIS.

The Marquis Posa! Right — that is the man
From whom I bring this letter.

ALVA.

Ha! What letter?

TAXIS.

A letter to be forwarded to Brussels.

ALVA *(attentively).*

To Brussels?

TAXIS.

And I bring it to the king.

ALVA.

Indeed! to Brussels! Heard you that, Domingo?

DOMINGO (*joining them*).
Full of suspicion!

TAXIS.
                    And with anxious mien,
And deep embarrassment he gave it to me.

DOMINGO.
Embarrassment!   To whom is it directed?

TAXIS.
The Prince of Orange and Nassau.

ALVA.
                              To William!
There's treason here, Domingo!

DOMINGO.
                              Nothing less!
In truth this letter must, without delay,
Be laid before the king.   A noble service
You render, worthy man — to be so firm
In the discharge of duty.

TAXIS.
                    Reverend sir!
'Tis but my duty.

ALVA.
                But you do it well.

LERMA (*coming out of the cabinet, addressing* TAXIS).
The king will see you.   [TAXIS *goes in*
                    Is the marquis come?

DOMINGO.
He has been sought for everywhere.

ALVA.
                              'Tis strange!
The prince is a state prisoner!   And the king
Knows not the reason why!

DOMINGO.
                    He never came
To explain the business here.

ALVA.

What says the king?

LERMA.

The king spoke not a word.   [*A noise in the cabinet.*

ALVA.

What noise is that?

TAXIS (*coming out of the cabinet*).

Count Lerma!   [*Both enter.*

ALVA (*to* DOMINGO).

What so deeply can engage them.

DOMINGO.

That look of fear! This intercepted letter!
It augurs nothing good.

ALVA.

He sends for Lerma!
Yet he must know full well that you and I
Are both in waiting.

DOMINGO.

Ah! our day is over!

ALVA.

And am I not the same to whom these doors
Flew open once? But, ah! how changed is all
Around me and how strange!
        [DOMINGO *approaches the cabinet door softly, and re-
        mains listening before it.*

ALVA (*after a pause*).

Hark! All is still
And silent as the grave! I hear them breathe.

DOMINGO.

The double tapestry absorbs the sounds!

ALVA.

Away! there's some one coming. All appears
So solemn and so still — as if this instant
Some deep momentous question were decided.

SCENE XXIII.

The PRINCE OF PARMA, *the* DUKES OF FERIA *and* MEDINA
SIDONIA, *with other* GRANDEES *enter — the preceding.*

PARMA.

Say, can we see the king?

ALVA.
                No!

PARMA.
                        Who is with him?

FERIA.

The Marquis Posa, doubtless?

ALVA.
                        Every instant
He is expected here.

PARMA.
                This moment we
Arrive from Saragossa.   Through Madrid
Terror prevails!   Is the announcement true?

DOMINGO.

Alas, too true!

FERIA.
                That he has been arrested.
By the marquis!

ALVA.
        Yes.

PARMA.
                And wherefore? What's the cause?

ALVA.

Wherefore?   That no one knows, except the king
And Marquis Posa.

PARMA.
                And without the warrant
Of the assembled Cortes of the Realm?

FERIA.

That man shall suffer, who has lent a hand
To infringe the nation's rights.

ALVA.

And so say I!

MEDINA SIDONIA.

And I!

THE OTHER GRANDEES.

And all of us!

ALVA.

Who'll follow me
Into the cabinet? I'll throw myself
Before the monarch's feet.

LERMA (*rushing out of the cabinet*).

The Duke of Alva!

DOMINGO.

Then God be praised at last!

LERMA.

When Marquis Posa
Comes, say the king's engaged and he'll be sent for.

DOMINGO (*to* LERMA; *all the others having gathered round
him, full of anxious expectation*).

Count! What has happened? You are pale as death!

LERMA (*hastening away*).

Fell villany!

PARMA *and* FERIA.

What! what!

MEDINA SIDONIA.

How is the king?

DOMINGO (*at the same time*).

Fell villany! Explain ——

LERMA.

The king shed tears!

DOMINGO.

Shed tears!

ALL (*together with astonishment*).

The king shed tears!
[*The bell rings in the cabinet,* COUNT LERMA *hastens in.*

DOMINGO.

Count, yet one word.

Pardon! He's gone! · We're fettered in amazement.

SCENE XXIV.

PRINCESS EBOLI, FERIA, MEDINA SIDONIA, PARMA,
DOMINGO, *and other grandees.*

EBOLI (*hurriedly and distractedly*).

Where is the king? Where? I must speak with him.

[*To* FERIA.

Conduct me to him, duke!

FERIA.

The monarch is
Engaged in urgent business. No one now
Can be admitted.

EBOLI.

Has he signed, as yet,
The fatal sentence? He has been deceived.

DOMINGO (*giving her a significant look at a distance*).

The Princess Eboli!

EBOLI (*going to him*).

What! you here, priest?
The very man I want! You can confirm
My testimony!

[*She seizes his hand and would drag him into the
cabinet.*

DOMINGO.

I? You rave, princess!

FERIA.

Hold back. The king cannot attend you now.

EBOLI.

But he must hear me; he must hear the truth —
The truth, were he ten times a deity.

DOMINGO.

Away! You hazard everything. Stand back.

EBOLI.

Man, tremble at the anger of thy idol.
I have naught left to hazard.

> [*Attempts to enter the cabinet;* ALVA *rushes out,*
> *his eyes sparkling, triumph in his gait. He*
> *hastens to* DOMINGO, *and embraces him.*

ALVA.

Let each church
Resound with high Te Deums. Victory
At length is ours.

DOMINGO.

What! Ours?

ALVA (*to* DOMINGO *and the other* GRANDEES).

Now to the king.
You shall hereafter hear the sequel from me.

ACT V.

SCENE I.

A chamber in the royal palace, separated from a large fore-court
by an iron-barred gate. Sentinels walking up and down. CAR-
LOS *sitting at a table, with his head leaning forward on his arms,*
as if he were asleep. In the background of the chamber are
some officers, confined with him. The MARQUIS POSA *enters,*
unobserved by him, and whispers to the officers, who immediately
withdraw. He himself steps close up to CARLOS, *and looks at*
him for a few minutes in silent sorrow. At last he makes a
motion which awakens him out of his stupor. CARLOS *rises,*
and seeing the MARQUIS, *starts back. He regards him for some*
time with fixed eyes, and draws his hand over his forehead as if
he wished to recollect something.

MARQUIS.

Carlos! 'tis I.

CARLOS (*gives him his hand*).

Comest thou to me again?
'Tis friendly of thee, truly.

MARQUIS.

Here I thought
Thou mightest need a friend.

CARLOS.

Indeed! was that
Thy real thought?   Oh, joy unspeakable!
Right well I knew thou still wert true to me.

MARQUIS.

I have deserved this from thee.

CARLOS.

Hast thou not?
And now we understand each other fully,
It joys my heart.   This kindness, this forbearance
Becomes our noble souls.   For should there be
One rash, unjust demand amongst my wishes,
Wouldst thou, for that, refuse me what was just?
Virtue I know may often be severe,
But never is she cruel and inhuman.
Oh! it hath cost thee much; full well I know
How thy kind heart with bitter anguish bled
As thy hands decked the victim for the altar.

MARQUIS.

What meanest thou, Carlos?

CARLOS.

Thou, thyself, wilt now
Fulfil the joyous course I should have run.
Thou wilt bestow on Spain those golden days
She might have hoped in vain to win from me.
I'm lost, forever lost; thou saw'st it clearly.
This fatal love has scattered, and forever,
All the bright, early blossoms of my mind.
To all the great, exalted hopes I'm dead.
Chance led thee to the king — or Providence, —
It cost thee but my secret — and at once
He was thine own — thou may'st become his angel:
But I am lost, though Spain perhaps may flourish.
Well, there is nothing to condemn, if not
My own mad blindness.   Oh, I should have known
That thou art no less great than tender-hearted.

MARQUIS.

No! I foresaw not, I considered not
That friendship's generous heart would lead thee on

Beyond my worldly prudence. I have erred,
My fabric's shattered — I forgot thy heart.

CARLOS.

Yet, if it had been possible to spare
Her fate — oh, how intensely I had thanked thee!
Could I not bear the burden by myself?
And why must she be made a second victim?
But now no more, I'll spare thee this reproach.
What is the queen to thee? Say, dost thou love her?
Could thy exalted virtue e'er consult
The petty interests of my wretched passion?
Oh, pardon me! I was unjust ——

MARQUIS.

Thou art so!
But not for this reproach. Deserved I one,
I merit all — and then I should not stand
Before you as I do. [*He takes out his portfolio.*
I have some letters
To give you back of those you trusted to me.

CARLOS (*looks first at the letters, then at the* MARQUIS, *in
astonishment*).

How!

MARQUIS.

I return them now because they may
Prove safer in thy custody than mine.

CARLOS.

What meanest thou? Has his majesty not read them?
Have they not been before him?

MARQUIS.

What, these letters!

CARLOS.

Thou didst not show them all, then.

MARQUIS.

Who has said
That ever I showed one?

CARLOS (*astonished*).

Can it be so?
Count Lerma ——

MARQUIS.

He! he told thee so! Now all
Is clear as day. But who could have foreseen it?
Lerma! Oh, no, he hath not learned to lie.
'Tis true, the king has all the other letters.

CARLOS (*looks at him long with speechless astonishment*).
But wherefore am I here?

MARQUIS.

For caution's sake,
Lest thou should chance, a second time, to make
An Eboli thy confidant.

CARLOS (*as if waking from a dream*).
Ha! Now
I see it all — all is explained.

MARQUIS (*goes to the door*).
Who's there?

SCENE II.

DUKE ALVA. *The former.*

ALVA (*approaching the PRINCE with respect, but turning
his back on the MARQUIS during the whole scene.*

Prince, you are free. Deputed by the king
I come to tell you so.
[CARLOS *looks at the* MARQUIS *with astonishment.
General silence.*
And I, in truth,
Am fortunate to have this honor first ——

CARLOS (*looking at both with extreme amazement, after a
pause, to the* DUKE).
I am imprisoned, duke, and set at freedom,
Unconscious of the cause of one or other.

ALVA.

As far as I know, prince, 'twas through an error,
To which the king was driven by a traitor.

CARLOS.

Then am I here by order of the king?

ALVA.

Yes, through an error of his majesty.

CARLOS.

That gives me pain, indeed.   But when the king
Commits an error, 'twould beseem the king,
Methinks, to remedy the fault in person.
I am Don Philip's son — and curious eyes
And slanderous looks are on me.   What the king
Hath done from sense of duty ne'er will I
Appear to owe to your considerate favor.
I am prepared to appear before the Cortes,
And will not take my sword from such a hand.

ALVA.

The king will never hesitate to grant
Your highness a request so just.   Permit
That I conduct you to him.

CARLOS.

Here I stay
Until the king or all Madrid shall come
To lead me from my prison.   Take my answer.
   [ALVA *withdraws.   He is still seen for some time linger-
   ing in the court and giving orders to the guards.*

SCENE III.

CARLOS *and* MARQUIS POSA.

CARLOS (*after the departure of the* DUKE, *full of expecta-
tion and astonishment, to the* MARQUIS).
What means all this?   Inform me, Roderigo —
Art thou not, then, the minister?

MARQUIS.

I was,
As thou canst well perceive ——
   [*Going to him with great emotion.*
O Carlos!   Now
I have succeeded — yes — it is accomplished —
'Tis over now — Omnipotence be praised,
To whom I owe success.

CARLOS.

Success ! What mean you ?
Thy words perplex me.

MARQUIS *(takes his hand)*.

Carlos ! thou art saved —
Art free — but I ——   [*He stops short*

CARLOS.

But thou ——

MARQUIS.

Thus to my breast
I press thee now, with friendship's fullest right,
A right I've bought with all I hold most dear.
How great, how lovely, Carlos, is this moment
Of self-approving joy ?

CARLOS.

What sudden change
I mark upon thy features !   Proudly now
Thy bosom heaves, thine eyes dart vivid fire !

MARQUIS.

We must say farewell, Carlos !   Tremble not,
But be a man !   And what thou more shalt hear,
Promise me, not by unavailing sorrow,
Unworthy of great souls, to aggravate
The pangs of parting.   I am lost to thee,
Carlos, for many years — fools say forever.
    [CARLOS *withdraws his hand, but makes no reply.*
Be thou a man : I've reckoned much on thee —
I have not even shunned to pass with thee
This awful hour — which men, in words of fear,
Have termed the final one.   I own it, Carlos,
I joy to pass it thus.   Come let us sit —
I feel myself grown weary and exhausted.
    [*He approaches* CARLOS, *who is in a lifeless stupor,
    and allows himself to be involuntarily drawn down
    by him.*
Where art thou ?   No reply !   I must be brief.
Upon the day that followed our last meeting
At the Carthusian monastery the king
Called me before him.   What ensued thou knowest.

And all Madrid. Thou hast not heard, however,
Thy secret even then had reached his ears —
That letters in the queen's possession found
Had testified against thee. This I learned
From his own lips — I was his confidant.
        [*He pauses for* CARLOS' *answer, but he still remains
            silent.*
Yes, Carlos, with my lips I broke my faith —
Guided the plot myself that worked thy ruin.
Thy deed spoke trumpet-tongued ; to clear thee fully
'Twas now too late : to frustrate his revenge
Was all that now remained for me ; and so
I made myself thy enemy to — serve thee
With fuller power — dost thou not hear me, Carlos,

CARLOS

Go on ! go on ! I hear thee.

MARQUIS.
                To this point
I'm guiltless. But the unaccustomed beams
Of royal favor dazzled me. The rumor,
As I had well foreseen, soon reached thine ears
But by mistaken delicacy led,
And blinded by my vain desire to end
My enterprise alone, I kept concealed
From friendship's ear my hazardous design.
This was my fatal error ! Here I failed !
I know it. My self-confidence was madness.
Pardon that confidence — 'twas founded, Carlos,
Upon our friendship's everlasting base.
        [*He pauses.* CARLOS *passes from torpid silence to
            violent agitation.*
That which I feared befel. Unreal dangers
Alarmed your mind. The bleeding queen — the tumult
Within the palace — Lerma's interference —
And, last of all, my own mysterious silence,   .
Conspired to overwhelm thy heart with wonder.
Thou wavered'st, thought'st me lost ; but far too noble
To doubt thy friend's integrity, thy soul
Clothed his defection with a robe of honor.

Nor judged him faithless till it found a motive
To screen and justify his breach of faith.
Forsaken by thy only friend — twas then
Thou sought'st the arms of Princess Eboli —
A demon's arms ! 'Twas she betrayed thee, Carlos!
I saw thee fly to her — a dire foreboding
Struck on my heart — I followed thee too late !
Already wert thou prostrate at her feet,
The dread avowal had escaped thy lips —
No way was left to save thee.

CARLOS.

                  No ! her heart
Was moved, thou dost mistake, her heart was moved

MARQUIS.

Night overspread my mind.   No remedy,
No refuge, no retreat was left to me
In nature's boundless compass.   Blind despair
Transformed me to a fury — to a tiger —
I raised my dagger to a woman's breast.
But in that moment — in that dreadful moment —
A radiant sunbeam fell upon my soul.
" Could I mislead the king ! Could I succeed
In making him think me the criminal !
However improbable, the very guilt
Will be enough to win the king's belief.
I'll dare the task — a sudden thunderbolt
May make the tyrant.start — what want I further ?
He stops to think, and Carlos thus gains time
To fly to Brussels."

CARLOS.

         And hast thou done this ?

MARQUIS.

I have despatched a letter to Prince William,
Saying I loved the queen, and had escaped
The king's mistrust in the unjust suspicion
Which falsely fell on thee — that I had found
Means, through the monarch's favor, to obtain
Free access to the queen.   I added, further,

That I was fearful of discovery —
That thou hadst learned my secret, and hadst sped
To Princess Eboli, with hopes through her
To warn the queen — that I had made thee prisoner —
And now that all seemed lost, I had resolved
To fly to Brussels.   This same letter I ——

CARLOS (*interrupts him, terrified*).

Hast surely not intrusted to the post!
Thou knowest that letters to Brabant and Flanders ——

MARQUIS.

Are given to the king ; and as things go
Taxis would seem to have discharged his duty.

CARLOS.

Heavens! then I'm lost.

MARQUIS.

How lost?   What meanest thou ?

CARLOS.

And thou, alas ! art lost together with me —
This dreadful fraud my father ne'er will pardon.

MARQUIS.

This fraud !   Thou'rt mad !   Who will disclose it to him ?

CARLOS (*regards him with a fixed look*).

Who !   Dost thou ask?   I will myself.

MARQUIS.

Thou ravest !

Stand back —

CARLOS.

Away !   For heaven's sake hold me not.
While I stay here, he's hiring the assassins.

MARQUIS.

Then is our time more precious — and we still
Have much to say.

CARLOS.

What !   Before all is finished ?
[*He makes another effort to go.   The* MARQUIS *holds
him by the arm, and looks at him impressively.*

MARQUIS.

Carlos ! was I so scrupulous — so eager —
When thou, a boy, didst shed thy blood for me?

CARLOS (*with emotion, and full of admiration*).
Kind Providence!

MARQUIS.

Reserve thyself for Flanders!
The kingdom is thy destiny — 'tis mine
To give my life for thee.

CARLOS (*takes his hand with deep sensibility*).

No, no! he will not,
Cannot resist a virtue so sublime.
I will conduct thee to him, and together,
Arm linked in arm, will we appear before him.
Then thus will I address him : " Father, see,
This is the way a friend acts towards his friend."
Trust me, 'twill move him — it will touch his heart.
He's not without humanity, — my father.
Yes, it will move him.   With hot tears, his eyes
Will overflow — and he will pardon us.
[*A shot is fired through the iron grating.* CARLOS
leaps up.

CARLOS.

Whom was that meant for ?

MARQUIS (*sinking down*).

I believe — for me.

CARLOS (*falling to the earth with a loud cry of grief*).
O God of mercy !

MARQUIS.

He is quick — the king .
I had hoped — a little longer — Carlos — think

Of means of flight — dost hear me? — of thy flight.
Thy mother — knows it all — I can no more.   [*Dies.*
    [CARLOS *remains by the corpse, like one bereft of*
      life. After some time the KING *enters, accom-*
      panied by many GRANDEES ; *and starts, panic-*
      struck, at the sight. A general and deep silence.
      The GRANDEES *range themelves in a semi-circle*
      round them both, and regard the KING *and his*
      SON *alternately. The latter continues without*
      any sign of life. The KING *regards him in*
      thoughtful silence.

SCENE IV.

The KING, CARLOS, *the* DUKES ALVA, FERIA, *and*
MEDINA SIDONIA, PRINCE OF PARMA, COUNT LERMA,
DOMINGO, *and numerous* GRANDEES.

KING (*in a gentle tone*).

Thy prayer hath met a gracious hearing, prince,
And here I come, with all the noble peers
Of this my court, to bring thee liberty.
    [CARLOS *raises his eyes and looks around him like*
      one awakened from a dream. His eyes are fixed
      now on the KING, *now on the corpse; he gives no*
      answer.
Receive thy sword again.   We've been too rash!
    [*He approaches him, holds out his hand, and as-*
      sists him to rise.
My son's not in his place; Carlos, arise!
Come to thy father's arms!   His love awaits thee.

CARLOS (*receives the embrace of the* KING *without any*
    consciousness. Suddenly recollects himself, pauses
    and looks fixedly at him).

Thou smell'st of blood — no, I cannot embrace thee!
    [*Pushes his father back. All the* GRANDEES *are*
      in commotion. CARLOS *to them : —*
Nay, stand not there confounded and amazed!
What monstrous action have I done?   Defiled
The anointed of the Lord!   Oh, fear me not.

I would not lay a hand on him. Behold,
Stamped on his forehead is the damning **brand**!
The hand of God hath marked him!

KING (about to go quickly).

Nobles! follow.

CARLOS.

Whither? You stir not from this spot.
> [*Detaining the* KING *forcibly with both hands, while
> with one he manages to seize the sword which the*
> KING *has brought with him, and it comes from the
> scabbard.*

KING.

What! Draw

A sword upon thy father?

ALL THE GRANDEES (drawing their swords).

Regicide!

CARLOS (holding the KING firmly with one hand, the
naked sword in the other).

Put up your swords! What! Think you I am mad?
I am not so : or you were much to blame
Thus to remind me, that upon the point
Of this my sword, his trembling life doth hover.
I pray you, stand aloof ; for souls like mine
Need soothing. There — hold back! And with the **king**
What I have yet to settle touches not
Your loyalty. See there — his hand is bloody!
Do you not see it? And now look you here!
> [*Pointing to the corpse.*
This hath he done with a well-practised hand.

KING (to the GRANDEES, who press anxiously around him).

Retire! Why do you tremble? Are we not
Father and son? I will yet wait and see
To what atrocious crime his nature ——

CARLOS.

Nature

I know her not. Murder is now the word!
The bonds of all humanity are severed,

Thine own hands have dissolved them through the realm.
Shall I respect a tie which thou hast scorned?
Oh, see! see here! the foulest deed of blood
That e'er the world beheld. Is there no God
That kings, in his creation, work such havoc?
Is there no God, I ask? Since mother's wombs
Bore children, one alone — and only one —
So guiltlessly hath died: And art thou sensible
What thou hast done? Oh, no! he knows it not:
Knows not that he has robbed — despoiled the world
Of a more noble, precious, dearer life
Than he and all his century can boast.

KING (*with a tone of softness*).
If I have been too hasty, Carlos — thou
For whom I have thus acted, should at least
Not call me to account.

CARLOS.
                    Is't possible!
Did you then never guess how dear to me
Was he who here lies dead? Thou lifeless corpse!
Instruct him — aid his wisdom, to resolve
This dark enigma now. He was my friend.
And would you know why he has perished thus?
He gave his life for me.

KING.
                    Ha? my suspicions!

CARLOS.
Pardon, thou bleeding corpse, that I profane
Thy virtue to such ears. But let him blush
With deep-felt shame, the crafty politician,
That his gray-headed wisdom was o'erreached,
E'en by the judgment of a youth. Yes, sire,
We two were brothers! Bound by nobler bands
Than nature ties. His whole life's bright career
Was love. His noble death was love for me.
E'en in the moment when his brief esteem
Exalted you, he was my own. And when
With fascinating tongue he sported with
Your haughty, giant mind, 'twas your conceit

To bridle him; but you became yourself
The pliant tool of his exalted plans.
That I became a prisoner, my arrest,
Was his deep friendship's meditated work.
That letter to Prince William was designed
To save my life. It was the first deceit
He ever practised. To insure my safety
He rushed on death himself, and nobly perished.
You lavished on him all your favor; yet
For me he died. Your heart, your confidence,
You forced upon him. As a toy he held
Your sceptre and your power; he cast them from him,
And gave his life for me.

      [*The* KING *stands motionless, with eyes fixed on
        the ground; all the* GRANDEES *regard him with
        surprise and alarm.*

                How could it be
That you gave credit to this strange deceit?
Meanly indeed he valued you, to try
By such coarse artifice to win his ends.
You dared to court his friendship, but gave way
Before a test so simple. Oh, no! never
For souls like yours was such a being formed.
That well he knew himself, when he rejected
Your crowns, your gifts your greatness, and yourself.
This fine-toned lyre broke in your iron hand,
And you could do no more than murder him.

ALVA (*never having taken his eyes from the* KING, *and
observing his emotion with uneasiness, approaches
him with apprehension*).

Keep not this deathlike silence, sire. Look round,
And speak at least to us.

CARLOS.

              Once you were not
Indifferent to him. And deeply once
You occupied his thoughts. It might have been
His lot to make you happy. His full heart
Might have enriched you; with its mere abundance
An atom of his soul had been enough

To make a god of you. You've robbed yourself —
Plundered yourself and me. What could you give,
To raise again a spirit like to this?

> [*Deep silence. Many of the* GRANDEES *turn
> away, or conceal their faces in their mantles.*

Oh, ye who stand around with terror dumb,
And mute surprise, do not condemn the youth
Who holds this language to the king, his father.
Look on this corpse. Behold! for me he died.
If ye have tears — if in your veins flow blood,
Not molten brass, look here, and blame me not.

> [*He turns to the* KING *with more self-possession
> and calmness.*

Doubtless you wait the end of this rude scene?
Here is my sword, for you are still my king.
Think not I fear your vengeance. Murder me,
As you have murdered this most noble man.
My life is forfeit; that I know full well.
But what is life to me? I here renounce
All that this world can offer to my hopes.
Seek among strangers for a son. Here lies
My kingdom.

> [*He sinks down on the corpse, and takes no part in
> what follows. A confused tumult and the noise
> of a crowd is heard in the distance. All is deep
> silence round the* KING. *His eyes scan the
> circle over, but no one returns his looks.*

KING.

What! Will no one make reply?
Each eye upon the ground, each look abashed!
My sentence is pronounced. I read it here
Proclaimed in all this lifeless, mute demeanor.
My vassals have condemned me.

> [*Silence as before. The tumult grows louder. A
> murmur is heard among the* GRANDEES. *They
> exchange embarrassed looks.* COUNT LERMA *at
> length gently touches* ALVA.

LERMA.

Here's rebellion!

ALVA (*in a low voice*).

I fear it.

LERMA.

It approaches! They are coming!

SCENE V.

An officer of the Body Guard. The former.

OFFICER (*urgently*).

Rebellion! Where's the king?
    [*He makes his way through the crowd up to the* KING.
                  Madrid's in arms!
To thousands swelled, the soldiery and people
Surround the palace; and reports are spread
That Carlos is a prisoner — that his life
Is threatened. And the mob demand to see
Him living, or Madrid will be in flames.

THE GRANDEES (*with excitement*).

Defend the king!

ALVA (*to the* KING, *who remains quiet and unmoved*).

        Fly, sire! your life's in danger.
As yet we know not who has armed the people.

KING (*rousing from his stupor, and advancing with
dignity among them*).

Stands my throne firm, and am I sovereign yet
Over this empire? No! I'm king no more.
These cowards weep — moved by a puny boy.
They only wait the signal to desert me.
I am betrayed by rebels!

ALVA.

        Dreadful thought!

KING.

There! fling yourselves before him — down before
The young, the expectant king; I'm nothing now
But a forsaken, old, defenceless man!

ALVA.

Spaniards! is't come to this?
> [*All crowd round the* KING, *and fall on their knees
> before him with drawn swords.* CARLOS *remains
> alone with the corpse, deserted by all.*

KING (*tearing off his mantle and throwing it from him*).
> There! clothe him now
With this my royal mantle; and on high
Bear him in triumph o'er my trampled corpse!
> [*He falls senseless in* ALVA'S *and* LERMA'S *arms.*

LERMA.

For heaven's sake, help!

FERIA.

> Oh, sad, disastrous chance!

LERMA.

He faints!

ALVA (*leaves the* KING *in* LERMA'S *and* FERIA'S *hands*).
> Attend his majesty! whilst I
Make it my aim to tranquillize Madrid.
> [*Exit* ALVA. *The* KING *is borne off, attended by all
> the grandees.*

Scene VI.

CARLOS *remains behind with the corpse. After a few moments
LOUIS MERCADO appears, looks cautiously round him, and
stands a long time silent behind the* PRINCE, *who does not
observe him.*

MERCADO.

I come, prince, from her majesty the queen.
> [CARLOS *turns away and makes no reply.*

My name, Mercado, I'm the queen's physician:
See my credentials.
> [*Shows the* PRINCE *a signet ring.* CARLOS *remains
> still silent.*
> And the queen desires
To speak with you to-day — on weighty business.

CARLOS.

Nothing is weighty in this world to me.

MERCADO.

A charge the Marquis Posa left with her.

CARLOS (*looking up quickly*).

Indeed! I come this instant.

MERCADO.

               No, not yet,
Most gracious prince! you must delay till night.
Each avenue is watched, the guards are doubled,
You ne'er could reach the palace unperceived;
You would endanger everything.

CARLOS.

               And yet ——

MERCADO.

I know one means alone that can avail us.
'Tis the queen's thought, and she suggests it to you
But it is bold, adventurous, and strange!

CARLOS.

What is it?

MERCADO.

             A report has long prevailed
That in the secret vaults, beneath the palace,
At midnight, shrouded in a monk's attire,
The emperor's departed spirit walks.
The people still give credit to the tale,
And the guards watch the post with inward terror.
Now, if you but determine to assume
This dress, you may pass freely through the guards
Until you reach the chamber of the queen,
Which this small key will open. Your attire
Will save you from attack. But on the spot,
Prince! your decision must be made at once.
The requisite apparel and the mask
Are ready in your chamber. I must haste
And take the queen your answer.

CARLOS.

               And the hour?

MERCADO.

It is midnight.

CARLOS.

Then inform her I will come.

[*Exit* MERCADO.

SCENE VII.

CARLOS *and* COUNT LERMA.

LERMA.

Save yourself, prince! The king's enraged against you.
Your liberty, if not your life's in danger!
Ask me no further — I have stolen away
To give you warning — fly this very instant

CARLOS.

Heaven will protect me!

LERMA.

As the queen observed
To me, this moment, you must leave Madrid
This very day, and fly to Brussels, prince.
Postpone it not, I pray you. The commotion
Favors your flight. The queen, with this design,
Has raised it. No one will presume so far
As to lay hand on you. Swift steeds await you
At the Carthusian convent, and behold,
Here are your weapons, should you be attacked.

[LERMA *gives him a dagger and pistols.*

CARLOS.

Thanks, thanks, Count Lerma!

LERMA.

This day's sad event
Has moved my inmost soul! No faithful friend
Will ever love like him. No patriot breathes
But weeps for you. More now I dare not say.

CARLOS.

Count Lerma! he who's gone considered you
A man of honor.

LERMA.

Farewell, prince, again!
Success attend you! Happier times will come —
But I shall be no more. Receive my homage!

[*Falls on one knee.*

CARLOS (*endeavors to prevent him, with much emotion*).

Not so — not so, count! I am too much moved —
I would not be unmanned!

LERMA (*kissing his hand with feeling*).
My children's king!
To die for you will be their privilege!
It is not mine, alas! But in those children
Remember me! Return in peace to Spain.
May you on Philip's throne feel as a man,
For you have learned to suffer! Undertake
No bloody deed against your father, prince!
Philip compelled his father to yield up
The throne to him; and this same Philip now
Trembles at his own son. Think, prince, of that!
And may Heaven prosper and direct your path!
[*Exit quickly.* CARLOS *about to hasten away by
another side, but turns rapidly round, and throws
himself down before the corpse, which he again
folds in his arms. He then hurries from the
room.*

Scene VIII.

The KING'S *Antechamber.*

DUKE ALVA *and* DUKE FERIA *enter in conversation.*

ALVA.

The town is quieted. How is the king?

FERIA.

In the most fearful state. Within his chamber
He is shut up, and whatso'er may happen
He will admit no person to his presence.
The treason of the marquis has at once
Changed his whole nature. We no longer know him.

ALVA.

I must go to him, nor respect his feelings.
A great discovery which I have made——

FERIA.

A new discovery!

ALVA.

A Carthusian monk
My guards observed, with stealthy footsteps, creep
Into the prince's chamber, and inquire
With anxious curiosity, about
The Marquis Posa's death. They seized him straight,
And questioned him. Urged by the fear of death,
He made confession that he bore about him
Papers of high importance, which the marquis
Enjoined him to deliver to the prince,
If, before sunset, he should not return.

FERIA.

Well, and what further?

ALVA.

These same letters state
That Carlos from Madrid must fly before
The morning dawn.

FERIA.

Indeed!

ALVA.

And that a ship at Cadiz lies
Ready for sea, to carry him to Flushing.
And that the Netherlands but wait his presence,
To shake the Spanish fetters from their arms.

FERIA.

Can this be true?

ALVA.

And other letters say
A fleet of Soliman's will sail for Rhodes,
According to the treaty, to attack
The Spanish squadron in the Midland seas.

FERIA.

Impossible.

ALVA.

And hence I understand
The object of the journeys, which of late
The marquis made through Europe. 'Twas no less
Than to rouse all the northern powers to arms
In aid of Flanders' freedom.

FERIA.
> Was it so?

ALVA.

There is besides appended to these letters
The full concerted plan of all the war
Which is to disunite from Spain's control
The Netherlands forever.   Naught omitted;
The power and opposition close compared;
All the resources accurately noted,
Together with the maxims to be followed,
And all the treaties which they should conclude.
The plan is fiendish, but 'tis no less splendid

FERIA.

The deep, designing traitor!

ALVA.
> And, moreover,

There is allusion made, in these same letters,
To some mysterious conference the prince
Must with his mother hold upon the eve
Preceding his departure.

FERIA.
> That must be

This very day.

ALVA.
> At midnight.   But for this

I have already taken proper steps.
You see the case is pressing.   Not a moment
Is to be lost.   Open the monarch's chamber.

FERIA.

Impossible!   All entrance is forbidden.

ALVA.

I'll open then myself; the increasing danger
Must justify my boldness.
> [*As he is on the point of approaching the door it
> opens, and the* KING *comes out.*

FERIA.
> 'Tis himself!

Scene IX.

The King. *The preceding.*

All are alarmed at his appearance, fall back, and let him pass through them. He appears to be in a waking dream, like a sleep-walker. His dress and figure indicate the disorder caused by his late fainting. With slow steps he walks past the GRANDEES *and looks at each with a fixed eye, but without recognizing any of them. At last he stands still, wrapped in thought, his eyes fixed on the ground, till the emotions of his mind gradually express themselves in words.*

KING.

Restore me back the dead! Yes, I must have him.

DOMINGO (*whispering to* ALVA).

Speak to him, duke.

KING.

He died despising me!
Have him again I must, and make him think
More nobly of me.

ALVA (*approaching with fear*).

Sire!

KING (*looking round the circle*).

Who speaks to me!
Have you forgotten who I am? Why not
Upon your knees, before your king, ye creatures!
Am I not still your king? I must command
Submission from you. Do you all then slight me
Because one man despised me?

ALVA.

Gracious king!
No more of him: a new and mightier foe
Arises in the bosom of your realm.

FERIA.

Prince Carlos ——

KING.

Had a friend who died for him;
For him! With me he might have shared an empire.

How he looked down upon me ! From the throne
Kings look not down so proudly. It was plain
How vain his conquest made him. His keen sorrow
Confessed how great his loss. Man weeps not so
For aught that's perishable. Oh, that he might
But live again ! I'd give my Indies for it !
Omnipotence ! thou bring'st no comfort to me :
Thou canst not stretch thine arm into the grave
To rectify one little act, committed
With hasty rashness, 'gainst the life of man.
The dead return no more. Who dare affirm
That I am happy ? In the tomb he dwells,
Who scorned to flatter me. What care I now
For all who live ? One spirit, one free being,
And one alone, arose in all this age !
He died despising me !

ALVA.

Our lives are useless !
Spaniards, let's die at once ! E'en in the grave
This man still robs us of our monarch's heart.

KING (*sits down, and leans his head on his arm*).
Oh ! had he died for me ! I loved him, too,
And much. Dear to me was he as a son.
In his young mind there brightly rose for me
A new and beauteous morning. Who can say
What I had destined for him ? He to me
Was a first love. All Europe may condemn me,
Europe may overwhelm me with its curse,
But I deserved his thanks.

DOMINGO.

What spell is this ?

KING.

And, say, for whom did he desert me thus ?
A boy, — my son ? Oh, no, believe it not !
A Posa would not perish for a boy ;
The scanty flame of friendship could not fill
A Posa's heart. It beat for human kind.
His passion was the world, and the whole course
Of future generations yet unborn.

To do them service he secured a throne —
And lost it. Such high treason 'gainst mankind
Could Posa e'er forgive himself? Oh, no;
I know his feelings better. Not that he
Carlos preferred to Philip, but the youth —
The tender pupil, — to the aged monarch.
The father's evening sunbeam could not ripen
His novel projects. He reserved for this
The young son's orient rays. Oh, 'tis undoubted,
They wait for my decease.

ALVA.

And of your thoughts,
Read in these letters strongest confirmation.

KING.

'Tis possible he may miscalculate.
I'm still myself. Thanks, Nature, for thy gifts;
I feel within my frame the strength of youth;
I'll turn their schemes to mockery. His virtue
Shall be an empty dream — his death, a fool's.
His fall shall crush his friend and age together.
We'll test it now — how they can do without me.
The world is still for one short evening mine,
And this same evening will I so employ,
That no reformer yet to come shall reap
Another harvest, in the waste I'll leave,
For ten long generations after me.
He would have offered me a sacrifice
To his new deity — humanity!
So on humanity I'll take revenge.
And with his puppet I'll at once commence.
[*To the* DUKE ALVA.
What you have now to tell me of the prince,
Repeat. What tidings do these letters bring?

ALVA.

These letters, sire, contain the last bequest
Of Posa to Prince Carlos.

KING (*reads the papers, watched by all present. He then lays them aside and walks in silence up and down the room*).

               Summon straight
The cardinal inquisitor ; and beg
He will bestow an hour upon the king,
This very night !

TAXIS.

          Just on the stroke of two
The horses must be ready and prepared,
At the Carthusian monastery.

ALVA.

                Spies
Despatched by me, moreover, have observed
Equipments at the convent for a journey,
On which the prince's arms were recognized.

FERIA.

And it is rumored that large sums are raised
In the queen's name, among the Moorish agents,
Destined for Brussels.

KING.

         Where is Carlos ?

ALVA.

With Posa's body.

KING.

           And there are lights as yet
Within the queen's apartments ?

ALVA.

              Everything
Is silent there. She has dismissed her maids
Far earlier than as yet has been her custom.
The Duchess of Arcos, who was last with her,
Left her in soundest sleep.

    [*An officer of the Body Guard enters, takes the* DUKE
        OF FERIA *aside, and whispers to him. The latter,
        struck with surprise, turns to* DUKE ALVA. *The
        others crowd round him, and a murmuring noise
        arises.*

FERIA, TAXIS, *and* DOMINGO (*at the same time*).
'Tis wonderful!

KING.

What is the matter!

FERIA.

News scarce credible!

DOMINGO.

Two soldiers, who have just returned from duty,
Report — but — oh, the tale's ridiculous!

KING.

What do they say?

ALVA.

They say, in the left wing
Of the queen's palace, that the emperor's ghost
Appeared before them, and with solemn gait
Passed on. This rumor is confirmed by all
The sentinels, who through the whole pavilion
Their watches keep. And they, moreover, add,
The phantom in the queen's apartment vanished.

KING.

And in what shape appeared it?

OFFICER.

In the robes,
The same attire he in Saint Justi wore
For the last time, apparelled as a monk.

KING.

A monk! And did the sentries know his person
Whilst he was yet alive? They could not else
Determine that it was the emperor.

OFFICER.

The sceptre which he bore was evidence
It was the emperor.

DOMINGO.

And the story goes
He often has been seen in this same dress.

KING.

Did no one speak to him?

OFFICER.

No person dared.
The sentries prayed, and let him pass in silence.

KING.

The phantom vanished in the queen's apartments!

OFFICER.

In the queen's antechamber.   [*General silence.*

KING (*turns quickly round*).

What say you?

ALVA.

Sire! we are silent.

KING (*after some thought, to the* OFFICER).

Let my guards be ready
And under arms, and order all approach
To that wing of the palace to be stopped.
I fain would have a word with this same ghost.

[*Exit* OFFICER. *Enter a* PAGE.

PAGE.

The cardinal inquisitor.

KING (*to all present*).

Retire!

[*The* CARDINAL INQUISITOR, *an old man of ninety, and blind, enters, supported on a staff, and led by two Dominicans. The* GRANDEES *fall on their knees as he passes, and touch the hem of his garment. He gives them his blessing, and they depart.*

SCENE X.

The KING *and the* GRAND INQUISITOR. *A long silence.*

GRAND INQUISITOR.

Say, do I stand before the king?

KING.

You do.

GRAND INQUISITOR.

I never thought it would be so again!

KING.

I now renew the scenes of early youth,
When Philip sought his sage instructor's counsel.

GRAND INQUISITOR.

Your glorious sire, my pupil, Charles the Fifth,
Nor sought or needed counsel at my hands.

KING.

So much happier he! I, cardinal,
Am guilty of a murder, and no rest —

GRAND INQUISITOR.

What was the reason for this murder?

KING.

'Twas

A fraud unparalleled ——

GRAND INQUISITOR.

I know it all.

KING.

What do you know? Through whom, and since what
time?

GRAND INQUISITOR.

For years — what you have only learned since sunset.

KING (*with astonishment*).

You know this man then!

GRAND INQUISITOR.

All his life is noted
From its commencement to its sudden close,
In Santa Casa's holy registers.

KING.

Yet he enjoyed his liberty!

GRAND INQUISITOR.

The chain
With which he struggled, but which held him bound,
Though long, was firm, nor easy to be severed.

KING.

He has already been beyond the kingdom.

GRAND INQUISITOR.

Where'er he travelled I was at his side.

KING (*walks backwards and forwards in displeasure*)
You knew the hands, then, I had fallen into;
And yet delayed to warn me!

GRAND INQUISITOR.

This rebuke
I pay you back.   Why did you not consult us
Before you sought the arms of such a man?
You knew him : one sole glance unmasked him to you.
Why did you rob the office of its victim?
Are we thus trifled with !   When majesty
Can stoop to such concealment, and in secret,
Behind our backs, league with our enemies,
What must our fate be then ?   If one be spared
What plea can justify the fate of thousands?

KING.

But he, no less, has fallen a sacrifice.

GRAND INQUISITOR.

No; he is murdered — basely, foully murdered.
The blood that should so gloriously have flowed
To honor us has stained the assassin's hand.
What claim had you to touch our sacred rights?
He but existed, by our hands to perish.
God gave him to this age's exigence,
To perish, as a terrible example,
And turn high-vaunting reason into shame.
Such was my long-laid plan — behold, destroyed
In one brief hour, the toil of many years.
We are defrauded, and your only gain
Is bloody hands.

KING.

Passion impelled me to it.
Forgive me.

GRAND INQUISITOR.

Passion! And does royal Philip
Thus answer me? Have I alone grown old?
[*Shaking his head angrily.*
Passion! Make conscience free within your realms,
If you're a slave yourself.

KING.

In things like this
I'm but a novice. Bear in patience with me.

GRAND INQUISITOR.

No, I'm ill pleased with you — to see you thus
Tarnish the bygone glories of your reign.
Where is that Philip, whose unchanging soul,
Fixed as the polar star in heaven above,
Round its own axis still pursued its course?
Is all the memory of preceding years
Forever gone? And did the world become
New moulded when you stretched your hand to him?
Was poison no more poison? Did distinction
'Twixt good and evil, truth and falsehood, vanish?
What then is resolution? What is firmness?
What is the faith of man, if in one weak,
Unguarded hour, the rules of ·threescore years
Dissolve in air, like woman's fickle favor?

KING.

I looked into his eyes. Oh, pardon me
This weak relapse into mortality.
The world has one less access to your heart;
Your eyes are sunk in night.

GRAND INQUISITOR.

What did this man
Want with you? What new thing could he adduce,
You did not know before? And are you versed
So ill with fanatics and innovators?
Does the reformer's vaunting language sound
So novel to your ears? If the firm edifice
Of your conviction totters to mere words,
Should you not shudder to subscribe the fate

Of many thousand poor, deluded souls
Who mount the flaming pile for nothing worse?

KING.

I sought a human being.   These Domingos——

GRAND INQUISITOR.

How ! human beings !   What are they to you?
Cyphers to count withal — no more !   Alas !
And must I now repeat the elements
Of kingly knowledge to my gray-haired pupil?
An earthly god must learn to bear the want
Of what may be denied him.   When you whine
For sympathy is not the world your equal ?
What rights should you possess above your equals?

KING (*throwing himself into a chair*).

I'm a mere suffering mortal, that I feel;
And you demand from me, a wretched creature,
What the Creator only can perform.

GRAND INQUISITOR.

No, sire ; I am not thus to be deceived.
I see you through.   You would escape from us.
The church's heavy chains pressed hard upon you ;
You would be free, and claim your independence.

[*He pauses.   The* KING *is silent*

We are avenged.   Be thankful to the church,
That checks you with the kindness of a mother.
The erring choice you were allowed to make
Has proved your punishment.   You stand reproved !
Now you may turn to us again.   And know
If I, this day, had not been summoned here,
By Heaven above ! before to-morrow's sun,
You would yourself have stood at my tribunal !

KING.

Forbear this language, priest.   Restrain thyself.
I'll not endure it from thee.   In such tones
No tongue shall speak to me.

GRAND INQUISITOR.

Then why, O king !
Call up the ghost of Samuel?   I've anointed

Two monarchs to the throne of Spain. I hoped
To leave behind a firm-established work.
I see the fruit of all my life is lost.
Don Philip's hands have shattered what I built.
But tell me, sire, wherefore have I been summoned?
What do I hear? I am not minded, king,
To seek such interviews again.

KING.

But one —
One service more — the last — and then in peace
Depart. Let all the past be now forgotten —
Let peace be made between us. We are friends.

GRAND INQUISITOR.
When Philip bends with due humility.

KING (*after a pause*).
My son is meditating treason.

GRAND INQUISITOR,
Well!
And what do you resolve?

KING.
On all, or nothing.

GRAND INQUISITOR.
What mean you by this all?

KING.
He must escape,
Or die.

GRAND INQUISITOR.
Well, sire! decide.

KING.
And can you not
Establish some new creed to justify
The bloody murder of one's only son?

GRAND INQUISITOR.
To appease eternal justice God's own Son
Expired upon the cross.

KING.

           And can you spread
This creed throughout all Europe?

GRAND INQUISITOR.

                  Ay, as far
As the true cross is worshipped.

KING.

                 But I sin —
Sin against nature. Canst thou, by thy power,
Silence her mighty voice.

GRAND INQUISITOR.

               The voice of nature
Avails not over faith.

KING.

             My right to judge
I place within your hands. Can I retrace
The step once taken?

GRAND INQUISITOR.

         Give him to me!

KING.

My only son! For whom then have I labored?

GRAND INQUISITOR.

For the grave rather than for liberty!

KING (*rising up*).

We are agreed. Come with me.

GRAND INQUISITOR.

               Monarch! Whither!

KING.

From his own father's hands to take the victim.
                  [*Leads him away.*

Scene XI.

Queen's Apartment.

CARLOS. *The* QUEEN. *Afterwards the* KING *and attendants.*
CARLOS *in monk's attire, a mask over his face, which he is just
taking off; under his arm a naked sword. It is quite dark.
He approaches a door, which is in the act of opening. The*
QUEEN *comes out in her night-dress with a lighted candle.* CAR-
LOS *falls on one knee before her.*

CARLOS.

Elizabeth!

QUEEN (*regarding him with silent sorrow*).
Do we thus meet again?

CARLOS.

'Tis thus we meet again!   [*A silence.*

QUEEN (*endeavoring to collect herself*).
Carlos, arise!
We must not now unnerve each other thus.
The mighty dead will not be honored now
By fruitless tears. Tears are for petty sorrows!
He gave himself for thee! With his dear life
He purchased thine. And shall this precious blood
Flow for a mere delusion of the brain?
Oh, Carlos, I have pledged myself for thee.
On that assurance.did he flee from hence
More satisfied. Oh, do not falsify
My word.

CARLOS (*with animation*)
To him I'll raise a monument
Nobler than ever honored proudest monarch,
And o'er his dust a paradise shall bloom!

QUEEN.

Thus did I hope to find thee! This was still
The mighty purpose of his death. On me
Devolves the last fulfilment of his plans,
And I will now fulfil my solemn oath.
Yet one more legacy your dying friend
Bequeathed to me. I pledged my word to him,

And wherefore should I now conceal it from you?
To me did he resign his Carlos — I
Defy suspicion, and no longer tremble
Before mankind, but will for once assume
The courage of a friend. My heart shall speak.
He called our passion — virtue! I believe him,
And will my heart no longer ——

CARLOS.

Hold, O queen!
Long was I sunk in a delusive dream.
I loved, but now I am at last awake:
Forgotten be the past. Here are your letters, —
Destroy my own. Fear nothing from my passion,
It is extinct. A brighter flame now burns,
And purifies my being. All my love
Lies buried in the grave. No mortal wish
Finds place within this bosom.
                    [*After a pause, taking her hand.*
                              I have come
To bid farewell to you, and I have learned
There is a higher, greater good, my mother,
Than to call thee mine own. One rapid night
Has winged the tardy progress of my years,
And prematurely ripened me to manhood.
I have no further business in the world,
But to remember him. My harvest now
Is ended.
      [*He approaches the* QUEEN, *who conceals her face.*
      Mother! will you not reply!

QUEEN.

Carlos! regard not these my tears. I cannot
Restrain them. But believe me I admire you.

CARLOS.

Thou wert the only partner of our league:
And by this name thou shalt remain to me
The most beloved object in this world.
No other woman can my friendship share,
More than she yesterday could win my love.

But sacred shall the royal widow be,
Should Providence conduct me to the throne.
   [*The* KING, *accompanied by the* GRAND INQUISITOR,
     appears in the background without being observed.
I hasten to leave Spain, and never more
Shall I behold my father in this world.
No more I love him. Nature is extinct
Within this breast. Be you again his wife —
His son's forever lost to him ! Return
Back to your course of duty — I must speed
To liberate a people long oppressed
From a fell tyrant's hand. Madrid shall hail
Carlos as king, or ne'er behold him more.
And now a long and last farewell —— [*He kisses her.*

QUEEN.

                   Oh, Carlos !
How you exalt me ! but I dare not soar
To such a height of greatness : — yet I may
Contemplate now your noble mind with wonder.

CARLOS.

Am I not firm, Elizabeth ? I hold thee
Thus in my arms and tremble not. The fear
Of instant death had, yesterday, not torn me
From this dear spot.   [*He leaves her.*
         All that is over now,
And I defy my mortal destinies.
I've held thee in these arms and wavered not.
Hark ! Heard you nothing !   [*A clock strikes.*

QUEEN.

            Nothing but the bell
That tolls the moment of our separation.

CARLOS.

Good night, then, mother ! And you shall, from Ghent,
Receive a letter, which will first proclaim
Our secret enterprise aloud. I go
To dare King Philip to an open contest.
Henceforth there shall be naught concealed between us !

You need not shun the aspect of the world.
Be this my last deceit.
   [*About to take up the mask — the* KING *stands between
    them.*

KING.

    It is thy last.
       [*The* QUEEN *falls senseless.*

CARLOS (*hastens to her and supports her in his arms*).
Is the queen dead?   Great heavens!

KING (*coolly and quietly to the* GRAND INQUISITOR).
              Lord Cardinal!
I've done *my* part. Go now, and do your own. [*Exit.*

DEMETRIUS

ACT I.

Scene I.

The Diet at Cracow.

On the rising of the curtain the Polish Diet is discovered, seated in the great senate hall. On a raised platform, elevated by three steps, and surmounted by a canopy, is the imperial throne, the escutcheons of Poland and Lithuania suspended on each side. The King *seated upon the throne; on his right and left hand his ten royal officers standing on the platform. Below the platform the* Bishops, Palatines, *and* Castellans *seated on each side of the stage. Opposite to these stand the Provincial* Deputies, *in a double line, uncovered. All armed. The* Archbishop of Gnesen, *as the primate of the kingdom, is seated next the proscenium; his chaplain behind him, bearing a golden cross.*

Archbishop of Gnesen.

 Thus then hath this tempestuous Diet been
 Conducted safely to a prosperous close;
 And king and commons part as cordial friends.
 The nobles have consented to disarm,
 And straight disband the dangerous Rocoss; *
 Whilst our good king his sacred word has pledged,
 That every just complaint shall have redress.
 And now that all is peace at home, we may
 Look to the things that claim our care abroad.
 Is it the will of the most high Estates
 That Prince Demetrius, who hath advanced
 A claim to Russia's crown, as Ivan's son,
 Should at their bar appear, and in the face
 Of this august assembly prove his right?

---

   * An insurrectionary muster of the nobles.

CASTELLAN OF CRACOW.
　　Honor and justice both demand he should;
　　It were unseemly to refuse his prayer.
BISHOP OF WERMELAND.
　　The documents on which he rests have been
　　Examined, and are found authentic. We
　　May give him audience.
SEVERAL DEPUTIES. 　　　　　　Nay! We must we must!
LEO SAPIEHA. ·
　　To hear is to admit his right.
ODOWALSKY. 　　　　　　　　　　And not
　　To hear is to reject his claims unheard.
ARCHBISHOP OF GNESEN.
　　Is it your will that he have audience?
　　I ask it for the second time — and third.
IMPERIAL CHANCELLOR.
　　Let him stand forth before our throne!
SENATORS. 　　　　　　　　　　　And speak!
DEPUTIES. 　Yes, yes! Let him be heard!
　　[*The Imperial* GRAND MARSHAL *beckons with his baton*
　　　to the doorkeeper, who goes out.
LEO SAPIEHA (*to the* CHANCELLOR).
　　　　　　　　　　　　Write down, my lord,
　　That here I do protest against this step,
　　And all that may ensue therefrom, to mar
　　The peace of Poland's state and Moscow's crown.
　　[*Enters* DEMETRIUS. *Advances some steps towards the*
　　　throne, and makes three bows with his head un-
　　　covered, first to the KING, *next to the* SENATORS,
　　　and then to the DEPUTIES, *who all severally answer*
　　　with an inclination of the head. He then takes up
　　　his position so as to keep within his eye a great
　　　portion of the assemblage, and yet not to turn his
　　　back upon the throne.
ARCHBISHOP OF GNESEN.
　　Prince Dmitri, son of Ivan! if the pomp
　　Of this great Diet scare thee, or a sight
　　So noble and majestic chain thy tongue,
　　Thou may'st — for this the senate have allowed —
　　Choose thee a proxy, wheresoe'er thou list,
　　And do thy mission by another's lips.

DEMETRIUS.

My lord archbishop, I stand here to claim
A kingdom, and the state of royalty.
'Twould ill beseem me should I quake before
A noble people, and its king and senate.
I ne'er have viewed a circle so august,
But the sight swells my heart within my breast
And not appals me. The more worthy ye,
To me ye are more welcome; I can ne'er
Address my claim to nobler auditory.

ARCHBISHOP OF GNESEN.

   .   .   .   The august republic
Is favorably bent.   .   .   .

DEMETRIUS.

Most puissant king! Most worthy and most potent
Bishops and palatines, and my good lords,
The deputies of the august republic!
It gives me pause and wonder to behold
Myself, Czar Ivan's son, now stand before
The Polish people in their Diet here.
Both realms were sundered by a bloody hate,
And, whilst my father lived, no peace might be.
Yet now hath Heaven so ordered these events,
That I, his blood, who with my nurse's milk
Imbibed the ancestral hate, appear before you
A fugitive, compelled to seek my rights
Even here in Poland's heart. Then, ere I speak,
Forget magnanimously all rancors past,
And that the Czar, whose son I own myself,
Rolled war's red billows to your very homes.
I stand before you, sirs, a prince despoiled.
I ask protection. The oppressed may urge
A sacred claim on every noble breast.
And who in all earth's circuit shall be just,
If not a people great and valiant, — one
In plenitude of power so free, it needs
To render 'count but to itself alone,
And may, unchallenged, lend an open ear
And aiding hand to fair humanity.

ARCHBISHOP OF GNESEN.

You do allege you are Czar Ivan's son;

And truly, nor your bearing nor your speech
Gainsays the lofty title that you urge,
But shows us that you are indeed his son.
And you shall find that the republic bears
A generous spirit.   She has never quailed
To Russia in the field !   She loves, alike,
To be a noble foe — a cordial friend.

DEMETRIUS.   Ivan Wasilowitch, the mighty Czar
Of Moscow, took five spouses to his bed,
In the long years that spared him to the throne.
The first, a lady of the heroic line
Of Romanoff, bare him Feodor, who reigned
After his father's death.   One only son,
Dmitri, the last blossom of his strength,
And a mere infant when his father died,
Was born of Marfa, of Nagori's line.
Czar Feodor, a youth, alike effeminate
In mind and body, left the reins of power
To his chief equerry, Boris Godunow,
Who ruled his master with most crafty skill.
Feodor was childless, and his barren bride
Denied all prospect of an heir.   Thus, when
The wily Boiar, by his fawning arts,
Had coiled himself into the people's favor,
His wishes soared as high as to the throne.
Between him and his haughty hopes there stood
A youthful prince, the young Demetrius
Iwanowitsch, who with his mother lived
At Uglitsch, where her widowhood was passed.
Now, when his fatal purpose was matured,
He sent to Uglitsch ruffians, charged to put
The Czarowitsch to death.
One night, when all was hushed, the castle's wing
Where the young prince, apart from all the rest,
With his attendants lay, was found on fire.
The raging flames ingulfed the pile; the prince
Unseen, unheard, was spirited away,
And all the world lamented him as dead.
All Moscow knows these things to be the truth.

ARCHBISHOP OF GNESEN.
Yes, these are facts familiar to us all.

The rumor ran abroad, both far and near,
That Prince Demetrius perished in the flames
When Uglitsch was destroyed. And, as his death
Raised to the throne the Czar who fills it now,
Fame did not hesitate to charge on him
This murder foul and pitiless. But yet,
His death is not the business now in hand !
This prince is living still ! He lives in you !
So runs your plea. Now bring us to the proofs !
Whereby do you attest that you are he ?
What are the signs by which you shall be known?
How 'scaped you those were sent to hunt you
 down
And now, when sixteen years are passed, and you
Well nigh forgot, emerge to light once more ?

DEMETRIUS.

'Tis scarce a year since I have known myself ;
I lived a secret to myself till then,
Surmising naught of my imperial birth.
I was a monk with monks, close pent within
The cloister's precints, when I first began
To waken to a consciousness of self.
My impetuous spirit chafed against the bars,
And the high blood of princes began to course
In strange unbidden moods along my veins.
At length I flung the monkish cowl aside,
And fled to Poland, where the noble Prince
Of Sendomir, the generous, the good,
Took me as guest into his princely house,
And trained me up to noble deeds of arms.

ARCHBISHOP OF GNESEN.

How ? You still ignorant of what you were ?
Yet ran the rumor then on every side,
That Prince Demetrius was still alive.
Czar Boris trembled on his throne, and sent
His sassafs to the frontiers, to keep
Sharp watch on every traveller that stirred.
Had not the tale its origin with you ?
Did you not give the rumor birth yourself ?
Had you not named to any that you were
Demetrius ?

DEMETRIUS.   I relate that which I know.
 If a report went forth I was alive,
 Then had some god been busy with the fame.
 Myself I knew not.   In the prince's house,
 And in the throng of his retainers lost,
 I spent the pleasant springtime of my youth.
                    In silent homage
 My heart was vowed to his most lovely daughter.
 Yet in those days it never dreamed to raise
 Its wildest thoughts to happiness so high.
 My passion gave offence to her bethrothed,
 The Castellan of Lemberg. He with taunts
 Chafed me, and in the blindness of his rage
 Forgot himself so wholly as to strike me.
 Thus savagely provoked, I drew my sword ;
 He, blind with fury, rushed upon the blade,
 And perished there by my unwitting hand.
MEISCHEK.
 Yes, it was even so.
DEMETRIUS.
 Mine was the worst mischance !   A nameless youth
 A Russian and a stranger, I had slain
 A grandee of the empire — in the house
 Of my kind patron done a deed of blood,
 And sent to death his son-in-law and friend.
 My innocence availed not ; not the pity
 Of all his household, nor his kindness — his,
 The noble Palatine's, — could save my life ;
 For it was forfeit to the law, that is,
 Though lenient to the Poles, to strangers stern.
 Judgment was passed on me — that judgment death
 I knelt upon the scaffold, by the block ;
 To the fell headsman's sword I bared my throat,
 And in the act disclosed a cross of gold,
 Studded with precious gems, which had been hung
 About my neck at the baptismal font.
 This sacred pledge of Christian redemption
 I had, as is the custom of my people,
 Worn on my neck concealed, where'er I went,
 From my first hours of infancy ; and now,
 When from sweet life I was compelled to part,

I grasped it as my only stay, and pressed it
With passionate devotion to my lips.
  [*The Poles intimate their sympathy by dumb show.*
The jewel was observed; its sheen and worth
Awakened curiosity and wonder.
They set me free, and questioned me; yet still
I could not call to memory a time
I had not worn the jewel on my person.
Now it so happened that three Boiars who
Had fled from the resentment of their Czar
Were on a visit to my lord at Sambor.
They saw the trinket, — recognized it by
Nine emeralds alternately inlaid
With amethysts, to be the very cross
Which Ivan Westislowsky at the font
Hung on the neck of the Czar's youngest son.
They scrutinized me closer, and were struck
To find me marked with one of nature's freaks,
For my right arm is shorter than my left.
Now, being closely plied with questions, I
Bethought me of a little psalter which
I carried from the cloister when I fled.
Within this book were certain words in Greek
Inscribed there by the Igumen himself.
What they imported was unknown to me,
Being ignorant of the language. Well, the psalter
Was sent for, brought, and the inscription read.
It bore that Brother Wasili Philaret
(Such was my cloister-name), who owned the book,
Was Prince Demetrius, Ivan's youngest son,
By Andrei, an honest Diak, saved
By stealth in that red night of massacre.
Proofs of the fact lay carefully preserved
Within two convents, which were pointed out.
On this the Boiars at my feet fell down,
Won by the force of these resistless proofs,
And hailed me as the offspring of their Czar.
So from the yawning gulfs of black despair
Fate raised me up to fortune's topmost heights.
And now the mists cleared off, and all at once
Memories on memories started into life

In the remotest background of the past.
And like some city's spires that gleam afar
In golden sunshine when naught else is seen,
So in my soul two images grew bright,
The loftiest sun-peaks in the shadowy past.
I saw myself escaping one dark night,
And a red lurid flame light up the gloom
Of midnight darkness as I looked behind me
A memory 'twas of very earliest youth,
For what preceded or came after it
In the long distance utterly was lost.
In solitary brightness there it stood
A ghastly beacon-light on memory's waste.
Yet I remembered how, in later years,
One of my comrades called me, in his wrath
Son of the Czar.   I took it as a jest,
And with a blow avenged it at the time.
All this now flashed like lightning on my soul,
And told with dazzling certainty that I
Was the Czar's son, so long reputed dead.
With this one word the clouds that had perplexed
My strange and troubled life were cleared away.
Nor merely by these signs, for such deceive;
But in my soul, in my proud, throbbing heart
I felt within me coursed the blood of kings;
And sooner will I drain it drop by drop
Than bate one jot my title to the crown.

ARCHBISHOP OF GNESEN.

And shall we trust a scroll which might have found
Its way by merest chance into your hands
Backed by the tale of some poor renegades?
Forgive me, noble youth!   Your tone, I grant,
And bearing, are not those of one who lies;
Still you in this may be yourself deceived.
Well may the heart be pardoned that beguiles
Itself in playing for so high a stake.
What hostage do you tender for your word?

DEMETRIUS.

I tender fifty, who will give their oaths, —
All Piasts to a man, and free-born Poles
Of spotless reputation, — each of whom

Is ready to enforce what I have urged.
There sits the noble Prince of Sendomir,
And at his side the Castellan of Lublin ;
Let them declare if I have spoke the truth.

ARCHBISHOP OF GNESEN.

How seem these things to the august Estates?
To the enforcement of such numerous proofs
Doubt and mistrust, methinks, must needs give
    way.
Long has a creeping rumor filled the world
That Dmitri, Ivan's son, is still alive.
The Czar himself confirms it by his fears.
— Before us stands a youth, in age and mien
Even to the very freak that nature played,
The lost heir's counterpart, and of a soul
Whose noble stamp keeps rank with his high claims.
He left a cloister's precincts, urged by strange,
Mysterious promptings ; and this monk-trained boy
Was straight distinguished for his knightly feats.
He shows a trinket which the Czarowitsch
Once wore, and one that never left his side;
A written witness, too, by pious hands,
Gives us assurance of his princely birth ;
And, stronger still, from his unvarnished speech
And open brow truth makes his best appeal.
Such traits as these deceit doth never don;
It masks its subtle soul in vaunting words,
And in the high-glossed ornaments of speech.
No longer, then, can I withhold' the title
Which he with circumstance and justice claims
And, in the exercise of my old right,
I now, as primate, give him the first voice.

ARCHBISHOP OF LEMBERG.

My voice goes with the primate's.

SEVERAL VOICES.   So does mine.

SEVERAL PALATINES.

And mine !

ODOWALSKY.   And mine.

DEPUTIES.   And all !

SAPIEHA.   My gracious sirs !
Weigh well ere you decide ! Be not so hasty !

It is not meet the council of the realm
Be hurried on to ——

ODOWALSKY.   There is nothing here
For us to weigh ; all has been fully weighed.
The proofs demonstrate incontestably.
This is not Moscow, sirs !   No despot here
Keeps our free souls in manacles.   Here truth
May walk by day or night with brow erect.
I will not think, my lords, in Cracow here,
Here in the very Diet of the Poles,
That Moscow's Czar should have obsequious slaves.

DEMETRIUS.

Oh, take my thanks, ye reverend senators !
That ye have lent your credence to these proofs;
And if I be indeed the man whom I
Protest myself, oh, then, endure not this
Audacious robber should usurp my seat,
Or longer desecrate that sceptre which
To me, as the true Czarowitsch, belongs.
Yes, justice lies with me, — you have the power.
'Tis the most dear concern of every state
And throne, that right should everywhere prevail,
And all men in the world possess their own.
For there, where justice holds uncumbered sway,
There each enjoys his heritage secure,
And over every house and every throne
Law, truth, and order keep their angel watch.
It is the key-stone of the world's wide arch,
The one sustaining and sustained by all,
Which, if it fail, brings all in ruin down.

    (*Answers of* SENATORS *giving assent to* DEMETRIUS.)

DEMETRIUS.

Oh, look on me, renowned Sigismund !
Great king, on thine own bosom turn thine eyes.
And in my destiny behold thine own.
Thou, too, hast known the rude assaults of fate ;
Within a prison camest thou to the world ;
Thy earliest glances fell on dungeon walls.
Thou, too, hadst need of friends to set thee free,
And raise thee from a prison to a throne.
These didst thou find.   That noble kindness thou

Didst reap from them, oh, testify to me.
And you, ye grave and honored councillors,
Most reverend bishops, pillars of the church,
Ye palatines and castellans of fame,
The moment has arrived, by one high deed,
To reconcile two nations long estranged.
Yours be the glorious boast, that Poland's power
Hath given the Muscovites their Czar, and in
The neighbor who oppressed you as a foe
Secure an ever-grateful friend. And you,
The deputies of the august republic,
Saddle your steeds of fire! Leap to your seats!
To you expand high fortune's golden gates;
I will divide the foeman's spoil with you.
Moscow is rich in plunder; measureless
In gold and gems, the treasures of the Czar;
I can give royal guerdons to my friends,
And I will give them, too. When I, as Czar,
Set foot within the Kremlin, then, I swear,
The poorest of you all, that follows me,
Shall robe himself in velvet and in sables;
With costly pearls his housings shall he deck,
And silver be the metal of least worth,
That he shall shoe his horses' hoofs withal.
  [*Great commotion among the* DEPUTIES. KORELA,
     Hetman of the Cossacks, declares himself ready to
     put himself at the head of an army.
ODOWALSKY.

How! shall we leave the Cossack to despoil us
At once of glory and of booty both?
We've made a truce with Tartar and with Turk,
And from the Swedish power have naught to fear.
Our martial spirit has been wasting long
In slothful peace; our swords are red with rust.
Up! and invade the kingdom of the Czar,
And win a grateful and true-hearted friend,
Whilst we augment our country's might and glory.
MANY DEPUTIES.

War! War with Moscow!
OTHERS.   Be it so resolved!
On to the votes at once!

SAPIEHA (*rises*).   Grand marshal, pleáse
    To order silence !   I desire to speak.
A CROWD OF VOICES.
    War ! War with Moscow !
SAPIEHA.   Nay, I will be heard.
    Ho, marshal, do your duty !
            [*Great tumult within and outside the hall.*
GRAND MARSHAL.   'Tis, you see,
    Quite fruitless.
SAPIEHA.   What?   The marshal's self suborned?
    Is this our Diet, then, no longer free ?
    Throw down your staff, and bid this brawling cease ;
    I charge you, on your office, to obey !
  [*The* GRAND MARSHAL *casts his baton into the centre*
        of the hall ; the tumult abates.
    What whirling thoughts, what mad resolves are
      these ?
    Stand we not now at peace with Moscow's Czar ?
    Myself, as your imperial envoy, made
    A treaty to endure for twenty years ;
    I raised this right hand, that you see, alof
    In solemn pledge, within the Kremlin's walls ;
    And fairly hath the Czar maintained his word.
    What is sworn faith ? what compacts, treaties, when
    A solemn Diet tramples on them all ?
DEMETRIUS.
    Prince Leo Sapieha !   You concluded
    A bond of peace, you say, with Moscow's Czar ?
    That did you not ; for I, I am that Czar.
    In me is Moscow's majesty ; I am
    The son of Ivan, and his rightful heir.
    Would the Poles treat with Russia for a peace,
    Then must they treat with me !   Your compact's null,
    As being made with one whose's title's null.
ODOWALSKY.
    What reck we of your treaty ?   So we willed
    When it was made — our wills are changed to-day.
SAPIEHA.
    Is it, then, come to this ?   If none beside
    Will stand for justice, then, at least, will I.
    I'll rend the woof of cunning into shreds,

And lay its falsehoods open to the day.
Most reverend primate! art thou, canst thou be
So simple-souled, or canst thou so dissemble?
Are ye so credulous, my lords? My liege,
Art thou so weak? Ye know not — will not know,
Ye are the puppets of the wily Waywode
Of Sendomir, who reared this spurious Czar,
Whose measureless ambition, while we speak,
Clutches in thought the spoils of Moscow's wealth.
Is't left for me to tell you that even now
The league is made and sworn betwixt the twain,—
The pledge the Waywode's youngest daughter's
 hand?
And shall our great republic blindly rush
Into the perils of an unjust war,
To aggrandize the Waywode, and to crown
His daughter as the empress of the Czar?
There's not a man he has not bribed and bought.
He means to rule the Diet, well I know ;
I see his faction rampant in this hall,
And, as 'twere not enough that he controlled
The Seym Walmy by a majority,
He's girt the Diet with three thousand horse,
And all Cracow is swarming like a hive
With his sworn feudal vassals. Even now
They throng the halls and chambers where we sit,
To hold our liberty of speech in awe.
Yet stirs no fear in my undaunted heart;
And while the blood keeps current in my veins,
I will maintain the freedom of my voice!
Let those who think like men come stand by me!
Whilst I have life shall no resolve be passed
That is at war with justice and with reason.
'Twas I that ratified the peace with Moscow,
And I will hazard life to see it kept.
ODOWALSKY.
     Give him no further hearing! Take the votes!
    [*The* BISHOP OF CRACOW *and* WILNA *rise, and descend
       each to his own side, to collect the votes.*
MANY.
     War, war with Moscow!

ARCHBISHOP OF GNESEN (*to* SAPIEHA).

                    Nöble sir, give way!
You see the mass are hostile to your views;
Then do not force a profitless division!

IMPERIAL HIGH CHANCELLOR (*descends from the throne to* SAPIEHA).

The king entreats you will not press the point,
Sir Waywode, to division in the Diet.

DOORKEEPER (*aside to* ODOWALSKY).

Keep a bold front, and fearless — summon those
That wait without. All Cracow stands by you.

IMPERIAL GRAND MARSHAL (*to* SAPIEHA).

Such excellent decrees have passed before;
Oh, cease, and for their sake, so fraught with good,
Unite your voice with the majority!

BISHOP OF CRACOW (*has collected the votes on his side*).

On this right bench are all unanimous.

SAPIEHA.

And let them to a man! Yet I say no!
I urge my veto — I break up the Diet.
Stay further progress! Null and void are all
The resolutions passed ——

  [*General commotion; the* KING *descends from the throne, the barriers are broken down, and there arises a tumultuous uproar.* DEPUTIES *draw their swords, and threaten* SAPIEHA *with them. The* BISHOPS *interpose, and protect him with their stoles.*

                    Majority?
What is it? The majority is madness;
Reason has still ranked only with the few.
What cares he for the general weal that's poor?
Has the lean beggar choice, or liberty?
To the great lords of earth, that hold the purse,
He must for bread and raiment sell his voice.
'Twere meet that voices should be weighed, not
    counted.
Sooner or later must the state be wrecked,
Where numbers sway and ignorance decides.

ODOWALSKY.

Hark to the traitor! ——

DEPUTIES.   Hew him into shreds!
    Down with him!
ARCHBISHOP OF GNESEN (*snatches the crucifix out of his
        chaplain's hand and interposes.*
                    Peace, peace!
    Shall native blood be in the Diet shed?
    Prince Sapieha! be advised!

                        [*To the* BISHOPS.
                    Bring him away,
    And interpose your bosoms as his shield!
    ˆThrough this side door remove him quietly,
    Or the wild mob will tear him limb from limb!
    [SAPIEHA, *still casting looks of defiance, is forced
        away by the* BISHOPS, *whilst the* ARCHBISHOPS OF
        GNESEN *and* LEMBERG *keep the* DEPUTIES *at bay.
        Amidst violent tumult and clashing of arms, the
        hall is emptied of all but* DEMETRIUS, MEISCHEK,
        ODOWALSKY, *and the Hetman of the Cossacks.*
ODOWALSKY.
    That point miscarried, —
    Yet shall you not lack aid because of this:
    If the republic holds the peace with Moscow,
    At our own charges we shall push your claims.
KORELA.
    Who ever could have dreamed, that he alone
    Would hold his ground against the assembled Diet?
MEISCHEK.
    The king! the king!
    [*Enter* KING SIGISMUND, *attended by the* LORD HIGH
        CHANCELLOR, *the* GRAND MARSHAL, *and several*
        BISHOPS.
KING.   Let me embrace you, prince!
    At length the high republic does you justice;
    My heart has done so long, and many a day.
    Your fate doth move me deeply, as, indeed,
    What monarch's heart but must be moved by it?
DEMETRIUS.
    The past, with all its sorrows, is forgot;
    Here on your breast I feel new life begin.
KING.
    I love not many words; yet what a king

May offer, who has vassels richer far
Than his poor self, that do I offer you.
You have been witness of an untoward scene,
But deem not ill of Poland's realm because
A tempest jars the vessel of the state.

MEISCHEK.

When winds are wild the steersman backs his helm,
And makes for port with all the speed he may.

KING.

The Diet is dissolved.   Although I wished,
I could not break the treaty with the Czar.
But you have powerful friends; and if the Pole,
At his own risk, take arms on your behalf,
Or if the Cossack choose to venture war,
They are free men, I cannot say them nay.

MEISCHEK.

The whole Rocoss is under arms already.
Please it but you, my liege, the angry stream
That raved against your sovereignty may turn
Its wrath on Moscow, leaving you unscathed.

KING.

The best of weapons Russia's self will give thee;
Thy surest buckler is the people's heart.
By Russia only Russia will be vanished.
Even as the Diet heard thee speak to-day,
Speak thou at Moscow to thy subjects, prince.
So chain their hearts, and thou wilt be their king.
In Sweden I by right of birth ascended
The throne of my inheritance in peace;
Yet did I lose the kingdom of my sires
Because my people's hearts were not with me.

Enter MARINA.

MEISCHEK.

My gracious liege, here, kneeling at your feet,
Behold Marina, youngest of my daughters;
The prince of Moscow offers her his heart.
Thou art the stay and pillar of our house,
And only from thy royal hand 'tis meet
That she receive her spouse and sovereign.
                              [MARINA *kneels to the* KING

KING.

Well, if you wish it, cousin, gladly I
Will do the father's office to the Czar.
                    [*To* DEMETRIUS, *giving him* MARINA's *hand.*
Thus do I bring you, in this lovely pledge,
High fortune's blooming goddess; and may these
Old eyes be spared to see this gracious pair
Sit in imperial state on Moscow's throne.

MARINA.

My liege, I humbly thank your grace, and shall
Esteem me still your slave where'er I be.

KING.

Rise up, Czaritza! This is not a place
For you, the plighted bridemaid of the Czar;
For you, the daughter of my foremost Waywode.
You are the youngest of your sisters; yet
Your spirit wings a high and glorious course,
And nobly grasps the top of sovereignty.

DEMETRIUS.

Be thou, great monarch, witness of my oath,
As, prince to prince, I pledge it here to you!
This noble lady's hand I do accept
As fortune's dearest pledge, and swear that, soon
As on my father's throne I take my seat,
I'll lead her home in triumph as my bride,
With all the state that fits a mighty queen.
And, for a dowry, to my bride I give
The principalities Pleskow and Great Neugart,
With all towns, hamlets, and in-dwellers there,
With all the rights and powers of sovereignty,
In absolute possession evermore;
And this, my gift, will I as Czar confirm
In my free city, Moscow. Furthermore,
As compensation to her noble sire
For present charges, I engage to pay
A million ducats, Polish currency.
So help me God, and all his saints, as I
Have truly sworn this oath, and shall fulfil it.

KING.

You will do so; you never will forget
For what you are the noble Waywode's debtor;

Who, for your wishes, perils his sure wealth,
And, for your hopes, a child his heart adores,
A friend so rare is to be rarely prized!
Then when your hopes are crowned forget not ever
The steps by which you mounted to the throne,
Nor with your garments let your heart be changed!
Think, that in Poland first you knew yourself, —
That this land gave you birth a second time.

DEMETRIUS.

I have been nurtured in adversity;
And learned to reverence the beauteous bond
Which links mankind with sympathies of love.

KING.

But now you enter on a realm where all —
Use, custom, morals — are untried and strange
In Poland here reigns freedom absolute;
The king himself, although in pomp supreme,
Must ofttime be the serf of his noblesse;
But there the father's sacred power prevails,
And in the subject finds a passive slave.

DEMETRIUS.

That glorious freedom which surrounds me here
I will transplant into my native land,
And turn these bond-serfs into glad-souled men;
Not o'er the souls of slaves will I bear rule.

KING.

Do naught in haste; but by the time be led!
Prince, ere we part, three lessons take from me,
And truly follow them when thou art king.
It is a king that gives them, old and tried,
And they may prove of profit to thy youth.

DEMETRIUS.

Oh, share thy wisdom with me! Thou hast won
The reverence of a free and mighty people;
What must I do to earn so fair a prize?

KING.   You come from a strange land,
Borne on the weapons of a foreign foe;
This first felt wrong thou hast to wash away.
Then bear thee like a genuine son of Moscow,
With reverence due to all her usages.
Keep promise with the Poles, and value them,

For thou hast need of friends on thy new throne:
The arm that placed thee there can hurl thee down.
Esteem them honorably, yet ape them not;
Strange customs thrive not in a foreign soil.
And, whatsoe'er thou dost, revere thy mother —
You'll find a mother ——

DEMETRIUS.   Oh, my liege!

KING.   High claim
Hath she upon thy filial reverence.
Do her all honor. 'Twixt thy subjects and
Thyself she stands, a sacred, precious link.
No human law o'errides the imperial power;
Nothing but nature may command its awe;
Nor can thy people own a surer pledge,
That thou art gentle, than thy filial love.
I say no more. Much yet is to be done,
Ere thou mak'st booty of the golden fleece.
Expect no easy victory!
Czar Boris rules with strong and skilful hand;
You take the field against no common man.
He that by merit hath achieved the throne,
Is not puffed from his seat by popular breath;
His deeds do serve to him for ancestors.
To your good fortune I commend you now;
Already twice, as by a miracle,
Hath it redeemed you from the grasp of death;
'Twill put the finish on its work, and crown you.

    [*Exeunt omnes but* MARINA *and* ODOWALSKY.

ODOWALSKY.
Say, lady, how have I fulfilled my charge?
Truly and well, and wilt thou laud my zeal?

MARINA.
'Tis, Odowalsky, well we are alone;
Matters of weight have we to canvass which
'Tis meet the prince know nothing of. May he
Pursue the voice divine that goads him on!
If in himself he have belief, the world
Will catch the flame, and give him credence too.
He must be kept in that vague, shadowing mist,
Which is a fruitful mother of great deeds,
While we see clear, and act in certainty.

He lends the name — the inspiration; we
Must bear the brain, the shaping thought, for him;
And when, by art and craft, we have insured
The needful levies, let him still dream on,
And think they dropped, to aid him, from the clouds.

ODOWALSKY.

Give thy commands : I live but for thy service.
Think'st thou this Moscovite or his affairs
Concern my thoughts ? 'Tis thou, thou and thy glory
For which I will adventure life and all.
For me no fortune blossoms; friendless, landless,
I dare not let my hopes aspire to thee.
Thy grace I may not win, but I'll deserve it.
To make thee great be my one only aim ;
Then, though another should possess thee, still
Thou wilt be mine — being what I have made thee.

MARINA.

Therefore my whole heart do I pledge to thee;
To thee I trust the acting of my thoughts.
The king doth mean us false. I read him through.
'Twas a concerted farce with Sapieha,
A juggle, all ! 'Twould please him well, belike,
To see my father's power, which he dreads deeply,
Enfeebled in this enterprise — the league
Of the noblesse, which shook his heart with fear,
Drawn off in this campaign on foreign bounds,
While he himself sits neutral in the fray.
He thinks to share our fortune, if we win ;
And if we lose, he hopes with greater ease
To fix on us the bondage of his yoke.
We stand alone. This die is cast. If he
Cares for himself, we shall be selfish too.
You lead the troops to Kioff. There let them swear
Allegiance to the prince, and unto me ; —
Mark you, to me ! 'Tis needful for our ends.
I want your eye, and not your arm alone.

ODOWALSKY.

Command me — speak —

MARINA.   You lead the Czarowitsch.
Keep your eye on him ; stir not from his side,
Render me 'count of every step he makes.

ODOWALSKY.

Rely on me, he'll never cast us off.

MARINA.

No man is grateful. Once his throne is sure,
He'll not be slow to cast our bonds aside.
The Russian hates the Pole — must hate him ever;
No bond of amity can link their hearts.

Enter OPALINSKY, BIELSKY, *and several Polish noblemen.*

OPALINSKY.

Fair patron, get us gold, and we march with you,
This lengthened Diet has consumed our all.
Let us have gold, we'll make thee Russia's queen.

MARINA.

The Bishop of Kaminieck and Culm
Lends money on the pawn of land and serfs.
Sell, barter, pledge the hamlets of your boors,
Turn all to silver, horses, means of war!
War is the best of chapmen. He transmutes
Iron into gold. Whate'er you now may lose
You'll find in Moscow twenty-fold again.

BIELSKY.

Two hundred more wait in the tavern yonder;
If you will show yourself, and drain a cup
With them, they're yours, all yours — I know them
    well.

MARINA.

Expect me! You shall introduce me to them.

OPALINSKY.

'Tis plain that you were born to be a queen.

MARINA.

I was, and therefore I must be a queen.

BIELSKY.

Ay, mount the snow-white steed, thine armor on,
And so, a second Vanda, lead thy troops,
Inspired by thee, to certain victory.

MARINA. My spirit leads you. War is not for women.
The rendezvous is in Kioff. Thither my father
Will lead a levy of three thousand horse.
My sister's husband gives two thousand more,

And the Don sends a Cossack host in aid.
Do you all swear you will be true to me?

ALL.   All, all — we swear! (*draw their swords.*)
Vivat Marina, Russiæ Regina!

[MARINA *tears her veil in pieces, and divides it among
them.   Exeunt omnes but* MARINA.

Enter MEISCHEK.

MARINA.
Wherefore so sad, when fortune smiles on us,
When every step thrives to our utmost wish,
And all around are arming in our cause?

MEISCHEK.
'Tis even because of this, my child!   All, all
Is staked upon the cast.   Thy father's means
Are in these warlike preparations swamped.
I have much cause to ponder seriously;
Fortune is false, uncertain the result.
Mad, venturous girl, what hast thou brought me to?
What a weak father have I been, that I
Did not withstand thy importunities!
I am the richest Waywode of the empire,
The next in honor to the king.   Had we
But been content to be so, and enjoyed
Our stately fortunes with a tranquil soul!
Thy hopes soared higher — not for thee sufficed
The moderate station which thy sisters won.
Thou wouldst attain the loftiest mark that can
By mortals be achieved, and wear a crown.
I, thy fond, foolish father, longed to heap
On thee, my darling one, all glorious gains,
So by thy prayers I let myself be fooled,
And peril my sure fortunes on a chance.

MARINA.
How?   My dear father, dost thou rue thy goodness?
Who with the meaner prize can live content,
When o'er his head the noblest courts his grasp?

MEISCHEK.
Thy sisters wear no crowns, yet they are happy.

MARINA.
What happiness is that to leave the home

Of the Waywode, my father, for the house
Of some count palatine, a grateful bride?
What do I gain of new from such a change?
And can I joy in looking to the morrow
When it brings naught but what was stale to-day?
Oh, tasteless round of petty, worn pursuits!
Oh, wearisome monotony of life!
Are they a guerdon for high hopes, high aims?
Or love or greatness I must have: all else
Are unto me alike indifferent.
Smooth off the trouble from thy brow, dear father!
Let's trust the stream that bears us on its breast,
Think not upon the sacrifice thou makest,
Think on the prize, the goal that's to be won —
When thou shalt see thy daughter robed in state,
In regal state, aloft on Moscow's throne,
And thy son's sons the rulers of the world!

MEISCHEK.

I think of naught, see naught, but thee, my child,
Girt with the splendors of the imperial crown.
Thou'rt bent to have it; I cannot gainsay thee.

MARINA.

Yet one request, my dearest, best of fathers,
I pray you grant me!

MEISCHEK.   Name thy wish, my child.

MARINA.

Shall I remain shut up at Sambor with
The fires of boundless longing in my breast?
Beyond the Dnieper will my die be cast,
While boundless space divides me from the spot;
Can I endure it? Oh, the impatient spirit
Will lie upon the rack of expectation
And measure out this monstrous length of space
With groans and anxious throbbings of the heart.

MEISCHEK.

What dost thou wish? What is it thou wouldst
    have?

MARINA.

Let me abide the issue in Kioff!
There I can gather tidings at their source.
There on the frontier of both kingdoms ——

MEISCHEK.
    Thy spirit's over-bold.   Restrain it, child!
MARINA.
    Yes, thou dost yield, — thou'lt take me with thee,
        then?
MEISCHEK.
    Thou rulest me.   Must I not do thy will?
MARINA.
    My own dear father, when I am Moscow's queen
    Kioff, you know, must be our boundary.
    Kioff must then be mine, and thou shalt rule it.
MEISCHEK.
    Thou dreamest, girl!   Already the great Moscow
    Is for thy soul too narrow; thou, to grasp
    Domains, wilt strip them from thy native land.
MARINA.
    Kioff belonged not to our native land;
    There the Varegers ruled in days of yore.
    I have the ancient chronicles by heart;
    'Twas from the Russian empire wrenched by force.
    I will restore it to its former crown.
MEISCHEK.
    Hush, hush!   The Waywode must not hear such
        talk.   [*Trumpet without.*
    They're breaking up.

ACT II.

SCENE I.

*A Greek convent in a bleak district near the sea Belozero. A train
    of nuns, in black robes and veils, passes over the back of the
    stage. MARFA, in a white veil, stands apart from the others,
    leaning on a tombstone. OLGA steps out from the train, remains
    gazing at her for a time, and then advances to her.*

OLGA.
    And does thy heart not urge thee forth with us
    To taste reviving nature's opening sweets?
    The glad sun comes, the long, long night retires,
    The ice melts in the streams, and soon the sledge
    Will to the boat give place and summer swallow.

The world awakes once more, and the new joy
Woos all to leave their narrow cloister cells
For the bright air and freshening breath of spring.
And wilt thou only, sunk in lasting grief,
Refuse to share the general exultation?

MARFA.

On with the rest, and leave me to myself!
Let those rejoice who still have power to hope.
The time that puts fresh youth in all the world
Brings naught to me; to me the past is all,
My hopes, my joys are with the things that were.

OLGA.

Dost thou still mourn thy son — still, still lament
The sovereignty which thou has lost? Does time,
Which pours a balm on every wounded heart,
Lose all its potency with thee alone?
Thou wert the empress of this mighty realm,
The mother of a blooming son. He was
Snatched from thee by a dreadful destiny;
Into this dreary convent wert thou thrust,
Here on the verge of habitable earth.
Full sixteen times since that disastrous day
The face of nature hath renewed its youth;
Still have I seen no change come over thine,
That looked a grave amid a blooming world.
Thou'rt like some moonless image, carved in stone
By sculptor's chisel, that doth ever keep
The selfsame fixed unalterable mien.

MARFA.

Yes, time, fell time, hath signed and set me up
As a memorial of my dreadful fate.
I will not be at peace, will not forget.
That soul must be of poor and shallow stamp
Which takes a cure from time — a recompense
For what can never be compensated!
Nothing shall buy my sorrow from me. No,
As heaven's vault still goes with the wanderer,
Girds and environs him with boundless grasp,
Turn where he will, by sea or land, so goes
My anguish with me, wheresoe'er I turn;
It hems me round, like an unbounded sea;
My ceaseless tears have failed to drain its depths.

OLGA. Oh, see! what news can yonder boy have brought
  The sisters round him throng so eagerly?
  He comes from distant shores, where homes abound
  And brings us tidings from the land of men.
  The sea is clear, the highways free once more.
  Art thou not curious to learn his news?
  Though to the world we are as good as dead,
  Yet of its changes willingly we hear,
  And, safe upon the shore, with wonder mark
  The roar and ferment of the trampling waves.
    [NUNS *come down the stage with a* FISHER BOY
XENIA — HELENA.
  Speak, speak, and tell us all the news you bring.
ALEXIA.
  Relate what's passing in the world beyond.
FISHER BOY.
  Good, pious ladies, give me time to speak!
XENIA.
  Is't war — or peace?
ALEXIA.   Who's now upon the throne?
FISHER BOY.
  A ship is to Archangel just come in
  From the north pole, where everything is ice.
OLGA.
  How came a vessel into that wild sea?
FISHER BOY.
  It is an English merchantman, and it
  Has found a new way out to get to us.
ALEXIA.
  What will not man adventure for his gain?
XENIA.
  And so the world is nowhere to be barred!
FISHER BOY.
  But that's the very smallest of the news.
  'Tis something very different moves the world.
ALEXIA.
  Oh, speak and tell us!
OLGA.   Say, what has occurred?
FISHER BOY.
  We live to hear strange marvels nowadays:
  The dead rise up, and come to life again.

OLGA.

 Explain yourself.

FISHER BOY.   Prince Dmitri, Ivan's son,

 Whom we have mourned for dead these sixteen years,

 Is now alive, and has appeared in Poland.

OLGA.

 The prince alive?

MARFA (*starting*).   My son!

OLGA.   Compose thyself!

 Calm down thy heart till we have learned the whole.

ALEXIA.

 How can this possibly be so, when he

 Was killed, and perished in the flames at Uglitsch?

FISHER BOY.

 He managed somehow to escape the fire,

 And found protection in a monastery.

 There he grew up in secrecy, until

 His time was come to publish who he was.

OLGA (*to* MARFA).

 You tremble, princess! You grow pale!

MARFA.   I know

 That it must be delusion, yet so little

 Is my heart steeled 'gainst fear and hope e'en now,

 That in my breast it flutters like a bird.

OLGA.

 Why should it be delusion? Mark his words!

 How could this rumor spread without good cause?

FISHER BOY.

 Without good cause? The Lithuanians

 And Poles are all in arms upon his side.

 The Czar himself quakes in his capital.

  [MARFA *is compelled by her emotion to lean upon*

   OLGA *and* ALEXIA.

XENIA.

 Speak on, speak, tell us everything you know.

ALEXIA.

 And tell us, too, of whom you stole the news

FISHER BOY.

 I stole the news? A letter has gone forth

 To every town and province from the Czar.

 This letter the Posadmik of our town

Read to us all, in open market-place.
It bore, that busy schemers were abroad,
And that we should not lend their tales belief.
But this made us believe them; for, had they
Been false, the Czar would have despised the lie.

MARFA.

Is this the calm I thought I had achieved?
And clings my heart so close to temporal things,
That a mere word can shake my inward soul?
For sixteen years have I bewailed my son,
And yet at once believe that still he lives.

OLGA.

Sixteen long years thou'st mourned for him as dead,
And yet his ashes thou hast never seen!
Naught countervails the truth of the report.
Nay, does not Providence watch o'er the fate
Of kings and monarchies? Then welcome hope!
More things befall than thou canst comprehend.
Who can set limits to the Almighty's power?

MARFA.

Shall I turn back to look again on life,
To which long since I spoke a sad farewell?
It was not with the dead my hopes abode.
Oh, say no more of this. Let not my heart
Hang on this phantom hope! Let me not lose
My darling son a second time. Alas!
My peace of mind is gone, — my dream of peace
I cannot trust these tidings, — yet, alas,
I can no longer dash them from my soul!
Woe's me, I never lost my son till now.
Oh, now I can no longer tell if I
Shall seek him 'mongst the living or the dead,
Tossed on the rock of never-ending doubt.
                    [*A bell sounds,* — *the sister* PORTERESS *enters.*

OLGA.

Why has the bell been sounded, sister, say?

PORTERESS.

The lord archbishop waits without; he brings
A message from the Czar, and craves an audience.

OLGA. Does the archbishop stand within our gates?
What strange occurrence can have brought him here?

XENIA.

Come all, and give him greeting as befits.
[*They advance towards the gate as the* ARCHBISHOP
*enters ; they all kneel before him, and he makes
the sign of the Greek cross over them.*

IOB. The kiss of peace I bring you in the name
Of Father, Son, and of the Holy Ghost,
Proceeding from the Father !

OLGA. Sir, we kiss
In humblest reverence thy paternal hand !
Command thy daughters !

IOB. My mission is addressed to Sister Marfa.

OLGA.

See, here she stands, and waits to know thy will.
[*All the* NUNS *withdraw.*

IOB. It is the mighty prince who sends me here ;
Upon his distant throne he thinks of thee ;
For as the sun, with his great eye of flame,
Sheds light and plenty all abroad the world,
So sweeps the sovereign's eye on every side ;
Even to the farthest limits of his realm
His care is wakeful and his glance is keen.

MARFA.

How far his arm can strike I know too well.

IOB. He knows the lofty spirit fills thy soul,
And therefore feels indignantly the wrong
A bold-faced villain dares to offer thee.
Learn, then, in Poland, an audacious churl,
A renegade, who broke his monkish vows,
Laid down his habit, and renounced his God,
Doth use the name and title of thy son,
Whom death snatched from thee in his infancy.
The shameless varlet boasts him of thy blood,
And doth affect to be Czar Ivan's son ;
A Waywode breaks the peace ; from Poland leads
This spurious monarch, whom himself created,
Across our frontiers, with an armed power :
So he beguiles the Russians' faithful hearts,
And lures them on to treason and revolt.
The Czar,
With pure, paternal feeling, sends me to thee.

Thou hold'st the manes of thy son in honor;
Nor wilt permit a bold adventurer
To steal his name and title from the tomb,
And with audacious hand usurp his rights.
Thou wilt proclaim aloud to all the world
That thou dost own him for no son of thine.
Thou wilt not nurse a bastard's alien blood
Upon thy heart, that beats so nobly; never!
Thou wilt — and this the Czar expects from thee —
Give the vile counterfeit the lie, with all
The righteous indignation it deserves.

MARFA (*who has during the last speech subdued the most
        violent emotion*).
What do I hear, archbishop? Can it be?
Oh, tell me, by what signs and marks of proof
This bold-faced trickster doth uphold himself
As Ivan's son, whom we bewailed as dead?

IOB. By some faint, shadowy likeness to the Czar,
By documents which chance threw in his way,
And by a precious trinket, which he shows,
He cheats the credulous and wondering mob.

MARFA.
What is the trinket? Oh, pray, tell me what?

IOB. A golden cross, gemmed with nine emeralds,
Which Ivan Westislowsky, so he says,
Hung round his neck at the baptismal font.

MARFA.
What do you say? He shows this trinket, this?
                        [*With forced composure.*
And how does he allege he came by it?

IOB. A faithful servant and Diak, he says,
Preserved him from the assassins and the flames,
And bore him to Smolenskow privily.

MARFA.
But where was he brought up? Where, gives he forth,
Was he concealed and fostered until now?

IOB. In Tschudow's monastery he was reared,
Unknowing who he was; from thence he fled
To Lithuania and Poland, where
He served the Prince of Sendomir, until
An accident revealed his origin.

MARFA.

> With such a tale as this can he find friends
> To peril life and fortune in his cause?

IOB. Oh, madam, false, false-hearted is the Pole,
> And enviously he eyes our country's wealth.
> He welcomes every pretext that may serve
> To light the flames of war within our bounds!

MARFA.

> And were there credulous spirits, even in Moscow,
> Could by this juggle be so lightly stirred?

IOB. Oh, fickle, princess, is the people's heart!
> They dote on alteration, and expect
> To reap advantage from a change of rulers.
> The bold assurance of the falsehood charms;
> The marvellous finds favor and belief.
> Therefore the Czar is anxious thou shouldst quell
> This mad delusion, as thou only canst.
> A word from thee annihilates the traitor
> That falsely claims the title of thy son.
> It joys me thus to see thee moved.   I see
> The audacious juggle rouses all thy pride,
> And, with a noble anger paints thy cheek.

MARFA.

> And where, where, tell me, does he tarry now,
> Who dares usurp the title of my son?

IOB. E'en now he's moving on to Tscherinsko;
> His camp at Kioff has broke up, 'tis rumored;
> And with a force of mounted Polish troops
> And Don Cossacks, he comes to push his claims.

MARFA.

> Oh, God Almighty, thanks, thanks, thanks, that thou
> Hast sent me rescue and revenge at last!

IOB. How, Marfa, how am I to construe this?

MARFA.

> Oh, heavenly powers, conduct him safely here!
> Hover, oh all ye angels, round his banners!

IOB. Can it be so?   The traitor, canst thou trust ——

MARFA.

> He is my son.   Yes! by these signs alone
> I recognize him.   By thy Czar's alarm
> I recognize him.   Yes! He lives! He comes!

Down, tyrant, from thy throne, and shake with fear
There still doth live a shoot from Rurik's stem;
The genuine Czar — the rightful heir draws nigh,
He comes to claim a reckoning for his own.

Iob. Dost thou bethink thee what thou say'st? 'Tis mad
    ness!

MARFA.

At length — at length has dawned the day of ven
    geance, —
Of restoration.   Innocence is dragged
To light by heaven from the grave's midnight gloom
The haughty Godunow, my deadly foe,
Must crouch and sue for mercy at my feet;
Oh, now my burning wishes are fulfilled!

Iob. Can hate and rancorous malice blind you so?

MARFA. Can terror blind your monarch so, that he
Should hope deliverance from me — from me —
Whom he hath done immeasurable wrong?
I shall, forsooth, deny the son whom heaven
Restores me by a miracle from the grave,
And to please him, the butcher of my house,
Who piled upon me woes unspeakable?
Yes, thrust from me the succor God has sent
In the sad evening of my heavy anguish?
No, thou escap'st me not.   No, thou shalt hear me
I have thee fast, I will not let thee free.
Oh, I can ease my bosom's load at last!
At last launch forth against mine enemy
The long-pent anger of my inmost soul!
        Who was it, who,
That shut me up within this living tomb,
In all the strength and freshness of my youth,
With all its feelings glowing in my breast?
Who from my bosom rent my darling son,
And chartered ruffian hands to take his life?
Oh, words can never tell what I have suffered,
When, with a yearning that would not be still,
I watched throughout the long, long starry nights,
And noted with my tears the hours elapse!
The day of succor comes, and of revenge;
I see the mighty glorying in his might,

Iob. You think the Czar will dread you—you mistake.
Marfa.
    He's in my power—one little word from me,
    One only, sets the seal upon his fate!
    It was for this thy master sent thee here!
    The eyes of Russia and of Poland now
    Are closely bent upon me. If I own
    The Czarowitsch as Ivan's son and mine,
    Then all will do him homage; his the throne.
    If I disown him, then he is undone;
    For who will credit that his rightful mother,
    A mother wronged, so foully wronged as I,
    Could from her heart repulse its darling child,
    To league with the despoilers of her house?
    I need but speak one word and all the world
    Deserts him as a traitor. Is't not so?
    This word you wish from me. That mighty service,
    Confess, I can perform for Godunow!
Iob. Thou wouldst perform it for thy country, and
    Avert the dread calamities of war,
    Shouldst thou do homage to the truth. Thyself,
    Ay, thou hast ne'er a doubt thy son is dead;
    And couldst thou testify against thy conscience?
Marfa.
    These sixteen years I've mourned his death; but yet
    I ne'er have seen his ashes. I believed
    His death, there trusting to the general voice
    And my sad heart — I now believe he lives,
    Trusting the general voice and my strong hope.
    'Twere impious, with audacious doubts, to seek
    To set a bound to the Almighty's will;
    And even were he not my heart's dear son,
    Yet should he be the son of my revenge.
    In my child's room I take him to my breast,
    Whom heaven has sent me to avenge my wrongs.
Iob. Unhappy one, dost thou defy the strong?
    From his far-reaching arm thou art not safe
    Even in the convent's distant solitude.
Marfa.
    Kill me he may, and stifle in the grave,
    Or dungeon's gloom, my woman's voice, that it

Shall not reverberate throughout the world.
This he may do; but force me to speak aught
Against my will, that can he not; though backed
By all thy craft — no, he has missed his aim!

IOB. Is this thy final purpose. Ponder well!
Hast thou no gentler message for the Czar?

MARFA.
Tell him to hope for heaven, if so he dare,
And for his people's love, if so he can.

IOB. Enough! thou art bent on thy destruction.
Thou lean'st upon a reed, will break beneath thee;
One common ruin will o'erwhelm ye both.   [*Exit*

MARFA.
It is my son, I cannot doubt 'tis he.
Even the wild hordes of the uncultured wastes
Take arms upon his side; the haughty Pole,
The palatine, doth stake his noble daughter
On the pure gold of his most righteous cause,
And I alone reject him — I, his mother?
I, only I, shook not beneath the storm
Of joy that lifts all hearts with dizzying whirl,
And scatters turmoil widely o'er the earth.
He is my son — I must, will trust in him,
And grasp with living confidence the hand
Which heaven hath sent for my deliverance.
'Tis he, he comes with his embattled hosts,
To set me free, and to avenge my shame!
Hark to his drums, his martial trumpets' clang!
Ye nations come — come from the east and south.
Forth from your steppes, your immemorial woods!
Of every tongue, of every raiment come!
Bridle the steed, the reindeer, and the camel!
Sweep hither, countless as the ocean waves,
And throng around the banners of your king!
Oh, wherefore am I mewed and fettered here,
A prisoned soul with longings infinite!
Thou deathless sun, that circlest earth's huge ball,
Be thou the messenger of my desires!
Thou all-pervading, chainless breeze that sweep'st
With lightning speed to earth's remotest bound,
Oh, bear to him the yearnings of my heart.

My prayers are all I have to give; but these
I pour all glowing from my inmost soul,
And send them up to heaven on wings of flame,
Like armed hosts, I send them forth to hail him.

Scene II.

*A height crowned with trees. A wide and smiling landscape occu-
pies the background, which is traversed by a beautiful river,
and enlivened by the budding green of spring. At various
points the towers of several towns are visible. Drums and
martial music without. Enter* Odowalsky, *and other officers,
and immediately afterwards* Demetrius.

Odowalsky.

Go, lead the army downward by the wood,
Whilst we look round us here upon the height.
                    [*Exeunt some of the officers.*

Enter Demetrius.

Demetrius (*starting back*).
Ha! what a prospect!
Odowalsky.   Sire, thou see'st thy kingdom
Spread out before thee. That is Russian land.
Razin.
Why, e'en this pillar here bears Moscow's arms;
Here terminates the empire of the Poles.
Demetrius.
Is that the Dnieper, rolls its quiet stream
Along these meadows?
Odowalsky.
That, sire, is the Desna;
See, yonder rise the towers of Tschernizow!
Razin.
Yon gleam you see upon the far horizon
Is from the roofs of Sewerisch Novogrod.
Demetrius.
What a rich prospect! What fair meadow lands!
Odowalsky.
The spring has decked them with her trim array;
A teeming harvest clothes the fruitful soil.
Demetrius.
The view is lost in limitless expanse.

Razin.

Yet is this but a small beginning, sire,
Of Russia's mighty empire. For it spreads
Towards the east to confines unexplored,
And on the north has ne'er a boundary,
Save the productive energy of earth.
Behold, our Czar is quite absorbed in thought.

Demetrius.

On these fair meads dwell peace, unbroken peace,
And with war's terrible array I come
To scatter havoc, like a listed foe!

Odowalsky.

Hereafter 'twill be time to think of that.

Demetrius.

Thou feelest as a Pole, I am Moscow's son.
It is the land to which I owe my life ;
Forgive me, thou dear soil, land of my home,
Thou sacred boundary-pillar, which I clasp,
Whereon my sire his broad-spread eagle graved,
That I, thy son, with foreign foemen's arms,
Invade the tranquil temple of thy peace.
'Tis to reclaim my heritage I come,
And the proud name that has been stolen from me.
Here the Varegers, my forefathers, ruled,
In lengthened line, for thirty generations ;
I am the last of all their lineage, snatched
From murder by God's special providence.

Scene III.

*A Russian village. An open square before a church.
The tocsin is heard.* Gleb, Ilia, *and* Timoska *rush
in, armed with hatchets.*

Gleb (*entering from a house*).
Why are they running?

Ilia (*entering from another house*).
Who has tolled the bell.

Timoska.
Neighbors, come forth ! Come all, to council come !
[*Enter* Oleg *and* Izor, *with many other peasants,
women and children, who carry bundles.*

GLEB.

    Whence come ye hither with your wives and children?
IZOR. Fly, fly! The Pole has fallen upon the land
    At Maromesk, and slaughters all he finds.
OLEG. Fly into the interior — to strong towns!
    We've fired our cottages, there's not a soul
    Left in the village, and we're making now
    Up country for the army of the Czar.
TIMOSKA.

    Here comes another troop of fugitives.
   [IWANSKA *and* PETRUSCHKA, *with armed peasantry,*
    enter on different sides.
IWANSKA.

    Long live the Czar! The mighty prince Dmitri!
GLEB. How! What is this!
ILIA.   What do you mean?
TIMOSKA.   Who are you?
PETRUSCHKA.

    Join all who're loyal to our princely line!
TIMOSKA.

    What means all this? There a whole village flies
    Up country to escape the Poles, while you
    Make for the very point whence these have fled,
    To join the standard of the country's foe!
PETRUSCHKA.

    What foe? It is no foe that comes; it is
    The people's friend, the emperor's rightful heir.

* * *

The POSADMIK (the village judge) enters to read a manifesto by Demetrius. Vacillation of the inhabitants of the village between the two parties. The peasant women are the first to be won over to Demetrius, and turn the scale.

* * *

Camp of DEMETRIUS. He is worsted in the first action, but the army of the Czar Boris conquers in a manner against its will, and does not follow up its advantages. Demetrius, in despair, is about to destroy himself, and is with difficulty prevented from doing so by Korela and Odowalsky. Overbearing demeanor of the Cossacks even to Demetrius.

Camp of the army of the CZAR BORIS. He is absent himself, and this injures his cause, as he is feared but not loved. His army is strong, but not to be relied on. The leaders are not unanimous, and partly incline to the side of Demetrius from a variety of motives. One of their number, Soltikow, declares for him from conviction. His adherence is attended with the most important results; a large portion of the army deserts to Demetrius.

BORIS in Moscow. He still maintains his position as absolute ruler, and has faithful servants around him; but already he is discomposed by evil tidings. He is with-held from joining the army by apprehension of a rebellion in Moscow. He is also ashamed as Czar to enter the field in person against a traitor. Scene between him and the archbishop.

Bad news pours in from all sides, and Boris' danger grows momently more imminent. He hears of the revolt of the peasantry and the provincial towns, — of the inac-tivity and mutiny of the army, — of the commotions in Moscow, — of the advance of Demetrius. Romanow, whom he has deeply wronged, arrives in Moscow. This gives rise to new apprehensions. Now come the tidings that the Boiars are flying to the camp of Demetrius, and that the whole army has gone over to him.

BORIS and AXINIA. The Czar appears in a touching aspect as father, and in the dialogue with his daughter unfolds his inmost nature.

BORIS has made his way to the throne by crime, but undertaken and fulfilled all the duties of a monarch; to the country he is a valuable prince and a true father of his people. It is only in his personal dealings with individuals that he is cunning, revengeful, and cruel. His spirit as well as his rank elevates him above all that surround him. The long possession of supreme power, the habit of ruling over men, and the despotic form of government, have so nursed his pride that it is impossible for him to outlive his greatness. He sees clearly what awaits him; but still he is Czar, and not degraded, though he resolves to die.

He believes in forewarnings, and in his present mood things appear to him of significance which, on other occasions, he had despised. A particular circumstance, in which he seems to hear the voice of destiny, decides him.

Shortly before his death his nature changes; he grows milder, even towards the messengers of evil, and is ashamed of the bursts of rage with which he had received them before. He permits the worst to be told to him, and even rewards the narrator.

So soon as he learns the misfortune that seals his fate, he leaves the stage without further explanation, with composure and resignation. Shortly afterwards he returns in the habit of a monk, and removes his daughter from the sight of his last moments. She is to seek protection from insult in a cloister; his son, Feodor, as a child, will perhaps have less to fear. He takes poison, and enters a retired chamber to die in peace.

General confusion at the tidings of the Czar's death. The Boiars form an imperial council and rule in the Kremlin. Romanow (afterwards Czar, and founder of the now ruling house) enters at the head of an armed force, swears, on the bosom of the Czar, an oath of allegiance to his son Feodor, and compels the Boiars to follow his example. Revenge and ambition are far from his soul;

he pursues only justice. He loves Axinia without hope, and is, without knowing it, beloved by her in return.

———

ROMANOW hastens to the army to secure it for the young Czar. Insurrection in Moscow, brought about by the adherents of Demetrius. The people drag the Boiars from their houses, make themselves masters of Feodor and Axinia — put them in prison, and send delegates to Demetrius.

———

DEMETRIUS in Tula, at the pinnacle of success. The army is his own; the keys of numerous towns are brought to him. Moscow alone appears to offer resistance. He is mild and amiable, testifies a noble emotion at the intelligence of the death of Boris, pardons a detected conspiracy against his life, despises the servile adulations of the Russians, and is for sending them away. The Poles, on the other hand, by whom he is surrounded, are rude and violent, and treat the Russians with contempt. Demetrius longs for a meeting with his mother, and sends a messenger to Marina.

———

Among the multitude of Russians who throng around Demetrius in Tula appears a man whom he at once recognizes; he is greatly delighted to see him. He bids all the rest withdraw, and so soon as he is alone with this man he thanks him, with full heart, as his preserver and benefactor. This person hints that Demetrius is under especial obligations to him, and to a greater extent than he is himself aware. Demetrius urges him to explain, and the assassin of the genuine Demetrius thereupon discloses the real facts of the case. For this murder he had received no recompense, but on the contrary had nothing but death to anticipate from Boris. Thirsting for revenge, he stumbled upon a boy, whose resemblance to the Czar Ivan struck him. This circumstance must be turned to account. He seized the boy, fled with him from Uglitsch, brought him to a monk, whom he succeeded in gaining over for his ends, and delivered to him the trinkets which he had himself taken from the murdered Demetrius. By means of this boy, whom he had never lost sight of, and whose steps he had attended upon all occasions without being observed, he is now revenged. His tool, the false Demetrius, rules over Russia in Boris' room.

During this narration a mighty change comes over Demetrius. His silence is awful. In the moment of the highest rage and despair, the assassin drives him to the extreme of endurance, when with a defying and insolent air he demands his reward. Demetrius strikes him to the earth.

Soliloquy of Demetrius. Internal conflict; but the feeling of the necessity for maintaining his position as Czar is triumphant.

The delegates from Moscow arrive, and submit themselves to Demetrius. They are received gloomily, and with a menacing demeanor. Among them is the Patriarch. Demetrius deposes him from his dignity, and soon afterwards sentences to death a Russian of rank, who had questioned the authenticity of his birth.

MARFA and OLGA await Demetrius under a magnificent tent. Marfa speaks of the approaching interview with more doubt and fear than hope, and trembles as the moment draws near which should assure her highest happiness. Olga speaks to her, herself without faith. During the long journey they have both had time to recall the whole circumstances; the first exultation had given place to reflection. The gloomy silence and the repulsive glances of the guards who surround the tent serve still further to augment their despondency.

The trumpets sound. Marfa is irresolute whether she shall advance to meet Demetrius. Now he stands before her alone. The little that was left of hope in her heart altogether vanishes on seeing him. An unknown some-

thing steps between them — Nature does not speak —
they are separated forever. The first impulse is an endeavor to approach; Marfa is the first to make a movement to recede. Demetrius observes it, and remains for
a moment paralyzed. Significant silence.

DEMETRIUS. Does thy heart say nothing? Dost thou
not recognize thy blood in me?

MARFA is silent.

DEMETRIUS. The voice of nature is holy and free; I
will neither constrain nor belie it. Had thy heart spoken
at the first glance then had mine answered it; thou
shouldst have found a pious, loving son in me. The claim
of duty would have concurred with inclination and heart-
felt affection. But if thou dost not feel as a mother for
me, then, think as a princess, command thyself as a queen!
Fate unexpectedly gave me to thee as a son; accept me
as a gift of heaven. Though even I were not thy son,
which I now appear to be, still I rob thy son of nothing.
I stripped it from thy foe. Thee and thy blood have I
avenged; I have delivered thee from the grave in which
thou wert entombed alive, and led thee back into the royal
seat. That thy destiny is linked with mine thou knowest.
With me thou standest, and with me must fall. All the
people's eyes are upon us. I hate deception, and what I
do not feel I may not show; but I do really feel a
reverence for thee, and this feeling, which bends my knee
before thee, comes from my heart.

[*Dumb show of* MARFA, *to indicate her internal emotion*.

DEMETRIUS. Make thy resolve! Let that which nature
will not prompt be the free act of thy will! I ask no hy-
pocrisy — no falsehood, from thee; I ask genuine feelings.
Do not seem to be my mother, but be so. Throw the
past from thee — grasp the present with thy whole heart!
If I am not thy son yet I am the Czar — I have power
and success upon my side. He who lies in his grave is
dust; he has no heart to love thee, no eye to smile upon
thee. Turn to the living.   [MARFA *bursts into tears*.

DEMETRIUS. Oh, these golden drops are welcome to
me. Let them flow! Show thyself thus to the people!

[*At a signal from* DEMETRIUS *the tent is thrown
open, and the assembled Russians become spec-
tators of this scene*.

Entrance of Demetrius into Moscow. Great splendor, but of a military kind. Poles and Cossacks compose the procession. Gloom and terror mingle with the demonstrations of joy. Distrust and misfortune surround the whole.

Romanow, who came to the army too late, has returned to Moscow to protect Feodor and Axinia. It is all in vain; he is himself thrown into prison. Axinia flies to Marfa, and at her feet implores protection against the Poles. Here Demetrius sees her, and a violent and irresistible passion is kindled in his breast. Axinia detests him.

DEMETRIUS as Czar. A fearful element sustains him, but he does not control it: he is urged on by the force of strange passions. His inward consciousness betokens a general distrust; he has no friend on whom he can rely. Poles and Cossacks, by their insolent licentiousness, injure him in the popular opinion. Even that which is creditable to him — his popular manners, simplicity, and contempt of stiff ceremonial, occasions dissatisfaction. Occasionally he offends, through inadvertency, the usages of the country. He persecutes the monks because he suffered severely under them. Moreover, he is not exempt from despotic caprices in the moments of offended pride. Odowalsky knows how to make himself at all times indispensable to him, removes the Russians to a distance, and maintains his overruling influence.

DEMETRIUS meditates inconstancy to Marina. He confers upon the point with the Archbishop Iob, who, in order to get rid of the Poles, falls in with his desire, and puts before him an exalted picture of the imperial power.

MARINA appears with a vast retinue in Moscow. Meeting with Demetrius. Hollow and cold meeting on both sides; she, however, wears her disguise with greater skill. She urges an immediate marriage. Preparations are made for a magnificent festival.

By the orders of Marina a cup of poison is brought to Axinia. Death is welcome to her; she was afraid of being forced to the altar with the Czar.

Violent grief of Demetrius. With a broken heart he goes to the betrothal with Marina.

After the marriage Marina discloses to him that she does not consider him to be the true Demetrius, and never did. She then coldly leaves him in a state of extreme anguish and dismay.

Meanwhile Schinskoi, one of the former generals of the Czar Boris, avails himself of the growing discontent of the people, and becomes the head of a conspiracy against Demetrius.

Romanow, in prison, is comforted by a supernatural apparition. Axinia's spirit stands before him, opens to him a prospect of happier times in store, and enjoins him calmly to allow destiny to ripen, and not to stain himself with blood. Romanow receives a hint that he may himself be called to the throne. Soon afterwards he is solicited to take part in the conspiracy, but declines.

Soltikow reproaches himself bitterly for having betrayed his country to Demetrius. But he will not be a second time a traitor, and adheres, from principle and against his feelings, to the party which he has once adopted. As the misfortune has happened, he seeks at least to alleviate it, and to enfeeble the power of the Poles. He pays for this effort with his life; but he accepts death as a merited punishment, and confesses this when dying to Demetrius himself.

Casimir, a brother of Lodoiska, a young Polish lady, who has been secretly and hopelessly attached to Demetrius, in the house of the Waywode of Sendomir, has, at his sister's request, accompanied Demetrius in the campaign, and in every encounter defended him bravely. In the moment of danger, when all the other retainers of Demetrius think only of their personal safety, Casimir alone remains faithful to him, and sacrifices life in his defence.

The conspiracy breaks out. Demetrius is with Marfa when the leading conspirators force their way into the room. The dignity and courage of Demetrius have a momentary effect upon the rebels. He nearly succeeds in disarming them by a promise to place the Poles at their disposal. But at this point Schinskoi rushes in with an infuriated band. An explicit declaration is demanded from the ex-empress; she is required to swear, upon the cross, that Demetrius is her son. To testify against her conscience in a manner so solemn is impossible. She turns from Demetrius in silence, and is about to withdraw. " Is she silent?" exclaims the tumultuous throng. " Does she disown him?" "Then, traitor, die!" and Demetrius falls, pierced by their swords, at Marfa's feet.